KANSAS FOLKLORE

Edited by
S. J. Sackett
and
William E. Koch

KANSAS FOLKLORE

UNIVERSITY OF NEBRASKA PRESS

LINCOLN: 1961

The editors wish to express their gratitude for the use of copyrighted material:

To Laura M. French for permission to reprint from *History of Emporia and Lyon County*, 1929.

To Nyle H. Miller for permission to reprint from the publications of the Kansas State Historical Society, 1901, 1902, 1944.

To Frank A. Root and William E. Connelley for permission to reprint from *The Overland Stage to California*, 1901.

To William Ansell Mitchell for permission to reprint from *Linn County, Kansas: A History*, 1928.

To Will E. Stoke for permission to reprint from *Episodes of Early Days in Central and Western Kansas*, 1926.

Publishers on the Plains

UNP

FOR KATHY DAGEL

This book is dedicated to the memory of Mrs. Kathy Dagel of Augusta, Kansas, whose untimely death deprived her fellow folklore enthusiasts of an energetic and accomplished collector and a superb performer.

CONTENTS

INTRODUCTION

Kansas is a big, open, new stretch of land where things have moved fast. Within their own life-span storytellers have seen the whole period of its development from territory to state, from frontier to continental crossroads. There are men and women in Kansas today who have traveled in oxcarts and jets, dwelt in dugouts and penthouses, been diverted by medicine shows and television programs.

In view of this background and recalling the physical characteristics of the plains region, it should come as no surprise that folklore material found in Kansas differs from that collected in long-settled, wooded, and mountainous sections of America—in New England, say, or the Hudson Valley, or the hills of Tennessee. On the wide, light-drenched prairie, other-worldly myths and fairy tales have lost out to realistic anecdotes, tall stories, and local legends. Kansans have sung, jested, bragged of the natural phenomena and the real personages affecting their lives or tickling their fancy—of crops and the weather and cowhands and buffalo-skinners—as well as the universal themes of love, work, religion, death.

Along with the many legends and stories, songs and sayings, brought in by the pioneers and easily recognized as imported, there is a great quantity of lore identifiably Kansan, created within the state's borders and revealing much about the land and its people. However, the folklorist searching for materials in Kansas must approach his problem with its history in mind. If he has been taught that a tale which has been printed is no longer folklore, let him remember that in the years from 1821 to 1936 sparsely settled Kansas had 4,368 newspapers, while in the same period New York, the state with the largest population, had only 3,309 and Pennsylvania a mere 2,519.[1] There has never been a time when things said by Kansans or believed by Kansans or

[1] Charles C. Howes, *This Place Called Kansas* (Norman: University of Oklahoma Press, 1952), p. 68.

hoped by Kansans did not make the newspapers. That Kansas yarns, or legends, or tall stories became newspaper items certainly does not eliminate them from the realm of folklore; they were alive in oral tradition before and after their appearance in print.

The studies presented here are, we believe, strong evidence that Kansas is fertile in material both interesting in itself and of potential value for future comparative studies. The work as a whole has been designed to stand as a representative survey; with this objective in view each contributor has selected specimens from a large body of materials, mostly primary sources, either collected in the field or firsthand accounts. Far more folklore has been collected than this book can begin to indicate, yet the amount is small compared to what has been gathered in those sections of the country where oral culture has been diligently researched for many more years than in Kansas.

Since each of the following studies defines the type of material with which it is concerned, no extended definition of folklore seems called for here. But because the recent quiet rebellion of scholars against using the term "folklore" to describe what Richard M. Dorson has called "fakelore" has brought charges that there is no commonly accepted definition, perhaps we should emphasize that there is unanimous agreement on two cardinal and fundamental points: to be designated as folklore, *material must have lived in oral tradition* (that is, must have been communicated from one person to another by word of mouth), *and the various materials*—songs, tales, legends, proverbs, or riddles—*must have been reported faithfully and accurately* (that is, are invalidated for serious study by any conscious embellishment, addition, or deletion by the compiler or collector).

It is our hope that the publication of KANSAS FOLKLORE will not only stimulate those already in the field to continue their efforts, but will also arouse interest in folkloristic activities among Kansans in general. Although perhaps not all are aware that it can be so labeled, everybody knows some folklore. A "field trip" need take one no farther than the attic for the composition book in which Great-Aunt Edith wrote down the songs she loved as a girl or the autograph album preserving the rhymed sentiments of her schoolmates; collecting may require no more than an attentive ear on a hot summer afternoon as Grandpa sits

by the air conditioner and recalls the summers of his boy-
hood—"If it stayed up right around a hunderd and ten for two,
three weeks, then we figured maybe we was in for a warm spell."
Far from being confined to New England or the South or the
Middle Atlantic States, folklore flourishes wherever there are
people with the heart to love a song or story and make it their
own. Kansas has these in plenty.

Grateful acknowledgment is made to the editor-collectors who
cooperated so splendidly; to Janet Conrow and Agnes Newbrey
for their valuable aid in preparing the typescript; to Mary Koch
for helping solve some knotty problems; and, above all, to those
Kansans who sang their songs, told their tales, and contributed
recipes or beliefs.

S. J. SACKETT
WILLIAM E. KOCH

KANSAS FOLKLORE

FOLKTALES

MARY FRANCES WHITE
Kansas State University

"Although the term 'folktale' is often used in English to refer to the 'household tale' or 'fairy tale' (the German Märchen) it is also legitimately employed in a much broader sense to include all forms of prose narrative, written or oral, which have come to be handed down through the years. In this usage the important fact is the traditional nature of the material." [1] Thus Stith Thompson defines for us the subject of this study. The definition is important because, although Märchen-type folktales are not commonly found in Kansas, many other types which are current in the state are included in the general category "folktale."

The pioneer period of Kansas history was prolific in both storytellers and incidents worthy of the telling. Border strife between abolitionists and pro-slavery men; Indian raids; the trail-town lawlessness and frontier justice—primitive, unpredictable, and infrequent; land speculation; the wind and the dust and the grasshoppers—all of these are the subjects of stories still being recounted. They take the form of historical reminiscences, folk anecdotes, and tall tales, and examples of each type are included in this study.

Most of the tales provide insight into the character of the narrator or the subject of the story, and into some phase of life on "the sod-house frontier." Crops, animal life, and the climate of Kansas figure in them prominently. We find vegetables of astounding dimensions, a profusion of jackrabbits and rattlers as well as more unusual animals, fish and game beyond measure and beyond belief, and—frequently the star actor—the capri-

[1] Stith Thompson, *The Folktale* (New York: The Dryden Press, 1946), p. 4.

cious Kansas weather in which the inhabitants take such perverse pride.

The tales are especially illuminating when they touch on the tribulations of the early settlers—harassed by Indians, victimized by land speculators and the whole breed of frontier sharp operators, routinely beset by plagues, droughts, and tornadoes. Yet, as these stories make abundantly clear, the Kansas settler faced up to adversity with dogged courage and wry humor; far from enduring hazards and hardships with a martyr's air, he confronted them with a grin. Time and again he would make a joke of misfortune, passing off a catastrophe as a minor annoyance or even hailing it as a blessing in disguise. Such an outlook was no small thing; it might almost be said that without the capacity to laugh at his troubles, the Kansas pioneer could not have survived.

Not all of the stories presented here are native to Kansas. The tall tale, for instance, is characteristic of the whole Midwest—indeed of any region in its period of exploration and settlement—and similar stories may be collected from any of our neighboring states; but their universality is precisely what makes them interesting to the student of folklore. To study the tales which were brought into the state and the slight changes which make them peculiarly Kansan is one of the functions of our folklorists. Three of the stories included are of Old World origin; they are representative of many introduced during the years after the Civil War when the railroad agents' promises of cheap land and the alluring descriptions in promotional brochures attracted immigrants from nearly every European country. These tales do not circulate widely in Kansas today, but there are communities in which they can still be heard.

Although there has been no major attempt to collect folktales in Kansas, many have been preserved for us in the pages of frontier newspapers. Early editors seemed to delight in them, and did an excellent job of retaining their pungency and anonymity. By virtue of publication they gained wider oral currency. Other stories were recorded in diaries, volumes of personal reminiscence, and county histories. Thus many Kansas folktales found their way into print. Since most of the periodicals and books in which they appeared are now unavailable, some of the most in-

teresting of these previously published tales are presented here,
together with stories recently collected from a living oral tradition in the state.[2]

TALES OF KANSAS WEATHER

WINDY TALE OF A KANSAS TENDERFOOT

[Abe Peters told A. T. McNeal this story of what happened to
a tenderfoot who was learning how to combat the Kansas wind.
Reprinted from the Kansas City *Star,* 13 August 1912.]

I have seen some hard winters out in western Kansas. There
are some things that an old resident learns out there from observation and experience. One is that when you are facing a hard
wind to keep your mouth shut. One day I was traveling with a
tenderfoot from the East. He was a long, slender man about 6 feet
3 inches long and about 6 inches wide. He had no more meat on
his bones than a fork handle and was about the most emaciated
looking person I ever saw. As I was saying, one day we started to
ride across the prairie when the wind came up in our faces, blowing at the rate of a hundred miles an hour or so. The tenderfoot
opened his mouth to say something to me. I heard him make a
curious noise and looked around to see what was the matter and
saw that he had inadvertently swallowed about six or seven barrels of wind. He looked like an inflated air cushion and seemed
to be about four times the size he was naturally. It seemed to set
him sort of crazy and he jumped out of the buggy. When he lit
on the ground he bounced into the air like a rubber ball and
then went bounding across the prairie like a tumbleweed before
the wind. At the end of three miles he fell into a canyon where
the wind couldn't hit him and stopped, but it was a week before
he was back to his normal size.

---

[2] Motif analyses of the stories in this study appear in the Appendix, page
239. They refer to parallel situations or events as listed in Stith Thompson,
Motif-Index of Folk-Literature (rev. ed.; Bloomington: Indiana University,
1957, six vols.). While the Appendix does not attempt to provide a complete
list of the motifs, enough are given so that the reader can find analogues in
collections of folktales from other U. S. regions and from other countries.

Harnessing the Winds

[Cyclones in Kansas often perform a service for mankind. "Give-a-dam" Jones, from near Verbruk, Kansas, vouches for this story of a twister, which appeared in the *Barton County Democrat*, 23 April 1893. There are several other versions.]

You know one of them little twisters we had last week up in our part of the county done me a good turn. I just had time to plow a couple of rounds 'fore unhitchin' for the day, an' left the plow stickin' in the ground—a little level patch betwixt some hills. An' in the morning—give-a-dam—one o' them little hell-roaring twisters didn't do a thing but grab that old plow and spun it 'round an' 'round, 'til the hull give-a-dam land I'd laid out was plowed up slick as if I'd done it myself. I don't give-a-dam if it'd turn up another patch.

Tall Cyclone Stories

[Among the tall tales swapped in the office of W. G. Tandy, former city commissioner of streets in Topeka, are many of the traditional stories about cyclones. This account, which appeared in the *Osborne County Farmer*, 20 January 1916, shows how good storytellers try to top each other.]

"I saw a cottonwood tree that stood in the way of a cyclone," said C. A. Porter, assistant city engineer. "The big wind had just gathered up a stack of wheat straw. The straws were blown right into the wood of that tree, just like each straw had been a nail and had been driven in. Straws were sticking with one end embedded in the wood so that tree looked like a huge mule-tail sticking out of the ground."

"I believe that, all right," replied B. F. Allen, inspector.

"That's nothing," spoke up A. R. Young, city engineer. "I saw a plow once which had been struck by a cyclone. It was an ordinary walking plow with a steel beam. When the farmer who was using it saw a storm coming, he unhitched and left the plow in the field. The cyclone hit that steel beam and whipped it right back between the handles—just bent it double and never moved the plow an inch from where it had been left."

"I'll believe anything I am told about a cyclone," declared Allen. "And speaking of that plow reminds me of what I saw up in Nebraska once. A farmer I know very well—in fact, he lived on the farm adjoining mine—was struck by lightning while he was plowing. Both he and his team were killed. He left a widow and a large family of small children. None of the children was large enough to go ahead and put in the crops and the poor woman had no money to pay for a hired man or to buy a team.

"As we were coming home from the cemetery after burying her husband, a number of us talked over her situation and decided that we neighbors would get together and plow the land and put in a crop for her. We noticed a big funnel-shaped cloud, but did not think much about it until we got near the field where the man had been killed.

"Well, sir, you can believe this or not, just as you please, but it is a fact—a whirlwind hit that plow, which was still standing in the furrow. The wind took that plow right straight down the furrow, just as straight as if a man was driving a team hitched to it. When the end of the furrow was reached the wind changed and turned that plow at right angles and plowed another furrow. When the next corner was reached the same thing happened, and that whirlwind just kept doing that way, and right before the eyes of all the people coming from the funeral that whole field was plowed—yessir—all in about a minute.

"Yep, and after that quarter-section was plowed, the wind hit the granary where the seed wheat was stored, turned the building over and scattered that wheat all over the field and covered it up. Yessir, I'll believe anything anyone tells me about a cyclone for I actually saw that."

"Didn't another cyclone come along about harvest time and harvest that wheat, thresh it, take it to the market and blow the exact amount of money back out of the bank to pay for it?" queried L. R. Lane.

"Ah, you are joking now, but what I have been telling I saw with my own eyes," insisted Allen.

"It was a cyclone that gave me my start in business," W. G. Tandy announced. "I was in the moving business. Two men in different parts of the town decided to trade houses. Each wanted to keep the lots he had, but wanted the other fellow's house, and

I took a contract to move them. The men decided to leave town and so went on a vacation to avoid the inconvenience which would result while the houses were being moved.

"While they were away and just before I started work, a cyclone came along one night and moved those houses for me. Didn't disturb another thing in the town and each house was set up just as nice and plumb as if I had done the work myself. I just sat down and wrote a telegram to the two men that the job was completed and I wanted my money. I never told them how the work had been done for me, and they never were able to figure out how I moved the wells and cellars along with the houses."

"Yes, cyclones certainly do some strange things," agreed Porter. "Tandy's experience reminds me of what happened to a contractor I know up in Marysville, Kansas. He had a contract to build a fine residence there. I drew the plans and specifications and the materials were all assembled. The stone for the foundation, the cement for the cellar, brick for the chimneys, lumber, shingles, window sashes, nails, and hardware were all on hand.

"Along came a cyclone and dug the cellar, laid the foundation, built the chimneys, sawed all the boards and put that house together. In fact built the entire house exactly according to the plans I had drawn. There wasn't even a nail or a screw missing. It even blew the paint out of the paint cans, mixed it and put on three coats and the decorative trimmings without splashing a drop. Then that cyclone went to town and visited an art store and came back with pictures with which it decorated the walls of every room in the house—hung every picture straight and without breaking a glass.

"But there was one thing about it I have never been able to figure out, and that is this: Even granting that that cyclone mixed the cement and poured sand and stone in the right proportions for concreting the foundation and cellar floor, how did that cyclone make the cement 'set' in time to support the weight of the house—the whole thing was done in five minutes, you know?"

IT'S HARD TO BELIEVE

[Any dry spell in Kansas is certain to revive stories of droughts, dust storms, and the sudden torrential rains that break a drought.

Many times these heavy rains are accompanied by electrical storms, hail, and violent wind. C. D. Shultz of Tribune, Kansas, tells this story of the experience he and his family had in a dust storm in the western part of the state. Reprinted from the Hutchinson *News-Herald,* 1 July 1951.]

It is hard to believe. As we were returning home from visiting relatives at Hutchinson and Pratt we were detoured by high water at Garden City. Just east of Lakin we ran into a dust storm that was as dark as the inside of a vinegar jug.

Well, it just happened to be raining at the same time, and it seemed that that dust had been wet up so often that it just got stubborn and refused to let the rain through. We drove along for a couple of miles under a solid ceiling like a fly hunting an escape, and as we drove the ceiling seemed to be settling and we wondered why that layer of dust was solid dirt for a depth of about twenty-five feet floating on that eight foot layer of compressed air and dust underneath, and water running along the top. It had settled down over a windmill until only the wheel was sticking out at the top, and the flowing water was turning the wheel.

Well, then we could see why that muck was slowly sinking because a few feet away at regular intervals a big bubble arose on the surface and a big puff of dust would rise. That windmill was pumping the dust out from underneath. Looked like a steam locomotive starting up a hill with a long freight. As I say, it's hard to believe.

CHANGEABLENESS OF KANSAS WEATHER

[Collected from George Evans of McFarland, Kansas, by P. J. Wyatt, 15 June 1956.]

It was related that in the early days we had some very hot weather, which we have most every year in Kansas. A farmer was driving a yoke of cattle, and-uh they became wearied on account of the heat, an' he found that he would have to do something— give them some water. This story represents the sudden changes that take place in Kansas, occasionally.

He rushed over to the well to get a bucket of water for his ox an' by the time he got to the wagon, his other ox had died with the heat, and-uh he looked around to his bucket, an' the weather had changed—the wind had changed to the north and his bucket was solid ice.

GROUND SQUIRREL DIGS HOLE IN DUST STORM

[Collected from George Evans of McFarland, Kansas, by P. J. Wyatt, 15 June 1956.]

Kansas is noted for high winds and hard storms; once in awhile, some cy-clones. We used to laugh about the whirlwinds.

I re-call a story by an old farmer that went out to do his chores and encountered a whirlwind. The dust was so thick he couldn't see his way, so he stopped to let it subside. When the sun came out in a short time, the—he noticed that the dust was so thick, that he saw a ground squirrel tryin' to make a hole for his dwelling.

THE BUCKSKIN CLOTHES THAT SHRANK

[Collected from Bob Daily of Alma, Kansas, by P. J. Wyatt, 18 June 1956.]

I got a new suit of buckskin clothes, and started out to see my girl, 'n' there was a big dew on, and I waded through weeds and grass. And when buckskin gets wet why it sticks and it'd get down under my feet, and I'd take my knife 'n' cut a rim off of the bottom of the leg. When I got there, why, I got in by the fire, 'n' begun to dry, 'n' the buckskin begun to shrink up. Pretty soon, all I had was just a little streak of buckskin above my knees.

FOLKTALES OF KANSAS ANIMALS

THE SANDHILL DODGER

[An animal which is a most wonderful example of the theory of adaptation to the environment is the sandhill dodger, known mainly to the inhabitants of the sandhill districts of Nebraska and Kansas. However, in other regions he has close relatives whose exploits are the basis of good stories. Lee Larabee of Liberal, Kansas, gave this account of the peculiar animal to the other members of the state fish and game commission a number of years ago. Reprinted from Topeka *Daily Capital,* 14 July 1927.]

They are getting rather uncommon now, . . . I always have

regretted that I didn't capture one for the museum. The animal
—it is a four-legged one—has run around those sandhills so
much that it has developed legs longer on one side than the
other. It runs with the two short legs next the hill, and makes
wonderful speed.

They are exceptionally intelligent, too. I remember once one
of our hands bet he could catch one with his rope. There were a
lot of bets placed on the event. You know the old cowboys would
bet—them days are gone forever, of course.

Well, we all went out to where one had been reported and sure
enough, we located it. Shorty went after it whooping and holler-
ing and swinging his rope. The dodger started around the hill,
and Shorty doubled his cries. Then we saw what an intelligent
animal the sandhill dodger is. Shorty met the animal at full
speed, and you'd never guess what it did.

Well, sir, when it saw Shorty coming toward him, the little
animal turned its nose right down its mouth, went right on
thru its entire body, and was headed the other way with its short
legs next the hill. Shorty never caught it.

THE HOOP SNAKE

[One of the most unpleasant features of life on the prairie was
the abundance of snakes. They would crawl through the open-
ings in the floor, slither up the walls of the sod-houses, and coil
under shocks of wheat. Along the trails were dens of snakes, with
hundreds of these reptiles crawling in all directions. Both bull
snakes and rattlesnakes were numerous. Other snakes reported
were the blow snake, which supposedly discharged a venom caus-
ing stupefaction and death to those who breathed it; the blue
racer, which traveled like lightning; and the glass snake, which
was so brittle that a slight blow broke it in two. The most interesting of all is the hoop snake, although not many people have
actually seen one. The following firsthand account of J. L. Harri-
son's experience with a Shunganunga hoop snake appeared in
the Public Letter Box, Topeka *Daily Capital*, 3 August 1914.]

Last week I wanted a mess of bullheads and as the raging
Shunganunga is a place for this beautiful game fish I went
thither.

When fishing in this limpid stream I always carry in addition to my tackle a baseball bat to guard against the ferocious snakes that infest the banks.

It was a good day for fishing for at the end of two hours I had a string of sixty-eight (68) bullheads.

Abhorring the name of gamehog I was satisfied then to quit. As I was rolling up my line a slight rustling in the weeds back of me attracted my attention. Presently there appeared a most strange object. In appearance it resembled a Ford automobile tire. It rolled gently down to the water's edge and assumed a horizontal position with a flop.

I realized instantly that I stood in the presence of a far-famed hoop snake!

The monster's head was the size of your fist. His eyes were beady and glittering, and just back of his nose tufts of whiskers projected similar to those of a rat.

I took in these details in a second, but having no love for any kind of snake I seized my trusty bat and struck him a terrific blow.

A most astonishing phenomenon resulted! Instantly the snake broke into seven distinct pieces which lay quiescent for a moment and then simultaneously upended themselves and walked off up into the bushes and disappeared.

Overcome with astonishment and awe I made a fatal mistake which I will regret as long as I live. I failed to follow to see whether as according to tradition the pieces reunited.

SHOOTING BLACKBIRDS

[Down in Barber county a group of men tried to outdo each other on lies about the crops. The first told the old story about the pumpkin vine that grew so fast it wore out the pumpkins dragging them over the ground. The second told of the man who took off his shoes and waded around in the Kansas mud and then lay down to sleep. When he awoke in the morning he found that both legs had sprouted, and his feet had grown so big that he couldn't wear anything less than a number eighteen shoe in place of the number seven that had fitted him the night before. The third told of the boy who climbed a Kansas cornstalk in sport and then was unable to get down because the stalk grew up faster than he could slide down. But it was the fourth man, Deacon Lester, who topped them all with this story about the blackbirds. Reprinted from Kansas City *Journal,* 9 September 1907.]

Blackbirds are bad down in Barber. They are worrying the farmers up and down the beautiful Medicine Valley. One day a farmer's boy rushed into the house and told his father that the dratted blackbirds were eating up all of the wheat. The old man grabbed his shotgun, but when he went to look for the shot he found that there was none in the house. He was a resourceful man, and in place of shot he loaded his gun with a handful of carpet tacks in each barrel. Then he rushed out to the field of grain. The birds saw him coming with blood in his eye and flew away only to light in a great cottonwood tree where they set up a tremendous chatter at the farmer. We might say that there are tremendous cottonwoods growing in the Medicine Valley. It is no uncommon thing to see a cottonwood there that will measure four feet in diameter.

The farmer was hot. He saw the birds congregated in the top of the huge cottonwood tree and turned loose at them with both barrels. When the smoke cleared away he heard the most infernal chatter from the birds that he had ever listened to, but they had not left the tree. Then he discovered that he had nailed them all fast to the limbs with the tacks from his gun. For a little while there was a wild fluttering of wings and then the farmer saw the cottonwood start from the ground. The blackbirds by one united effort pulled it up by the roots and flew away with it. The farmer watched the tree slowly vanishing in the upper air until it became a mere speck in the sky and then disappeared from sight. Then with the expression, "Well, I will be doggoned," he turned toward his humble home.

QUICK WIT

[Collected from Mrs. Gladys Green of Emporia, Kansas, by Mary Frances White, 18 July 1958. It had been told to Mrs. Green by Myrna Cline of Peck, Kansas.]

Grandma arrived at the neighbors' just as their two boys were taking the stock out on the prairie to graze. She and the neighbor lady were going to make soap. The two women became absorbed in their work and were startled when the boys came galloping into the yard, screaming something about a snake.

The little boy had jumped off the horse and was walking in the grass when he heard the buzzing of the rattler. He became terrified and started to run just as the snake struck him in the heel.

The neighbor lady became hysterical. The men were gone and the nearest doctor was 25 miles away. Grandma told the little boy to sit down and the larger one to catch her a chicken. She ran into the house and grabbed up a knife and a razor.

She cut an "X" across the boy's heel, grabbed a chicken and cut it open behind and below the wing. Then she inserted the boy's foot into the body cavity of the live chicken. The chicken died quickly, its meat turning a greenish-black. When Grandma was finished 12 dead chickens lay in the yard.

That boy not only lived, but wasn't really sick from the bite of that poison snake. But every spring about that same time, there were a few weeks' time when the muscles in his heel drew up until he had to walk on his toe.

THE CAT HE COULDN'T KILL

[Collected from Bob Daily of Alma, Kansas, by P. J. Wyatt, 18 June 1956.]

The old cat got to catchin' chickens, 'n' I took her down to the crick 'n' drowned her, 'n' next mornin', why, she was settin' on the porch. I took 'er out 'n' shot 'er, 'n' next mornin', she was back on the porch. 'N' I took 'er out, 'n' chopped 'er head off. Got up the next morning, 'n' she was sittin' on the porch with 'er head in 'er mouth.

CHICKENS GET READY TO BE MOVED

[Collected from E. B. Smith of Willard, Kansas, by P. J. Wyatt, 13 June 1956.]

Well, he'd done so much movin' around, this farmer that was always buying and selling farms, that 'is chickens got so used to bein' caught 'n' tied up, that ever' time they drove the wagon in the yard, why, all they done was run out t'wards the wagon, 'n' lay down an' crossed their feet, ready fur 'im to tie up an' throw um in, 'n' that was all thur was to it.

FOLKTALES OF HUNTING AND FISHING IN KANSAS

Two in One

[Collected from Mrs. Gladys Green of Emporia, Kansas, by Mary Frances White, 18 July 1958. Mrs. Green learned this story from Myrna Cline, who had learned it from her great-grandmother, Mrs. J. V. Green, Mrs. Gladys Green's mother-in-law.]

Grandma and Grandpa moved to Thomas County from Maryville, Missouri, in the summer of 1886. It was too late to plant a spring garden, so Grandma put out a fall garden. It consisted mostly of turnips and pumpkins.

The turnips and pumpkins came up green and were very inviting looking to the antelope herds. The antelope loved to graze on the turnip tops and soon became a nuisance. Grandpa had tried to shoot them many times, but he could not get close enough to shoot, because they would run as soon as they saw him approaching.

Grandpa put a wagon near the turnip patch so he could use it for a cover so that he could get within shooting distance of the antelopes. He also placed a forked stick so that he could just leave the gun propped up on the stick and the wagon box. That way all he had to do was slip quietly outside, aim the gun, and fire at the grazing animals.

Early one morning the whole household was hustling about getting Uncle Andrew off to catch the train at Monument. He was returning to Missouri for a visit. Uncle Lee was to take him in a spring wagon to the station eight miles away.

After they were gone and all was quiet about the place, Grandpa saw the antelope herd approach and start grazing in the turnip patch. Carefully he slipped out and started for the wagon. At the wagon he carefully drew a bead on a nice young buck. But glancing up he noticed another animal coming up behind the first. He held his fire until only one antelope was visible. Quickly he pulled the trigger . . . one antelope dropped where it stood, the other leaped ahead for a step or so and then fell dead.

Uncle Loge and Grandpa began to dress the animals at once. They discovered the bullet had gone completely through the heart of the first and had lodged in the heart of the second animal.

Grandpa saddled the fastest horse in the corral. While Grandmother and her brother finished dressing the other antelope, he grabbed an old tablecloth and wrapped one carcass in it. Mounting the horse, he took off to catch Uncle Andrew, who was just mounting the train steps as Grandpa pulled up in a sliding stop. He jumped off the horse and handed Uncle Andrew the meat to take to their parents in Missouri.

ALL THE GEESE THAT RESULTED FROM ONE SHOT

[Collected from Henry Clark of Paxico, Kansas, by P. J. Wyatt, 30 June 1956.]

Well, we was livin' out on a farm, 'nd we was pretty hard up out there, an' didn't have no ammanition much—just one shell, so I thought I'd go out 'n' see if I could git something with that one shell.

Aw-w-w-w, I went down the river there, an' I saw a gre-e-a-t big bunch of ducks and-uh pheasants, and-uh all kinds of-uh quail, and-uh sagehens. And then I run over there and chopped this tree down, and there was a coon and a possum in the tree, and killed all them pheasants and things, 'nd one of 'em got crippled, and jumped in the crick, and I jumped in the crick to git 'im. I didn't want none of um to get away.

Got my pants full of fish, 'n' turtles 'n' crawdads, 'n' stepped on a big frog, com'n' out. 'Nd when I got out, 'nd got um all piled up, I didn't have no way to take um home.

So I went down there—I seen the old gray mare down there, 'n' I went down there, an' grabbed that old gray mare 'n' give 'er a big kick, 'n' she jumped out of 'er hide, 'n' I had a sack to carry um home in.

'Nd the old gray mare prit-near froze to death the next day, before I got her hide back!

A FISH STORY

[Collected from George Evans of McFarland, Kansas, by P. J. Wyatt, 15 June 1956.]

A farmer made an artificial lake an' planted fish in it, so the story goes, 'n' in due time, he went down to fish. The pond, or lake, was p'rhaps three-quarters of a mile square, or in circumference—I ferget which.

The farmer fished, 'n' got pretty tired of fishing, but finally got a bite. He couldn't land his catch, so he looked, an' finally saw that it was a pretty good-sized fish. He went home 'n' got a team and a rope 'n' fixed up a hook an' hooked the fish again, 'n' hitched the team on, 'n' pulled it out. The team couldn't pull it, however, but the fish gave a flop 'n' came out itself. It lowered the lake about two feet. So, that-uz all the fishing he could do at once.

FOLKTALES OF KANSAS AGRICULTURE

PUMPKINS AND CORN

[As people trailing to the West began to homestead the land in Kansas, they were delighted to find that the soil was even richer and more fertile than they had expected. Stories about its productiveness soon began to circulate. Reprinted from Coolidge *Border Ruffian*, 10 July 1886.]

There is no doubt . . . that Missouri is a great country, but it will not compare for a moment with Kansas.

Think of the Kansas pumpkins! Gentlemen, when I was on a farm in that glorious country I once lost three valuable cows. For three weeks I searched for them in vain and was returning home in disgust when I suddenly heard the tinkle of a cowbell.

Investigation showed that the cows were inside of a pumpkin, eating calmly and enjoying their commodious quarters. How did they get in, you say? Well, the pumpkin vines grew rapidly there, and dragged a pumpkin over the rough ground until a hole was worn in the side, through which the cows entered. I afterwards had it cured and used it for a wagon shed.

Is it a good country for corn, you ask? Stranger, you'll never know what a corn country is until you go to Kansas.

When the husking is done in the fall the men go out with mallets and wedges and split up the cornstalks for shipment to the East as telegraph poles or saw them off in lengths to be used as car wheels.

When the men are husking they carry along stepladders, which they place near the cornstalk. Two men then climb up and cut off the ears with a crosscut saw, letting them fall to the ground. Four horses are then hitched to each ear, and it is dragged to the crib.

Big farms there? I should say so. Why, when I started one spring to plow a furrow the entire length of the farm, I had a boy follow me to plant the corn, and when I got to the end of the furrow and started for home, I found that the corn the boy had planted was ripe, so I just husked my way home and got there just in time to spend New Year's.

INTELLIGENT INSECTS

[Mr. D. W. McVey of Xenia, Ohio, questioned some of the reports he had heard about the crops in Kansas, specifically those about the sweet alfalfa and the shortage of pumpkins because the vines grew so fast that they wore the pumpkins out dragging them over the ground. Tom McNeal, veteran Kansas storyteller and newspaper editor, soon set him straight about these reports. Reprinted from Kansas City *Star,* n.d., clipping in Kansas State Historical Society Library.]

The stories about the pumpkins are chestnuts. They did not originate in Kansas and we repudiate them. To begin with, no vine is strong enough to drag a Kansas pumpkin. The great difficulty in raising pumpkins in Kansas is to keep the pumpkin from pulling the vine out of the ground. It is true that Kansas alfalfa probably beats any in the world both for yield and sweetness. A Kansas beekeeper says that one trouble about raising bees near alfalfa is that they gather too much honey. He had a large swarm of bees located a mile from an alfalfa field. One day he watched the workers go out to gather honey but didn't see any coming back. He didn't understand it and went over toward the alfalfa field to see what was the trouble. About half way over he met the bees walking back to the hive. They had loaded up with honey till they couldn't fly and had to walk and carry the load. He said that he had to use over two quarts of glycerine on the blistered feet of those bees. The intelligent insects soon became accustomed to the treatment and would lie on their backs while he rubbed glycerine on their sore feet. This took so much time that it ruined the profits of the business.

GREAT WHEAT COUNTRY

[When strangers made slighting remarks about the state or its crops, particularly wheat, Kansans did not take the criticism lying down. This conversation between a farmer and a Schouarie granger is reprinted from the Caldwell *Post,* 18 December 1879.]

"Let's see, they raise some wheat in Kansas, don't they?" asked a Schouarie granger of a Kansas man.

"Raise wheat! Who raises wheat? No sir; decidedly no sir. It raises itself. Why, if we undertook to cultivate wheat in that state, it would run us out. There wouldn't be any place to put our houses."

"But I've been told that grasshoppers take a good deal of it."

"Of course they do. If they didn't I don't know what we would do. The cussed stuff would run all over the state and drive us out—choke us up. Those grasshoppers are a godsend; only there ain't half enough of them."

"Is that wheat nice and plump?"

"Plump! Why, I don't know what you call plump wheat, but there are seventeen in our family, including ten servants, and when we want bread, we just go out and fetch a kernel of wheat and bake it."

"Do you ever soak it in water first?"

"Oh no; that wouldn't do. It would swell a little, and then we couldn't get it in our range oven."

TALL SUNFLOWERS

[Whenever Kansas has a good growing summer, tales about the plant life flourish, too. Naturally there are stories about the sunflower, the state flower. This typical example is reprinted from the Kansas City *Star,* 28 August 1938.]

About the year the Kansas Pacific started building west, the sunflowers grew so high and thick that they were cut up and used as firewood. One farmer, whose entire corn crop was shaded out by them, made a small fortune sawing up sunflower stalks for railroad ties.

This farmer also built a log barn out of the sunflower stalks and kept his cow in it. The cow would wander away, so one night he tied her to a sunflower stalk. Next morning she was

gone. He looked for her quite a while until he heard her bawl
from up in the sky. Then he perceived that the sunflower stalk
had grown during the night so that the cow hung by her halter
forty feet in the air. And he had to chop the stalk down before
he could milk that morning.

BIG STRAWSTACK

[Collected from Clarence Anderson of Utica, Kansas, by S. J.
Sackett, 8 November 1957. Mr. Anderson, a farmer of Swedish
descent, invents and tells Ole Olson stories which are famous all
over Lane County.]

You see, Ole come from the old country and one day he said to
me: "Andy, I sure like Western Kansas, because everything's so
big out here. I feel kind of big myself."

"I been noticin' that, Ole. You know, Ole, I think you got a
touch of the big head. That ain't so good."

"Oh, no, I only wanted to do something, the biggest in the
world. You know."

"Yeah. Well, now I know you got it. You know, last year I tried
—and I planted a thousand acres of wheat and wanted to be kind
of a big shot. You know what I got? Nothin' but straw. It's risky,
Ole."

"Well, let's make the biggest straw pile in the world," he says.

"Ole, heavens, don't call it a pile, but I'll tell you what we'll
do. If you'll stack it, we'll make the biggest strawstack in the
world. But you got to stay up there. Don't you come down till
you're finished. Okay?"

We started to thrash out west of the house there. We thrashed
and we thrashed while Ole stayed up there. One day he come
down. I says, "Ole, don't you like it up there?"

"Oh," he says, "I've got to come down and get some air."

Well, I knew it was pretty high, but I didn't hardly think the
air was getting thin up there. But you know, I noticed it was frost
on his shoulders. It was cold up there too, you know. Air on his
shoulders, you know. But, well, we was famous. Everybody could
come to see the biggest strawstack in the world. They tromped on
my garden, my fences and—oh my goodness, and besides I says,
"Ole, I told you that would get us into trouble." I says, "I haven't
got no place to farm. That bloomin' stack takes up the whole

farm. People are just tromping all over my garden, my fences. Say, what'll we do?"

"Well, I think of somethin'."

We was famous having the biggest strawstack in the world. Well, he come home from town one day and says, "Andy, I went to buy me a hat; they didn't have none to fit me."

"Oh, I know that."

"My head wasn't too big; the hat was too small. Can I make my own hat?"

"What are you going to make it out of? I suppose out of—"

"Can I make it out of that straw? Can I use all I want?"

"Yes, sure, all you want. Oh, plenty of straw."

Well, he went out there that morning, and you know toward evening a cloud come up. Oh boy, oh boy. I thought we had one of those gully-washers for sure—darker and clouds, you know—but you know when I looked closely it was Ole and his big hat coming in from the west. He had a hat.

I said, "How much straw did you use?"

"Well, you said I could use all I wanted; I used all of it."

Oh, what a hat! "Well," I said, "we got rid of the strawstack, but now what'll we do with the hat? We're no better off, Ole." But then I happened to think. "Ole, quick. You go down to that ravine, see, north of the tracks there, that big long draw that goes out into the pasture," and I said, "when you hear me whistle real loud, then you sit down right quick, and then come to the house."

You know, Ole went down there, and I gave a whistle, I could whistle before I got my falsies. The Missouri Pacific even took off its streamers, you know, and put on them other honkers, I out-whistled 'em so bad. I could whistle in those days. And he stopped and he started coming to the house.

Ole never knew what become of that hat. One corner of that hat went on that hill over there, and the other one went over on this one. Well, for several years, you know, the drought, you know, in the thirties, the cattle roamed under the shade of that hat, and it was nice grazing and cool. Finally, you know, even the grass got scarce there and the cattle come to nibble on that hat, and it took them three more years to eat that hat up.

So I'm sorry I can't show you the hat.

GRASSHOPPERS STARVED TO DEATH

[Collected from Clarence Anderson of Utica, Kansas, by S. J. Sackett, 8 November 1957.]

You see, Ole, he is from the old country. He don't quite understand things in Western Kansas. I think he played a pretty dirty trick on the grasshoppers. After all, the grasshoppers was here long before he was here. Even before my grandpa was here; and my grandpa was here—he was—my grandad—they helped build the Union Pacific out here at Ellis and— Oh, I can tell you some stories about that. But, anyway, he played a dirty trick on them.

You see, you know how the grasshoppers are, they are awful bad about taking the wheat—the young wheat coming up. And they do like that young wheat coming up, and so he filled up the drill boxes and the drill and he went out. Well, it looked like he was drilling wheat to beat the band all over the field and edges you know. But listen, he shut the mechanism so he wasn't putting wheat in the ground. Oh no! But he made the furrows and everything and wouldn't you know, the grasshoppers came from everywhere, the neighbors' and everywhere. They sat there waitin' for that wheat to come up until they starved to death.

KANSAS HISTORY IN ANECDOTE

NEVER OUT OF RATTLESNAKE OIL

[Thousands of wagon trains and stages traveled the trails across Kansas carrying freight and passengers to the West. Their supplies were procured at one of the five or six starting points, such as Atchison, Westport, or Independence. As this story illustrates, pride in filling orders was characteristic of frontier merchants. Reprinted from Frank A. Root and William Elsey Connelly, *The Overland Stage to California* (Columbus, Ohio: Long's College Book Company, 1950), p. 579. Originally published in Topeka, Kansas, 1901, by the authors.]

Being the starting-point west for the overland California stagecoaches in the '60's, Atchison naturally furnished many interesting incidents. During the period of four-horse Concord stages there, one of the "Overland" boys visited a prominent drug-store on Commercial street to have a few drugs, medicines, etc., put up.

The customer had a memorandum from which he called, one by one, the articles as wanted, and, to each one inquired for, the druggist, whom we will call Jim Gould for short, nodded in the affirmative and promptly put it up for the customer.

"Now," said the anxious 'Overlander,' as he had reached the bottom of his list, "I want something that I don't think can be found in Atchison."

"What is it?" inquired Jim, the druggist, anxiously.

"I want a half-pint of rattlesnake oil."

"I've got it," quickly answered Jim. "I always keep it; never allow myself to be out."

"Glad to hear it; but I thought I would have to send to St. Louis or Chicago for it," said the customer, greatly pleased to know he could get such an important article so near home.

Jim took a half-pint bottle, went into the back room, and, in a few minutes, returned with the "rattle-snake" (?) oil. Jim filled the customer's order and wrapped up everything neatly in a secure package, and the Overland customer paid the bill and departed. He had not been gone fifteen seconds before Jim turned around and with a "smile that was childlike and bland," said to me (the only person in the room beside himself) : "I never allow myself to be out of anything when running a drug-store. I have everything that is wanted. I draw 'lard oil,' 'bear's oil,' and 'rattlesnake oil' out of one and the same barrel."

SAVING THE FAMILY'S MONEY

[Charles H. Withington came to Kansas in 1853 and settled at Council Grove. In 1854 he established the first store in Lyon County and in southern Kansas not connected officially with an Indian post. During 1855 and 1856 "Withington's" was headquarters for most of the immigrants who came to this section of the territory. Mr. Withington helped the new people to find claims and acted as guide, often neglecting his own business to assist them. The Andersons who figure in the following story were a notorious gang of robbers. Reprinted from Laura M. French, *History of Emporia and Lyon County* (Emporia: Emporia Gazette Printers, 1929) , pp. 177–179.]

Mr. Withington, before leaving home one morning on business, told Mrs. Withington he disliked to leave her alone, as he had heard the Andersons were headed in their direction, and no

telling what day they would swoop down upon them. Mrs. Withington said she could manage them, and that she wasn't afraid.
She was washing that day, her washtub in the narrow strip of
shade made by the cabin, when she saw the little band of men
on horseback coming over a hill. She knew them, personally, and
when the leader ordered her to prepare dinner for them, she replied, "Mr. Anderson, you have eaten many a good meal in my
house, to which you have been welcome, but I take no orders
from you or any other man. When you ask me, respectfully and
decently, to get dinner for you, I'll do it, and not before." The
leader apologized, and politely asked Mrs. Withington if she
would prepare dinner for him and his men. She got up the best
dinner she could, and after the meal the leader said:

"Now, Mrs. Withington, we'll have no more fooling. I want
that bag of gold that is hidden somewhere about this place, and I
am going to have it, and the quicker you get it for me the better
it will be for you."

"Help yourself," said Mrs. Withington, "but don't expect me
to assist you in your search."

For a long time the robbers searched, ripping open feather-
beds and pillows, emptying trunks and drawers, tearing up the
carpet, while Mrs. Withington calmly went on with her washing.
Finally the men threatened her, telling her she would have to
tell them where the gold was hidden or they would not be respon-
sible for the consequences. She looked the leader straight in the
eye.

"You call yourself a brave man," she said, "yet you threaten a
defenseless woman. Go ahead—shoot me if you will, but I will
not tell you where to find that gold."

It was getting late and the robbers feared that Mr. Withington
might come, accompanied by other men who would put up a
fight, so they left after Mrs. Withington defied them. After Mr.
Withington arrived, Mrs. Withington lifted the bag of gold from
the bottom of the washtub, where it had reposed all this time
under dirty suds and soiled clothing.

COUNTING THE INDIANS

[When the white man began to explore and settle the western
territory of which Kansas was a part, he found a number of dif-

ferent Indian tribes. While there are many accounts of tragic encounters between the Indians and the early settlers, this one has an amusing twist to it. Reprinted from Max Greene, *The Kanzas Region* (New York: Fowler and Wells, 1856), pp. 26–28.]

It is related by Sage, that, on one occasion, being out with his friend Grin, in search of a fertile stampede at which to recruit their teams, they had wandered some miles out of sight of the caravan, when, upon descending the ridge of a mound into the hollow beyond, they were summarily confronted by a party of Pawnees. Without pausing to reflect, the traders turned their horses' heads, and galloped back the way they had come. The red-skins gave rapid chase, and their arrows began to whistle on the still air.

"There are five hundred of the devils!" exclaimed Grin to his companion.

"There are not forty," said Sage.

"Twenty dollars on it that there are forty," was rejoined.

"Twenty dollars then is the figure," said Sage.

And not slacking their speed for an instant, the hands of the doughty disputants were grasped in confirmation of the bet.

"And now, how are we to know who wins?" was the query.

"I'll count them!" said Grin; and "suiting the action to the word," the veteran of the woods wheeled full upon the face of the assailants, and extending the forefinger of his left hand, while his right grasped a revolver, deliberately began counting, "One, two, three, four," and so on.

Amazed at this turn of affairs, and not knowing what to make of it, the foremost Pawnee, almost within scalping distance, drew in his pony; the others came to a halt; then seized with dismay at the assurance which enabled a lone man upon the prairie to breast the full tide of their charge, and not being able to surmise what invisible danger was about to burst upon them, their hearts failed them, and, hurry-skurry, they bolted off at every point.

"Eighteen, nineteen, twenty, twenty-one, twenty-two"; and the lank finger of the trader slowly wagged in the direction of the receding forms, as Sage, taking a curve, came around to his aid.

"Thirty-seven, thirty-eight, thirty-nine!" he uttered with animation, as the last dusky figure dodged behind the crest of the mount; and turning, with a complacent smile,—"There must have been forty; who wins?"

"Make it a draw game, and I'll stand treat," answered Sage: and the chums amicably continued together their quest for water and grass.

CORN ROWS

[Glib-tongued promoters of new towns in Kansas Territory resorted to all the tricks in advertising to lure people to the state. Town sites were said to be spread over the state as thickly as fleas on a dog's back. Reprinted from Will E. Stoke, *Episodes of Early Days in Central and Western Kansas* (Great Bend, Kansas: Privately printed, 1926), I, 110.]

A traveler in Kansas, crossing a prairie the other day, came upon a man with a plow, who seemed to be preparing the land for agricultural purposes.

"My friend," said the traveler, addressing the long whiskered man in high top boots, shirt sleeves and a broad brimmed hat, "ain't you laying off them corn rows quite a distance apart?"

"Corn rows? How come?"

"Yes, those rows over there on the prairie!"

"Gosh-all-hemlocks, stranger," exclaimed the Kansas man, as he spat at a prairie dog hole a couple of yards away and scored a bull's eye, "is it possible you hain't heard of it yet?"

"Heard of what?" asked the traveler.

"Why, this here boom. Man alive, where you been? Them ain't corn rows over there. They's streets an' alleys, an' this here's a city. You are right now a-straddlin' the corner uv Commercial Street and Emporium Avenue where we aim to build the hotel with forty rooms. No, sir, this here ain't no corn patch, not by a durn sight."

SWEET REVENGE

[When a stagecoach driver got into a town at the end of his run, he often became involved in all the deviltry going on. Reprinted from G. D. Greeman, *Midnight and Noonday, or Dark Deeds Unraveled* (Caldwell, Kansas: Privately printed, 1892), pp. 271–274.]

The incident which I am going to relate, happened during the first few months after Caldwell's connection with Wichita by the stage line. The driver of the stage was a young man addicted to the habit of drinking whiskey. The settlers in and around Caldwell made the necessary arrangements to have a little pleasure, by giving a public ball, all men invited who cared to "trip the light fantastic toe" and the consequences were that the larger proportion of the crowd, were a class of disorderly and drinking people.

The stage driver was in town, on the evening of the ball, and he, being a lover of that fascinating art, known as dancing, concluded to avail himself of the present opportunity, and seek the company of some young lady to accompany him as a partner to the ball room.

He had been drinking since his arrival in town and the result was that when the hour came for him to appear for the young lady, he was very much intoxicated. The young lady was working at the City Hotel.

The young lady declined to accept the honor of his company, on account of his drunkenness. He considered her refusal as an insult, and as a solace, he went to the saloon and sought to drive evil thoughts and care from his mind, by filling himself full of whiskey. He was so drunk the following morning that a new stage driver was in demand and the stage made its accustomed trip, but with a new driver however.

About noon some one went to the stage driver and told him if he did not stop drinking, and "sober up" he would be discharged as stage driver. This information had the desired effect upon the driver, and about five o'clock in the afternoon, he was sober enough to go to the hotel and get his supper.

As he entered the door of the hotel, he saw the young lady, who had refused to go to the ball with him, go into the back yard, with a pan of dish water to empty into a swill barrel. He quietly approached unknown to her and as she was in the act of emptying the water into the barrel, he took hold of her feet and gently dropped her head first into the barrel of swill, then turned and ran away.

I was standing in the door of the blacksmith shop, and saw the whole proceeding, and, in company with a man, who was also a blacksmith, I ran across the street to get the girl out of the barrel.

The barrel was overflowing with dishwater and refuse from the kitchen; the girl was kicking and struggling to get out of her predicament, when we arrived on the scene. Had I not understood the blacksmith's trade and been accustomed to handling kicking animals, I should have used much hesitancy in venturing so near the barrel. We saw it useless to attempt to pull her out, by the feet, so we tipped the barrel over, girl and all. She was nearly drowned, and wallowed around in the dish water and finally succeeded in gaining "terra firma." When she wiped the greasy water out of her eyes sufficiently to see us, she began to "read our title clear," and almost tore up the ground in her rage. We protested our innocence and related the circumstances to her; she kept up her abusive talk, until quite a crowd of people arrived on the scene. Some of the people laughed, and I could not help but laugh to see the girl standing with her dress bedaubed with dishwater, her hair filled with coffee grounds, potato parings and dirty grease. The men became very indignant over the affair and had not the landlady come to our rescue, confirmed our statement, we would have, probably, been used in a rough manner by the bystanders. But when they found the stage driver had put the girl into the barrel, they went to a saloon, found him, and the trouble was settled by treating the crowd to all the whiskey they wanted to drink.

HE GOOT HORSE

[Anyone who acquired property by trading needed to be alert during the transaction to be sure the trader did not get the better of him. Reprinted from Will E. Stoke, *Episodes of Early Days in Central and Western Kansas*, pp. 187–188.]

A man came riding up the street on a tough looking but apparently sound and serviceable mule. A big German settler accosted him with:

"How you trade mit me for horse?"

The other looked about for the horse, and asked: "What kind of a horse? Where is it?"

"Oh, he goot horse—he no look so goot, but he goot horse."

The German brought around his horse leading him, again saying: "He not look goot, but you c'n ride him. How you trade?"

The man sized up the animal, which was a fair sized horse, apparently not old, and said, as a venture: "Give you five dollars to boot."

"All right, I trade," said the German, "he no look so goot but he fine horse."

The man forked over the five, skinned the saddle off the mule and put it on the horse, mounted and started off. After a few steps the horse stumbled over a bump in the ground and fell. The rider got up, jerked the horse to his feet and again looked him over. This time he got in front of the animal, and immediately discovered the trouble.

"Why, you blamed Dutchman, this horse is blind," he exclaimed.

"Well, dat's all right; I did tell you two, three times, he no 'look goot.' Vat you tink, he no look' goot?"

"Ain't it the truth," said the man, and he led his blind horse away, knowing he had been bested by the other man.

JUSTICE JOYCE

[The administration of justice on the frontier passed through several phases. First there were vigilance committees; then came the lawyers, legislation was enacted, and courts were established. Some of the early-day legal lights were remarkable characters and their courtroom procedures were no less remarkable. This story about a witty Irishman who was a justice of the peace in Hays, Kansas, is reprinted from Robert Marr Wright, "Personal Reminiscences of Frontier Life in Southwestern Kansas," *Kansas Historical Collections*, VII (1901–1902), 74.]

One day, near Hays City, two section-hands (both Irish) got into an altercation. One came at the other with a spike hammer. The other struck him over the head with a shovel, fracturing his skull and instantly killing him. There was no one present. The man who did the deed came, gave himself up, told a reasonable story and was very penitent. Citizens went out and investigated, and concluded it was in self-defense. When the Irishman was put on trial, Justice Joyce asked the prisoner the usual question, "Are you guilty, or not guilty?" "Guilty, your honor," answered the prisoner. "Shut your darned mouth," said Joyce; "I discharge you for want of evidence."

HANGING THE JURY

[In the days when Polk Cline was practicing law in Rush County, part of the lawyer's technique was stacking the jury against the other fellow. Reprinted from "Twice Told Tales," *Kansas Magazine*, Ser. 3, IV (November, 1910), 103. "Twice Told Tales" was a regular feature, one or two brief stories being given in each issue. Many appeared without reference to the original source.]

One time a Russian accused of horse stealing retained Polk Cline to defend. "The proof was evident, the presumption great." The Cossack had been caught with the horse in his possession. The county was poor. The County Attorney, anxious for re-election, hated to make big cost bills. If the jury could be hung a time or two, he would dismiss the case rather than pile up a bill of costs.

The jury was empanelled in the evening and dismissed to try the case the next day. Polk went to one of the jurors whom he knew to be "practical" and said to him: "Bill, if you'll hang that jury I'll give you fifteen dollars." "All right," said Bill, "I'll do it."

The case was tried with the usual jockeying, objections, and Black Hill speeches and the jury retired. After being out thirty-six hours they reported they could not agree and were dismissed. The practical juror came to Polk's office and collected his fifteen dollars. "Polk," he said, "I had a devil of a time hanging that jury. 'leven of them damn fools wanted to acquit that feller."

FOR MECHANICAL PURPOSES

[The Prohibition era was the source of many amusing incidents and episodes. The following story tells of the distinguished Kansas lawyer who found himself out of beer one Saturday night. Reprinted from "Twice Told Tales," *Kansas Magazine*, Ser. 3, IV (December, 1910), 85.]

It was in the days when one had to "sign up" for beer and allege that it was for "medical, mechanical or scientific purposes." The druggist had the beer but insisted that the purchaser must sign up, and asked what disease he should put in the affidavit. Bill studied. He never had had anything but the mumps and the measles and he wasn't sure that was a specific for either. A bright thought struck him. "You have the right to sell for mechanical purposes," said he. "Yes," said the druggist. "Well, I want this for mechanical purposes." So the druggist filled out the affidavit "for mechanical purposes." Bill got the beer and was leaving when the druggist said, "By the way, what mechanical purpose do you use beer for?" Bill fixed the beer under his arm, looked the druggist firmly in the eye and said, "I want it to grease a buggy with."

THE FLYING JAYHAWK

[The mythical Jayhawk of Kansas at times is a practical joker. According to Kirke Mechem, "The following is an army pilot's account, in 1944, of a weird flight 'in a B-777, one of the new seven-motor bombers.' This plane, strangely enough, had been christened 'The Flying Jayhawk.' On its fuselage there was a painting of the sponsor, going into action with three pairs of dice. Clutched in its right claw there were a three and a four, in its left a two and a five, while from its beak it rolled out a six and a one. This interview is from the Wichita *Beagle*." Reprinted from Kirke Mechem, "The Mythical Jayhawk," *Kansas Historical Quarterly*, XIII (February, 1944), 11–13.]

We were on a routine flight returning to Wichita, loafing along at 8,000 feet. A little this side of Hutchinson I heard a swishing sound above the roar of the plane. Then something passed us, a sort of shadow, going like a bat out of hell. As it went by it kind of wailed, though maybe it was more like a loud swoosh. From the sound I figured it for one of those new jet-propelled jobs. Then I heard Sergeant Goober's voice in my ear phone.

"Good God, Lieutenant! Look!" he yelled. "It's got feathers!"

By that time it was too far away for me to make out. But it was plain that it was the biggest and fastest thing I'd ever seen in the air. My heart did an outside loop—laugh if you want to—but for a second it came over me that this was some secret plane the Nazis had suddenly turned loose on us. Then Goober's voice came in again.

"Lieutenant!" he said, "It's stopped!"

He was right. It had stopped dead, in the air! Then it started forward. Then it let down its left claw.

Yeah, I said claw! Foot. Leg. Whatever you want to call it. But it wasn't a wheel. That's the only thing the whole crew agrees on. Bright and shiny—yellow—but no part of any normal landing gear. And it kept on letting it down. Every once in a while it would knife up into the air and maybe do a couple of impossible rolls, as if calling attention to itself. Then it would swoosh down and dangle that yellow left claw at us again.

This kept up till we were over Wichita. But when we approached the airport it zoomed up out of sight. For a second I thought it had left us. But as I circled the field I could hear the swoosh louder than ever and I realized that it was right above us. Then, as I settled in for a landing, Goober came into my ear with a shriek.

"Lieutenant! Lieutenant!" he yelled. "It's sending its claws into us!"

My first thought was to give her the gun. Why I didn't I'll never know. Instead, I made a normal landing and the swooshing sound faded away. Then the plane suddenly toppled over sideways. I had landed with the left wheel gone!

Well, that's my story. If I'm stuck with it so is Goober and the rest of the crew. Goober says this whatever-it-was looked exactly like the picture of the Jayhawk we've got on the plane. I wouldn't know, I don't see so well. Besides, Goober is a K.U. man and has funny ideas. Too funny, and could be he's giving 'em to me. You see, when I came out of the hangar, still wiping off the sweat, right in front of me, sitting on a fence, was a bird the size of a wren, exactly the same! Big yellow beak and all, except this one had on boots! I stopped, popeyed. The bird looked at me a second then let out a squawk like a Bronx cheer. When he flew off he made a faint swooshing sound, like a baby sky-rocket.

FIGHTING A GRIZZLY

[Kansas Territory at one time extended to the foot of the Rocky Mountains. In those very early days before the western lands had been settled, grizzly bears wandered down from the mountains to the prairie and on occasion attacked trappers and explorers. The following story is still told to hunters gathered around the campfire at the close of day. Reprinted from Charles Brandon Boynton and T. B. Mason, *A Journey Through Kansas*

(Cincinnati: Moore, Wilstach, Keys and Company, 1855),
pp. 177–179.]

Grizzly bears grow as *large as the law allows.* Some of them
will weigh eighteen hundred, and if a man should see one of
these critters walking up to him on his hind feet and swinging his
fore-paws, he would be apt to think he was *going to the Legisla-
tur'* mighty quick. Even an Indian is often terribly scared by one
of these bears. We camped one evening, just at sunset, by the
side of a small creek in the prairie, and a little beyond was tall
prairie-grass and some small bushes. One of the younger Indians
strayed over among these, looking for game. In a few moments
we heard first his gun, then the war-whoop, then a yell which
was prolonged to a continuous scream. Then the scared Indian
broke cover on a clean run, loping for life, and close at his heels
a grizzly bear that shuffled and shook as he ran, as if he hadn't
a bone in his body. A Frenchman seized his gun and ran to meet
them, and fired at the bear without stopping him; and then he
too turned, and the two came on in double quick time, the bear
striking and snapping at their rear. In a moment more he was
in the reach of all our guns, and we brought him to a dead halt.
But not the poor Indian. He ran through the camp, giving the
war-whoop at every leap, and went far beyond into the prairie,
before he could be brought up and made to know where he was.
An old hunter is never anxious to 'scrape acquaintance' with a
grizzly bear. One who knows them will not shoot at one from
choice, except with at least an ounce ball, and when he feels entirely certain of a dead shot. The hunters are willing to give them
a wide berth, unless they have greatly the advantage. I saw in the
mountains a man whose arms and chest were stripped nearly
bare of flesh, and who was covered with scars elsewhere, from a
battle with one of these bears. He was a Frenchman, and he and
a companion were hunting and traveling alone, and were, of
course, strongly bound to each other. They met unexpectedly,
one day, a grizzly bear, who at once attacked them. They both
fired, and having only wounded the animal, they both turned
and ran. After having gained some distance ahead, one looked
back and saw that the bear had caught his companion, and that
he was making desperate efforts to defend himself with his hunter's knife, while the bear was tearing his flesh in the most horrid

manner. His regard for his companion overcame his love of life, and he resolved to aid him or die with him. He ran back, and as he could not wait to reload his gun, he attacked the bear with his knife and hatchet. After a desperate conflict, in which both were dreadfully mangled, the bear fell partly upon one and died. For a long time neither was able to rise. The flesh upon the arms and chest and face of the one first overtaken by the bear was torn into strings, or stripped entirely off, so that the bones lay bare, yet no artery was cut. The other was at length able to crawl on his belly to a spring at some distance, and obtain some water for himself and his friend. For days he crawled thus back and forth for water, unable to rise upon his feet; and when their little stock of food was gone, they cut pieces from the bear and ate them raw, drinking water from the spring. Often, he told me, the wolves would come and eat on one side of the bear while they lay on the other. The one least hurt recovered so as to nurse his companion, whose frightful wounds began to heal, and in the end they were relieved by a party of trappers. The one I saw had very little meat left on him. Better let a grizzly alone if you can't put an ounce ball through the vitals.

FOLKTALES FROM OTHER LANDS

ZAVOLANA SMRT (DEATH IS CALLED)

[Collected from Mrs. Maurine Ehrlich of Atwood, Kansas, by Donald Chandler, 29 June 1957. Mrs. Ehrlich learned the story from her mother at Jennings, Kansas, about 1925. Her mother, Anna Haflina Shimmick, was born in Kanin, Czechoslovakia. According to Mrs. Ehrlich, this story was often told to children when they made the remark, "I wish I were dead."]

A feeble, white-haired old man trudged haltingly behind a wheelbarrow filled with dried wood and twigs. He was shaking with the cold for the wind was sharp and his worn clothes were thin.

The tottering man had no children to help him with his work. As he paused to rest his aching arms, he muttered, "Oh! What a burden my life is. If only death would come, to relieve me of my troubles."

Hardly had he spoken until death appeared, scythe in hand, and asked, "Why did you call? Poor man, what do you want?"

The frightened old gentlemen replied, "I called to ask if you would be so kind as to push my wheelbarrow home for me."

THE GIRL WHO WAS SCARED TO DEATH

[Collected from Mrs. Ivan Westerhaus, of Marion, Kansas, by Bettie Nebergall, her daughter, 7 July 1958. Mrs. Westerhaus learned this story from her mother, Mrs. Katherine Breidenstein, who was born in Lauderbach, Germany.]

Several young people were at a party and were eager to find something different to do. Someone offered the dare that no one would volunteer to go to a cemetery and drive a stick into a grave. After a long silence, one young girl said she would go and would return in a very short time. She went to the grave, plunged the stick into the grave and turned away. In the dark she had driven the stick through her long skirt. When she turned to run she could not move. Horrified that death's hand had reached out from the grave to stop her, she collapsed and died. Her friends found her still pinned to the grave.

THE LITTLE GLASSMAN

[Collected from Mrs. Ruth Thomas of Osawatomie, Kansas, by Jean Koerner of Kansas State University, in 1959. Mrs. Thomas explained that this story of the good and bad spirits of the Black Forest in Germany is an old, old one, and that it was told by mothers to their children.]

The good spirit is known as the Little Glassman. He is very tiny and can change himself into any other form at will to hide from those who are seeking him. He is gentle and kind and tries to help all the people who need him. There is also a legend that anyone who was born at midnight, or rather between twelve on Saturday and one on Sunday night, could, if he found the Little Glassman, have granted any three wishes he would make. The first two the Little Glassman must grant, but if the third one was foolish, he might refuse to grant it and save the wish for some time when the person really needed it and asked for something worth while.

The evil spirit is the Hollander Michael, a huge woodsman

with high hip boots, who rollicks, roisters, and fights. He never appears except during a terrific storm when the trees of the Black Forest are broken and wrecked and many homes are harmed. Those who seek him must go out in this storm to find him.]

Many years ago there lived in the Black Forest a poor widow whose husband had been killed working as a woodcutter there. She had only herself and a son whose name was Peter. She supported herself and the boy by gathering fallen wood and selling it for kindling. When Peter was about seventeen, his mother became very ill and the doctor could do nothing for her. Peter was one of the children who had been born at the right time on Saturday night, so he went into the forest to find the Little Glassman and ask that his mother be spared. He walked into the forest to the place where the Little Glassman should be found and searched and searched. At last he saw a tiny being, who looked almost like a squirrel, dart behind the bole of a huge tree. Hurriedly, Peter repeated the verse which goes with the request for the little spirit to show himself to the Sunday's child. Immediately the Little Glassman came out from behind the bole of the tree and asked Peter what he wished. Peter first asked that his mother get well, and this the Little Glassman granted gladly; then he asked what the second wish was. Peter waited and thought and eventually made the wish that he would always have as much money in his pockets as one of the very wealthy young men of the neighborhood had. The Little Glassman was very angry at this and granted it but said, "I will not give you your third wish, as you may some day need something much worse than you do now, and so you will have to wait for that." Peter was quite angry and went away vowing that he would never look for the Little Glassman again.

He returned to his home and found his mother much improved. He had already reached in his pockets and found a large amount of money there, so he was very happy. The years went by and Peter and his mother lived a much more pleasant life. Peter met and fell in love with a beautiful girl by the name of Elizabeth. They were married and lived in a new home near his mother. Since there was always money in his pocket, Peter made no attempt to work and continued to run about and have a good time. His mother was very unhappy about this, but it bothered

Peter not at all. Elizabeth, too, was rather unhappy about Peter's not caring about having something useful to do, but since she loved him, she overlooked it, and tried to be as happy as possible. They had two lovely children, a boy and a girl.

Suddenly one evening when Peter had been gambling with some of the other young men, he reached in his pocket for some money and it was empty. Peter was startled and could not believe it. He felt again in all his pockets, and sure enough they were empty. He went home and the next day he heard that the man whom he had made his wish about had lost all *his* money. Peter was most unhappy and went out to look for work, but there was little work to be found, especially as he had done nothing to gain experience. At last in desperation he decided to go to the Hollander Michael since he felt that he did not want to return to the Little Glassman. He journeyed far into the forest and stayed at a woodcutter's cottage until a storm came. As soon as one started, he went out into the wood. The wind howled and shrieked, the rain fell in torrents, and the trees snapped and broke about him. He was frightened but he went on. He finally found a gigantic woodsman of striking appearance working with others and asked if he were the Hollander Michael. When he was answered in the affirmative, he requested that he might talk to him.

When he told Michael what he wanted, he was told that he might have money, but he would have to give the Hollander his heart and have it replaced with a glass one. Moreover, when needed, he must go with the Hollander and cut down logs, which they would float down the river to the sea and sell to lumber mills. Peter agreed and was taken to a cabin where his heart was removed and replaced with a glass one.

He returned to his home and from that time on he had no cares or worries. He spent money freely and caroused with other rowdies. His mother died of a broken heart and Elizabeth was very unhappy. The children were afraid of their father, but nothing worried Peter. At last Elizabeth became very ill and was expected to die. This finally worried Peter enough, in spite of the glass heart, so that he decided to return again to the Little Glassman and ask for his third wish.

He went into the forest and hunted and hunted everywhere. At last, weary and worn out, he lay down at the foot of a huge oak tree. He awakened to hear what he thought was a squirrel scampering up the tree. Remembering the last time, he hastily repeated his verse and sure enough the Little Glassman was there. He asked what Peter wanted, and when Peter told him, he took a small cross from his pocket and gave it to Peter. He told him that he was to find the Hollander Michael, and when he did, he was to tell him that he did not believe that he had ever had his own heart replaced with a glass one. To tempt the Hollander, he was to tell him he would not believe that he had a glass heart unless he put the old one back so that he could tell the difference. When the old heart was in, he was to take the cross out and hold it before him. When Peter returned to Elizabeth and was his old self, the Little Glassman promised Peter that she would get well because that was the reason she was letting herself die.

Peter did as he was told, and the Hollander Michael faded away as soon as he saw the cross. Peter went home and Elizabeth got well. Peter found a job at which he made an adequate living, and the little family lived happily from then on.

LEGENDS

WILLIAM E. KOCH and MARY FRANCES WHITE
Kansas State University

To ascertain that the narratives presented in this study were legends in the true sense of the word, we have applied three criteria: they must be said to have occurred at a certain place and time, for this is evidence that they have been popularly accepted as historical truth; they must contain some supernatural element or other embellishment which would distinguish them from oral history; and they must include at least one established folk motif to demonstrate that they are made of the type of material that is the very essence of folklore.

The first of these criteria—popular acceptance as historical truth—is set up as a means of differentiating the legend from the Märchen-type folktale. Unlike the folktale, which moves in an unreal world and functions primarily as entertainment, the legend is considered by its narrators to be true and is told with historical intent.

The second criterion—presence of a supernatural element or other embellishment—determines whether we are dealing with a legend or with a historical reminiscence. The historical reminiscence is spoken history. As eyewitness testimony and as a source of local color and other background information, it can be an important aid to the historian; moreover, it performs a valuable auxiliary service in chronicling aspects of life which are not always conveniently recorded by the historian. The legend often begins as spoken history; however, as it is told and retold it accumulates trappings, frequently of a supernatural character, which enrich its narrative interest but damage its reliability.

The third test becomes necessary when a legend is derived from printed sources, as are several included here. The professional collection of folklore in the oral tradition is a recent development, and it was in earlier times that the tradition flourished. Today the people who might have been informants are dead, and their knowledge cannot be recovered from a living source. As a consequence, the folklorist must turn to printed accounts which have captured and reflect an oral tradition. In doing so, however, he must constantly guard against using materials which had their only life on the printed page. With experience, he develops the capacity to sense whether or not an account has the feel of folk materials. Once he has detected the presence of an oral tradition in a printed narrative, he seeks objective tests to confirm this subjective judgment. One test is to determine whether the story contains folk motifs such as those found in tales which demonstrably exist in oral tradition.[1] If it can be shown that the story appears in different versions, it is additional confirmation.

In selecting materials from printed sources for inclusion in this study, we have exercised some care. Of the dozen legends which were not obtained firsthand from living people, all but three are reprinted from the earliest available accounts. To avoid presenting material with which the reader may be familiar, we have drawn mostly on newspapers and magazines. When variants of a story are included, one is a contemporary version.

GHOST LEGENDS

TAKALUMA, THE PHANTOM INDIAN

[Floyd Benjamin Streeter recounts the story told to him by the man who met and talked to a ghost late at night, 23 January 1879. Mr. Streeter does not identify this man, but he gives the story in the language of his informant, a cowboy. Reprinted from *The Aerend,* IV (Winter, 1933), 157–159.]

I am a graduate of a college of the East and am not given to indulgences of absurd fancies, and yet the experience I met with last Thursday night was so remarkable in its character that I am almost inclined to believe it an hallucination, notwithstanding it is still so vividly engraved on the tablets of my memory.

[1] Motif analyses of these legends, referring to Stith Thompson's *Motif-Index of Folk-Literature,* will be found in the Appendix, beginning on page 242.

I was engaged in herding cattle by the Saline River in the northern part of Ellis County, Kansas, and on the night mentioned I was belated several miles down the Saline from my camp in Oak Canyon. Not desiring to remain away from camp over night, I urged my jaded horse along up the river until I came to the crossing below Phil Mock's claim, when he suddenly came to a standstill and resisted every effort to induce him to move. Just then the most terrible yell that ever waked the midnight stillness of earth greeted my ears, and looking forward, in the murky gloom I beheld an apparition that chilled the very marrow of my bones. A large powerful-looking Indian—the most perfect specimen of manhood my eyes ever beheld—stood before me. To grasp my revolver and fire at the red man was but the work of an instant; but the result was the most startling shock my nervous system has ever received. The Indian stood erect, unharmed, laughed a low mocking laugh, and then in tones of purest English said: "Does the White Man think his bullet can harm the spirit of Takaluma, the great chief of Inciennes, that has wandered by this beautiful water for more than a thousand years? White Man, I have but little time to talk and I would tell you a tale of wrong and ask you to see that it is redressed."

By this time my fear had merged into a feeling of curiosity and recklessness, and I remarked that if he desired to talk, I would dismount and build a fire. I did so, and the Phantom-Indian, or whatever it was, continued.

"If White Man would be satisfied that I am a spirit from another world, let him feel of this hand my substance."

I did so, and as sure as the whale swallowed Jonah, my hand swept through space. Having thus satisfied myself as to the real phantom character of the form that stood before me, I told him to proceed.

"My people," he continued, "came from the West as many suns ago as the trees of the forest have leaves. They crossed the great water when it was but a little stream between the land of Nod, where dwell the almond-eyed Chinee (heathen Chinee) whose chronology contains an account of the Great Water which destroyed all living things, and of a fertile land beyond. My people in search of this land traveled East for many moons, until coming into this valley. Charmed with its beauty and satisfied with the abundance of game, they built their wigwams and made it their home. Soon, however, a pestilence made its appearance among them, which gathered them all to the happy hunting grounds. Their wigwams decayed and nothing remains to mark the place where once dwelt a mighty people. For years their rest was undisturbed, but at last the white man came, and with his plowshare disturbed the rest of my people."

Just here it occurred to me that he was very familiar with the language, habits, and occupations of the white man, and I propounded a question as to how he had obtained all this store of knowledge, to which he replied that association with the spirits of other nations had advised him; his people had spoken the Hebrew language. He continued:

"A few months ago the bones of my father were exhumed and his skull carried away by a resident of this valley. Since then, for an hour each night, I am compelled to wander and search for it, and I ask you to use your influence to have it returned to its resting place. Well know I the party who desecrated my father's grave, but I have not the power to enter habitations. But should the skull not be returned before two more moons shall have waned, then woe to the robbers of the dead, for a spirit will be sent in search of it, with full power to effect an entrance anywhere. My hour is up. I must now return to the mound of my damp sepulchre. Farewell!"

It is to be hoped that the person who carried away the skull of this Indian heeded the warning and returned it so that it is not necessary for spirits to continue their prowling around on cold nights.

A PHANTOM TRAIN ON THE KANSAS PACIFIC

[Allegedly there were a dozen eyewitnesses to the occurrence described here by Mr. J. F. Timmons, a Wyandotte County farmer. Edwardsville was twelve miles west of Kansas City on the Kansas Pacific Railroad. Reprinted from the Atchison *Globe,* 7 August 1878.]

Edwardsville, July 31, 1878.—Last Tuesday morning, the section men on the K. P. road on my farm, seeing the storm coming up very fast, got their handcar on the track and started full speed for Edwardsville. They had run but a little ways when the entire crowd at the same time saw coming around the curve east of Edwardsville what they supposed to be a locomotive at full speed. They jumped down and took their car off the track as fast as possible, when they saw it was not a locomotive. Whatever it was came down the track giving off a volume of dense smoke with occasional flashes resembling a headlight in the center of smoke. It came three-fourths of a mile from where they first saw it, then turned off the track at a pile of cordwood, went round it once, then went off in a southwesterly direction, through a thick wood. The section men came running to my house evidently much frightened and bewildered by what they saw. What was it?

THE MIDNIGHT HARVESTER

[Mr. Henry Swanzey, living on a farm between Iowa Point and Highland in Doniphan County, had a strange experience which caused a good deal of excitement in the neighborhood. This account appeared in the local paper at the time. The appearance of a benevolent revenant to complete an unfinished task is a common folk motif. Reprinted from Sol Miller, "A Wonderful Tale," *Commonwealth* (Topeka), 7 August 1885.]

Mr. Swanzey had been harvesting, and at sundown had turned out for the night. As is usual on such occasions, the machine, a self-binder, was left at a corner nearest the house, handy for the next day's work. All the grain that had been cut that day had been shocked up and no bundles left lying on the ground. About midnight, Mr. Swanzey woke up, and through the still night air he thought he heard the noise as of a reaper in motion. At first he paid no attention to it but as he became more awake and the noise more distinct and regular, he concluded he would see what it was. He got up and went out of the house, and the noise of the machine indicating that it was in the field, he went in that direction. On arriving at the place where he had left the machine, he was somewhat surprised to see that it was gone, and as he heard it on the opposite side of the field, concluded to wait until it came around. As it made the turn coming down the end, he was more astonished to see hitched to it four fine large white horses, and driving them a person he did not know, although he thought he recognized an old-time neighbor, who had been dead for several years. When the horses got within thirty yards of him he called out to the driver and wanted to know who he was and what he meant by such proceedings. No sooner had he spoken than the team stopped, the driver got down from his seat and began to unhitch them. The farmer was getting alarmed, and giving a yell, started toward the machine, but before he got there horses and driver suddenly disappeared, and apparently into the ground. The farmer then went back to the house, and calling one of his sons and hired hands, went back to the field to examine more closely into the mysterious proceedings; but beyond the fact that the machine was some fifty yards from where it was left the evening before, and that three rows of bundles were found around the field, nothing was to be seen or heard. There is not a person in the neighborhood who has four white horses, and the question is, who and what was it that was doing the harvesting?

THE RUNAWAY TRACTOR

[Mechanization does not deter marvels in folklore. Collected from Donald White of Bennington, Kansas, in 1960, by Janet White, a Kansas State student.]

My great-uncle bought a farm a number of years ago on which was a house believed to be haunted in early days, but in later years the ghost stories had nearly been forgotten. Then a few years ago while working in a field on this farm he observed a storm approaching, so he drove the tractor to the house and parked it for the night. Later that evening the storm came up in full force with wind, rain, and lightning. As the storm began to fade it seemed they could hear a tractor running. Upon looking out the door they saw the tractor, which had been left the evening before, was running and moving in circles. My uncle went out and stopped the tractor. They investigated to see if someone had attempted to start the tractor to use it to pull themselves out of the mud, but there were no tracks about at all. Since it had rained, any tracks would have been plainly visible.

To this day there are no definite facts as to what started the tractor.

It is assumed that lightning struck the starter and caused the tractor to start; it evidently had been left in gear with the steering wheel turned in such a way as to cause it to travel in a circle.

Why this should have happened on a farm which had a haunted house is mysterious.

THE HAUNTED STONE HOUSE

[In stories such as the one which follows, the interest depends not only on the events but on associations with specific landmarks and locales. In Manhattan, Kansas, for example, a certain house on Manhattan Avenue is supposed to be haunted; it is said that flashing lights have been seen in the cupola. Reprinted from the *Sherman County News,* 2 December 1887.]

About three miles from Gaylord is an old stone house which has not been occupied for three or four years. The gentleman who is authority for the story states that about a week since, he in company with a friend was returning home from town at a late hour. While passing the house mentioned, they were startled by screams of distress and groans of agony. The voice, sounding like that of a female, issued from within the building. Starting in that direction to render assistance and prevent, as they supposed, a murder, they were not a little astonished to see the house suddenly illuminated with various colored lights in which were visible several human forms, among them being that of a woman struggling for liberty. The gentlemen for an instant were so startled that they could not move from the spot. Before they recovered, the lights disappeared as suddenly as they came and the mysterious sound ceased. Not being armed, they were loth to enter the building and decided to reach home, prepare themselves, and return to investigate. As the hour was late and they had some distance to travel, they did not get back until early dawn the next morning. A close search revealed no trace of a struggle and nothing could be found to indicate that the building had been occupied for months. Knowing that it was not imagination on their part, they agreed to again visit the spot after nightfall and wait a reoccurrence of the mystery. About 11 o'clock the next night, they were stationed in a ravine near the house to await developments. After the elapse of an hour, or about 12 o'clock, they were made aware that the building was occupied, and but a few moments passed before their ears were again greeted by a repetition of the screams and groans heard the night previous. Suddenly leaping from their hiding places, they ran toward the building, and had just reached the doorsteps when it was again brightly illuminated, and before their eyes stood the same forms and that of the woman as witnessed on the first occasion. One of the gentleman discharged his revolver, in his excitement, directly into the room, when as suddenly as the report the light and figures disappeared as if into the ground. Lanterns, which had been prepared for the occasion, were made, but to no avail. Becoming considerably agitated, the gentlemen made haste to get away from the spot. Hardly had they gone a dozen yards when they were made aware that the building was again lighted up, and on looking back, the form of a woman was seen in the doorway beckoning them to return. So startling was the revelation, however, that they made haste to get away from the spot as rapidly as possible. A watch has been kept every night since and at about the usual hour the same scene occurs nightly. The gentlemen cannot fathom the secret of these strange freaks and are greatly worked up over the matter. They do not desire to frighten those who live in that vicinity; therefore we refrain from giving the location. It is stated that a party will be quietly made up from town one night this week to visit the building and investigate the truthfulness of the story.

OLD JOE'S GHOST

[As narrated to Eileen Cozine in 1956 by Fred Meyer, then around seventy years old, of Jewell County. The type of unusual animal in the tale is commonly referred to as the "Waumpus" or "Waumpus Cat" and lives in the memory of many people who were reared in the rural areas of this country. The prank of slipping a loaded .22 cartridge in the pipe bowl of an unsuspecting person was standard procedure in the early days. Few, if any, fatalities ever resulted.]

One autumn when I was a small boy, my parents were building an addition to their little homestead house. The building was being done by a young carpenter, Newt Carey, who lived about two and a half miles away. Each morning he came to work in a farm wagon drawn by a team of horses.

One morning he failed to arrive at the usual hour. When he arrived several hours late he was in a state of high excitement. It

happened as he was driving by the home of Joe X that a young
girl who was working there came running frantically to the road
and begged him to come to the house to help them, for an awful
thing had happened.

Now Joe was the neighborhood tippler. While he was an honest hardworking man when sober, he was so addicted to the use
of whiskey that it was a rare week in which he was sober more
than half of the time. The family consisted of a son David, a lad
of about twelve, and several smaller children, the youngest a
newborn babe of less than a week. The girl whose terrifying cries
attracted Newt's attention was the daughter of a neighbor whose
services had been to attend to the household duties until such
time as Mrs. X, who was still confined to her bed, would be able
to resume her household responsibilities. The day after the arrival of the new baby Old Joe, as he was familiarly known, had
suddenly and mysteriously disappeared. No one knew anything
of his whereabouts.

Now the "awful thing" to which the girl referred came about
in this way. Under the house was a small dark cellar. The only
entrance to this part of the residence was through a trap door
in the kitchen floor. As the girl was preparing breakfast, she
heard a strange noise in the cellar. While somewhat frightened,
she managed to gather courage enough to raise the trap door just
a bit, and she was shocked to see a great black woolly object
which looked to her like the uncombed head of a great giant.
She shrieked in fright and immediately closed the trap door and
pulled an organ which was standing near by over it. This evidently displeased the apparition, for he immediately set up a
loud bellowing sound and proceeded to thump on the trap door
and kitchen floor with his head and to thrash about, upsetting
boxes and bottles stored in the cellar. It was at this point that
the girl ran for help, and seeing Mr. Carey coming down the
road, implored his aid. When he arrived, he could hear the
strange object still thrashing about in the cellar. He decided it
was too much for him to tackle alone since he was unarmed, so
he hastily gave the alarm to neighbors, and within an hour several
frightened men armed with shotguns, axes, and butcher knives
had assembled. By this time the noise had ceased. Some of the
bolder, stronger men opened the trap door and, carrying a lan-

tern, went into the cellar. Aside from the fact that the contents of the shelves had been scattered around, there was nothing unusual to be seen or heard. Since Mrs. X and the children were very much afraid, some of the men stayed throughout the day and others came to sit up for the night. Nothing happened until about midnight when in one of the partition walls could be heard a weird scraping, scratching noise. This kept up for several minutes. Then there would be quiet for a while after which similar sounds could be heard in another part of the house. In the weeks that followed there would be several days and nights during which there would be no unusual happenings, and then they would reoccur with renewed vigor. This kept up throughout the winter. The neighbors would sit up until several nights had passed with no demonstration; then they would cease coming.

In the meantime a number of steps were taken to clear up the mystery. The commonly accepted theory was that Old Joe had been murdered and that his ghost was haunting the place. But where was the body? An old abandoned well which had been filled with brush and trash was cleared out, for some were sure that the body was hidden there, but they found nothing. Every ditch, brush patch, and strawstack in the immediate community was carefully searched but of no avail.

Another theory advanced was that Old Joe himself was lurking about and during the night would sneak up to the house and by some means or other cause these strange noises to scare the family and others who might be there. Or perhaps it was some prankster who took delight in scaring people. And if it were a person, they would make it hot for him, whoever he might be, if they ever caught him. To facilitate this they arranged for the village constable or someone deputized by him to be there to arrest the culprit if he were ever apprehended. One night when the regular constable was present, the group of men were passing the time away at a game of pitch. It was customary on occasions such as this for some of the men to bolster up their courage by means of nips from a bottle of whiskey. It was only natural that after a few hours of this that some of them should get to the point when their thinking was a bit confused. On this particular night the constable laid his pipe down on the table for a minute while he shuffled his cards. He picked his pipe up and relighted it, only to have a blast of gunpowder explode in his face. Both frightened and angered, he arose in his might and thundered out, "I arrest you in the name of the law." He then proceeded to nail the warrant which he carried in his pocket to the kitchen door.

To the simple country folk, many of whom were quite superstitious, there was but one explanation of these goings on. The house was haunted. For some unknown reason the ghost or ghosts frequented this house. Old Joe's mysterious departure likely entered in. Would the ghosts confine their activity to this one house, or might they not call on other homes in the community? Housewives shuddered at the thought of staying alone at night, and children dreaded to go outside or into a dark room. Even though the men acted bold and brave, inwardly they felt jittery while walking along a lonely road or by vacant houses at night. At every neighborhood gathering ghosts were the principal topic of conversation, and tales grew in weirdness as they were told over and over again.

As spring approached, the activity of the ghosts became less frequent and finally faded out altogether. Then one warm spring evening Old Joe came trudging down the road toward his home and family. After he took over again there were no more ghosts.

As time wore on, the real plan and procedure gradually came to light. Old Joe had mortgaged his crop to pay debts he had incurred to buy whiskey. Winter was coming on. The family would be without food, fuel, and money to buy other necessities. There was not even any money with which to buy whiskey. With Old Joe around, the neighbors would not likely be very sympathetic. With his being gone and the family in trouble, they would provide for their needs. So Old Joe planned for two things: to mysteriously disappear and to make it appear that the family was in dire trouble. What worse trouble could anyone have than having to live in a haunted house? Old Joe guessed right. All winter long neighbors from far and near brought in meat, flour, eggs, and other foods. The men chopped wood, and if someone noticed that a child needed a new dress or that his shoes were worn out, the word got out and soon their need was supplied. Old Joe had gone to a Nebraska town where he managed to work enough to pay for his board and whiskey. He often chuckled to himself as he read in the newspaper stories which were headlined as "The Devil Seen Alive," "Peace Officer's Pipe Explodes," etc. Credit for the skillful execution of the hoax belongs to the boy David. Just how much of the ghost activity was due to his own imitation and how much was the result of Old Joe's coaching is not known, but the fact remains that the whole thing was carried out with cleverness and precision.

The "awful thing" that appeared in the cellar on that first morning was David himself with the woolly part of an old buffalo robe over his head. He managed to skip out of the cellar and hide the robe while the neighbors were gathering.

The strange noises heard in the walls of the house were made by devices which he manipulated from his bed. The house was a one and a half story building, the upper story of which was not finished. By means of strong cords he would let a device down between the walls of the rooms, and operate it puppet fashion at will. From his sleeping quarters he had access to the walls of every room in the house.

The explosion of the constable's pipe was brought about by his unobtrusively picking up the pipe from the table, and when no one was looking he slipped a loaded cartridge in the refilled pipe.

The events of this story happened a long time ago and I now am an old man. I have never believed in ghosts but even yet as I drive down a country road past a desolate farmhouse, I often feel a cold creepy chill running down my back and find myself recalling that "awful thing" in the dark cellar and the strange noises in the walls of the home of the neighborhood drunk.

THE SHERIFF'S CLAY PIPE

[The scene of the previous narrative was Jewell County; Washington, the county in which the following story is laid, adjoins Jewell. "The Sheriff's Clay Pipe" is certainly, therefore, a shortened version of "Old Joe's Ghost." In this account a member of the posse, rather than an accomplice, drops the .22 cartridge into the law officer's pipe. The sheriff in each of the stories seems to be considered a dupe. It was because ghosts do not operate in the daytime or in lighted places that it was necessary to "blow out the lantern." Collected from a Kansas State University student, a resident of Jewell County, in 1958.]

Our neighbors who lived one-half mile north of us on a farm in Washington County, Kansas, were bothered by weird sounds at night, so they called in the sheriff to find the ghost. The sheriff came with his warrant of arrest and a posse of neighbors to help in the arrest, my father, who told me the story, being one of them. They gathered around the kitchen table to wait for the intruder, but all was quiet. Thinking that the light might be keeping the ghost away, they blew out the lantern and continued to wait but still no sounds until about one o'clock in the morning when a shot was heard and the sheriff's clay pipe was shattered and knocked from his mouth. The sheriff jumped to his feet and shouted, "There he is down the cellar, he shot at me." The lantern was quickly lighted and they all rushed down the cellar, but no ghost was to be found and there was no hole in the floor from the shot.

It was later learned that the shot was from a .22 rifle shell that had been placed in the sheriff's pipe by one of the posse while it was lying on the table in the dark. It was also learned, much later, that the sounds were made by one of the boys of the family by a set of strings and weights in the wall that were operated by him from his bed in the attic.

PLACE-NAME LEGENDS

LEGENDS OF MARAIS DES CYGNES

[The Marais des Cygnes River, called the Sage and Osage on early maps, rises in Wabaunsee County in east-central Kansas, and flows east and south near the towns of Ottawa, Osawatomie, and LaCygne to the state line. After it crosses into Missouri, it is always known as the Osage River and forms part of the man-made Lake of the Ozarks.

The legend of the Marais des Cygnes is one of the most persistent in Kansas folklore. An account of why and where the river was named usually is included in the various versions. In actuality the name probably derives from the Osage appellation *Maxackautsi*, "the spot abounding in wild swans," translated as *Marais des Cygnes* (literally "swans' marsh") by early French traders. That the word marsh should be applied to a river is not too easily explained, but the problem seems not to have concerned the raconteurs in the least. There are many variant pronunciations and designations: *Maradasine, Maradazine, Miry Desein, Miry,* and *Swan,* to list a few.

The river's name is linked with a well-known event in early Kansas history. Not far from its banks in May, 1858, border ruffians lined up and killed five men and wounded five. "Le Marais du Cygne," one of John Greenleaf Whittier's most famous anti-slavery poems, sternly protested what was called the "Marais des Cygnes Massacre," and promised revenge.

Interesting similarities and differences appear in the following three versions of the legend. The tribe to which the hero belongs is not named in Version A; in Version B he is a Comanche, and in Version C a Cheyenne. There is no agreement on the tribe in other recorded versions. In Versions A and B the heroine's abduction by the hero is motivated by her father's refusal to consent to the marriage. In Version C there is no parental conflict; the young Cheyenne suitor is accepted and leaves the camp simply to go on a hunt. Whereas in Versions A and C the canoe is swamped in flood waters, in Version B "an angry thing seized the boat and pulled it down." In Versions A and B two swans rise from the depths of the water and float away, but in Version C a "magic flight" is the manner of departure. Other versions collected but not included usually speak of flight. In Version C, the "lover's leap" motif is suggested. In both Versions B and C the legend is said to be an Osage story told to Evangeline. A study of many versions of this legend might possibly show it to be related directly to one of the episodes in the famous and delightful European "Swan Maiden" tale, but it seems unlikely.

The patent fabrications and stylistic ornaments superimposed by white men on a traditional Indian tale are revealed in these three versions. Mrs. McDowell's account (Version A), however, is quite satisfyingly natural and shows no attempt to stylize.]

Version A

[Narrated in 1957 by Mrs. J. W. McDowell of LaCygne, Kansas. In 1856, Eli Cox, Mrs. McDowell's grandfather, brought his bride to Kansas from Illinois in a covered wagon drawn by oxen. They settled in Linn County where LaCygne is now located. This legend was a favorite in the family. To quote Mrs. McDowell: "I well remember his (the grandfather's) taking me upon his knee, lighting his clay pipe, and entertaining me in this way. This is one of the stories I liked best."]

Long years before the white man came to Kansas, when the Indians lived happily upon the land, a very handsome young brave fell in love with a beautiful princess, the daughter of the tribal chief. He wished to marry the princess, but the chief refused to give his consent. One day when the river was overflowing its banks from much rain, and so wide that the brave thought his canoe could not be overtaken, he and the princess got into his canoe and he began to paddle downstream, carried rapidly by the swift current of the flooding waters. However, the chief soon discovered their flight, called his warriors to battle, and in their own canoes they gave chase, gaining very rapidly upon the two lovers. Just as it seemed that capture was inevitable, the young brave's canoe overturned and sank beneath the water, carrying with it him and his beautiful princess. The warriors watched for them to rise to the surface of the water, but never saw them again. Instead, some great distance on down stream two lovely, graceful white swans suddenly appeared upon the flooding waters and were carried swiftly downstream away from danger. Ever after, the river was known as the River of the Swan, and when the white men came and built a town near the spot where these things occurred, they called it the City of the Swan.

Version B

[As a boy living near LaCygne, Kansas, in 1871, William Ansel Mitchell learned this version of the legend from John Roubidoux, a chief of the Miami tribe (*Linn County, Kansas: A History* [Kansas City: Campbell-Gates, 1928], pp. 318–320). Although the Miami are woodland Indians, many of them had been moved to the area in which the Osages were living. In this version the river is named by Evangeline of the Acadian legend, who supposedly was spending several months with the Osages. Longfellow makes no mention of this episode in his "Evange-

line," published in 1847, but does speak of a Shawnee woman
who tells Evangeline a sorrowful tale of her murdered husband,
a *coureur de bois*.]

One day, during the routine of village work, Evangeline saw
several young boys and girls approach Sona, the Wise Mother
of the tribe, and in excited whisperings they were telling of
some unusual event.

"They have seen Coman and Osa," said the Wise Mother.
Evangeline sensed a tribal romance and to the Wise Mother she
said, "Tell me about it."

"It is," said the Wise Mother, "a long story of long ago. It es-
tranged two big tribes who have never since been friendly. It is
the story of a young war chief of the greatest prairie tribe and a
beautiful young princess of our people. Coman was the young
chieftain and he celebrated the close of a great buffalo hunt by
appearing at our village with twenty of his young and handsome
braves, all dressed in feather bonnets and beaded finery and
mounted on powerful horses. They carried ceremonial banners,
signifying peace and joy. Their visit was a great event, all our
young people, especially the maidens, dressing in their finest
to do honor to their proud guests. Osa, our princess, granddaugh-
ter of White Hair, was the comeliest among the maidens, young
and pretty and arrayed in the finest new buckskin decorated
elaborately in bead designs designating her royal station in the
tribe.

"Coman was entranced by her. He sought her constantly. Osa
manifested her admiration and attachment for him. They made
it a long and merry season and when the frost came and the
visitors must return to their prairie tribe, the parting was not a
happy one, as White Hair refused to give Osa to the great prairie
chief. Osa rebelled and threatened to follow him. The winter
was a bad one and our young people hard to manage after their
great festival with the visiting braves. But when the flood waters
were running out, and there were flowers and green leaves everywhere, on a bright May morning there appeared on that bank
across the river twenty horsemen in war bonnets and carrying
beautiful ceremonial banners. At their head was Coman, dressed
in his proudest trappings. He led a beautiful horse without a
rider, and a second glance showed it was to carry a woman.

Coman gave that beautiful and graceful salutation known as the peace sign and dismounting, got into one of our canoes to cross to us. With some difficulty he got across, but showed that he was better as a horseman than as a boatman.

"Osa was radiant as she met him. Her luggage was brought and Coman insisted they go.

"Coman was exultant in his triumph and addressing White Hair, he said: 'Coman is a great chief of a great people. We have the Land of the Sky. We have the great mountains where Manitou makes his home and mixes medicine for all his people. The eye never sees the end of our domain. Our warriors vanquish all opponents. Our lodges are filled with a great and happy people who own the hordes of buffalo on the plains, which give us both meat and clothing. Our war horses are numberless. When the Comanches put on their war bonnets it is a sight to thrill the world. Our people offer a royal welcome to Osa as the bride of Coman.'

"But White Hair was not convinced and said: 'It is not wise that it should be so. Osa is a daughter of the forest. Her home is in a land of plenty. The land produces corn and melons, and as the seasons go there are berries, persimmons, pawpaws, grapes and plums. The whole tribe could live on the pecans, walnuts and hickory nuts the forests give to us. The great trees shelter us from the storms and the heat of summer. They furnish fuel for our fires in winter. There are buffalo and deer and bear, and fish in the waters. The Osages are rich and happy and grow wise in their contentment.

" 'Why should Osa go to your country where you see far and see nothing? It is a deceptive country which smiles in the spring time and then burns up the grass and leaves the earth bare. It frowns in the winter and covers the earth with snow. It has no trees. It has no water. The buffalo and deer desert it.

" 'Your people are cruel and blood-thirsty because of the cruel country you live in. Osa should not go to live among you. The Great Spirit has placed this river between us and the sullen roar of its flood waters voices his anger.'

"Osa had an expression of dismay as she witnessed the dignified refusal of her grandfather, but stepping into the canoe she showed her decision to go with her chosen man. Coman turned the canoe into the stream and the waiting people on each side were thrilled with the beauty of the scene and its significance. With strong, confident stroke Coman forced the canoe into the flood when some angry thing below seized the boat and drew it downward out of sight. In a flash the two lovers disappeared. No trace was ever seen of them or their boat. As the horrified people looked upon the scene, a miracle happened. At the place where the lovers disappeared there was seen on the water two great white swans which swam away together through peaceful waters under a canopy of vines and flowers and wild rice.

"These swans were seen today by the children. They always return here. Their story is in the great epic poem of the Osages."

The assemblage of young people, who always listened to this story when told by the Wise Mother, arose and beckoned them to follow, going to the great cliff at the top of Timbered Mound, from which Evangeline, as she looked over the shimmering waters of lakes and river and the green valley, spread her arms as though to embrace them and said:

"C'est le marais des cygnes."
It is the marsh of the swans.

Version C

[Reprinted from the Ottawa *Campus,* XVIII (January, 1902), 191, which credited the information to Bruce Dennis of La-Cygne, Kansas.]

About the year 1786, Evangeline Bellefontaine left the Acadian settlement in Louisiana and came northward searching for her lover, Gabriel Lejeunesse, as so beautifully related by Longfellow. Crossing the Ozark Mountains, Evangeline learned from the Osage Indians the pretty Indian legend of the swans, and it was she who gave the river the name "Le Marais des Cygnes," the river of the swans. The legend as it comes from the Osages is as follows: In the early days an Indian chief, Makota, dwelt with his tribe in a beautiful spot on the banks of the river. The chief's only daughter, Nanonie, a beautiful girl of eighteen, was loved by all the young men of the tribe, but she, loving a life of freedom, gently refused all suitors. One day a young Cheyenne chief appeared and asked permission to build his lodge in the edge of the village. The request being granted, he soon became a general favorite of the tribe. He also became a frequent visitor to the old chief's lodge, and gradually won the admiration of Nanonie.

Winter passed, spring came, and the young couple were often seen strolling along the banks of the beautiful stream. It was well known that Makota was pleased with the love affair, the nuptials of which were soon to be celebrated. Just before the event, Danookee, the lover chief, started on a hunt. He parted from Nanonie on the bank of the river, promising to return in three days. But the days passed into weeks, and the weeks into months of lonely expectation, but Danookee came not. Nanonie grew pale and strangely silent, and with heavy tread and heavier heart she daily visited the spot where she had parted from her lover, and there stood gazing into the deep, quiet stream.

Autumn and winter passed, and with another spring Nanonie roamed hours on the river bank waiting for her lover who never returned. Her step became slower, her heart more sorrowful, and the beautiful Nanonie was fading away. One evening at dusk, having returned from the river bank, as she sat brooding in silence in her father's lodge, she suddenly sprang to her feet and ran to the river, crying in agonizing accents, "Danookee, Danookee!" Following her to the dark water's edge, the tribe beheld her body sinking beneath the surface of the water. Several braves sprang after her but she could not be found. Soon all was quiet and as the Indians with lighted torches stood mournfully looking into the dark waters, a sudden light shone over the stream, and there arose to its surface two beautiful swans. For a moment they remained motionless; then spreading their white wings they soared upward together, disappearing in the darkness. " 'Tis the spirits of Danookee and Nanonie," quoth they, "flying to the happy hunting grounds," and with a feeling of awe they returned to their native lodges, henceforth to tell the story of "The River of the Swans."

Legends of Waconda Springs

[Waconda Springs pool, in Mitchell County, north-central Kansas, is an ideal setting for a "lover's leap" type of legend. A physiographic phenomenon, this curious salt pool is fed from an unknown underground source and lies in a hollow mound some thirty feet high and sixty feet across. For centuries before the advent of the white man, the Plains Indians worshiped it as a supernatural force and found its waters beneficial. Sir William Johnson, who may have been the first white man to look on the pool, visited it in 1767, and it has continued to attract adventurers, geologists, historians, and travelers. A sanatorium and health resort was established there in 1906, and the spring water is still bottled and sold. The continued existence of this Kansas spa is problematic, however: if the proposed Glenn Elder Dam is constructed, Waconda will be in its flood area.

While there may have been an Indian tale of simple sacrifice connected with the spot, Waconda, the name given to the maiden of the legend in some versions, is probably a white man's appellation. According to one source,[2] *Waconda* is a Kaw word meaning God or chief divinity; the Sioux word for God, *Wakontanka*, is similar. Possibly there may be a connection between the Berkshires' "Wahconah Falls" Indian legend and the Kansas legend of Waconda Springs; in the New England legend, however, it is the male whose name is Wahconah. In some versions of the Kansas legend the maiden's name is Turtle Dove. In versions not included here, the quite common "footrace for the maiden's hand" motif appears: the loser throws himself into the pool and the maiden, too, sacrifices herself rather than marry the unloved winner. Some versions, for example Version C, show literary embellishment by popular writers.

Regardless of the findings of ethnohistorians, the cluster of romantic versions of the Waconda Springs place-name legend has satisfied thousands of present-day readers. Few books on Kansas history fail to mention the Springs, and it is the subject of at least two serious studies as well as numerous magazine and newspaper feature stories. There also have been poetic and musical treatments of the tale.

The legend probably has had a more vigorous oral tradition than any other local Kansas legend concerned with Indians.]

Version A

[Reprinted from Mabel Bingham, "The Legend of Waconda," *The Aerend,* IV (Spring, 1933), 125.]

[2] *Kansas: A Guide to the Sunflower State,* ed. Harold Evans (New York: The Viking Press, 1959), p. 328.

At one time two Indian braves were in love with a beautiful Indian maid, Waconda. In order to decide which brave should have the maiden, her father set some task for them to perform to prove which was the more worthy of his dusky daughter. Waconda was in love with one of the braves, but the other she despised. The lover of Waconda lost, so he jumped into the spring. Knowing she could not be happy without her lover, she followed him to a watery grave on the hunting grounds of the Great Spirit. Since then the spring has been called Waconda in honor of the maid who died with her lover.

Version B

[From a Kansas Historical Marker on U. S. Highway 24, three-quarters of a mile north of the spring.]

Many moons ago, so runs the Indian legend, Waconda, a beautiful Princess, fell in love with a brave of another tribe. Prevented from marriage by a blood feud, this warrior embroiled the tribes in battle. During the fight an arrow struck him as he stood on the brink of a spring and he fell mortally wounded into the waters. Waconda, grief stricken, plunged after him. Believing her soul still lived in the depths, the tribes for countless ages carried their sick to drink the healing waters. Here they celebrated their victories and mourned their losses, never neglecting to throw into the spring some token for the Great Spirit.

Version C

[Reprinted from a Waconda Springs Health Resort brochure.[3]]

Legend tells us that Waconda was the name of a beautiful Indian maid, the daughter of a tribal chief. She was the pride of her mother's tepee, the idol of her father's heart, a delight to the eyes of the young men of her tribe and the joy of all her people.

Waconda, one day, determined to explore the country, had wandered unafraid, some distance from the camp. Her ear caught a sound. It was a human cry, a call for help, and coming from a clump of bushes. She crept forward quietly until she could see the crumpled figure of a man. He was alone. Unafraid

[3] Dick Mann, associate editor of *Capper's Farmer,* gave valuable assistance on Waconda Springs history.

now, she rose and ran swiftly to him. His eyes were closed. "You are hurt. Can I help?" she asked. "Oh gentle maiden, if I could but have water. I—I am so weak from loss of blood."

"A moment and you shall have it."

Hurrying to the sparkling pool of the Great Spirit Spring, she carried as much water as her deerskin pouch would hold. The young warrior drank gratefully and tried to lift himself. "No, no, do not move. See, the blood starts, I will get more water now, and will bathe and bind your wounds." She bandaged as skillfully as she was able the deep cuts in thigh and arm from which so much blood had drained and then lifted the injured man into a more comfortable position.

"Who are you, gentle one? I would know whom to thank for so much kindness from a stranger."

But upon disclosing their names and tribes they found that their people were blood enemies. However, the call of youth was stronger than tribal loyalty and the young people talked until the sun was low. "I will bring you food," she said, "and when our hunters return will have my father bring you to our camp that you may be better cared for." "No, no! I could not enter helpless into an enemy camp. Do not be angry, oh Waconda, and do not trouble yourself about the food. Already I have taken from your hands far more than one should accept from an enemy," said the young warrior. "You are foolish, young warrior," Waconda said. "I am not your enemy. That is but our fathers' affair. I will bring the food." "My life is yours, oh Waconda of the gentle spirit," declared the injured warrior. "Whatever you ask of me, that I will do."

In the morning he was gone, but since the two hunting camps were not a great distance apart the young chief came into the vicinity again and again. Waconda met him often, at first by chance, and then by plan until the two learned to love one another. One day the young chief said, "Tomorrow, oh beloved, I go to your father to offer him many swift dogs, fine robes and other gifts that you may come and dwell with me forever in my lodge."

"I would indeed go with you gladly, oh Takota, but I fear it is hopeless. Go, however," said Waconda, "perhaps the Gods will be kind."

But they were not. The great chief, Waconda's father, listened courteously to the young man's suit and sadly to his daughter's pleading. He wished his daughter's happiness, but the tribal law against intermarriage with blood enemies was an ancient and much honored one. He could do nothing but call a council of the chiefs of both tribes and present the case for their decision.

During the council, feeling ran high between the two tribes. Angry words were spoken. And so instead of smoking the pipe of peace a challenge of war was issued and accepted and the Indians met for battle in the beautiful Solomon valley. At last the battle centered upon the little hillock whose age-old pool reflected alike the cloud-flecked blue of the sky and the fearfully-painted bodies of the warriors.

Waconda and her women stood watching not far away. Suddenly an arrow from the bow of one of her own kinsmen pierced the heart of her gallant young lover who had been fighting daringly and bravely at the pool's edge. He caught his breast, gave a despairing cry, and toppled backward into the blue-green water. Waconda darted to the spot. Flinging her arms aloft and calling upon her Gods to give back her lover, she plunged in after him. But the pool was deep and the waters closed over the sweethearts. Neither was seen again.

In awe the fighting warriors drew away and silently went to their camps. And ever afterwards, in memory of this daring and heroic sacrifice, the Red Men called this pool Waconda, the Spring of the Great Spirit, believing that the devoted shade of the Indian maid dwelt there with that of her lover. They worshiped there and made sacrifices of things they held most dear.

The Legend of Ogeese Creek

[From a letter written by C. E. Cory to Esther Clark Hill, 1 October 1931 (copy on file, Kansas State Historical Society Manuscript Collection). Ogeese Creek is in Neosho County, Kansas.]

Along in the early years of the last century, actually before there was such a place as Kansas, when the Chouteau Brothers had trading posts scattered over this region, they and their husky young French followers were the first white inhabitants. They hunted and trapped and bought furs of the Indians all over what is now South Kansas. That fact accounts for so many French streams' names. When settlement came, the fur traders disappeared. Occasionally, some of the employees at the trading post had selected a farm, married an Indian maiden, built a cabin and become a permanent citizen. One of these young Frenchmen, a born pioneer, was Jean Auguste (pronounced O-giest), whose home was a small tributary of the Neosho river, opposite Erie, Kansas. By popular usage, the stream became Auguste Creek; but of course the English speaking early settlers could not master the French pronunciation; they were too busy with other things. They did not care. They just called it Ogeese.

After while came the first publisher of a local map. He knew all about quadrants, and transits and levels; but he knew nothing of place-names, and cared less. He heard the popular name for the stream, and marked it on his map "Ogeese Creek." Other map makers followed; the name got into the public records, and probably will stay there.

LEGENDS OF VIOLENCE

THE BENDER LEGEND

[Narrated by Percy DePuy of Manhattan, Kansas, in 1958. Mr. DePuy was born twenty years after the Bender murders but within fifty miles of where they were committed. His account testifies to the persistence of the tragedy in folk memory. Except for the fact that there were four Benders instead of three, the details of his account are basically correct.

The homestead-claim on which lived John Bender and his wife and their son and daughter was situated some ten or fifteen miles northwest of Parsons, in Labette County, Kansas. It was here between the spring of 1871 and the spring of 1873 that a series of the most revolting murders in the annals of American crime was committed. In 1873 no less than eight mutilated bodies were found buried in the Bender orchard. Other missing persons were traced to the area and students of the case believe there probably were even more victims. The Bender family themselves vanished completely; no one knows what finally happened to them—

a circumstance which adds to the fascination that the story has for the folk imagination.

The hundreds of newspaper stories and magazine features about the Benders contribute many interesting side lights and speculations. John Bender, for instance, might have been the old man arrested for murder in Idaho in 1884 who bled to death trying to amputate enough of his foot so that he could remove a leg shackle. Kate Bender, the daughter, is said to have died in San Francisco.

The application of the term "legend" to this event is justified because of the mysterious disappearance of the Bender family and because of Kate Bender's reputation as a clairvoyant and "healer" with supernatural powers. In the archives of the Kansas State Historical Society is a printed handbill, reported to be one distributed in southeast Kansas. It reads as follows:

Prof. Miss Katie Bender—
Can heal all sorts of diseases; can cure Blindness, Fits, Deafness, and all such diseases, also Deaf and Dumbness. Residence 14 miles east of Independence, on the road from Independence to Osage Mission, one and one half mile South East of Norahead Station.
June 18, 1872   KATIE BENDER]

When I was quite small, we had no rural telephones and no motion picture shows to attend. Our family took newspapers and magazines and drew many books from the Carnegie Library in Girard. Consequently, we read more than most of our neighbors did. Winter evenings were long! For entertainment, families would visit back and forth in the evenings. Two or more families would collect at one of their houses. They might eat popcorn and apples and play such games as Flinch and Authors. Sometimes the old folks would just sit and gossip and the kids would stop their games to listen. There was a great deal of gossip among the neighbors, even in the summertime. A death, especially an unusual death, would become the subject of many conversations. After the story of an unusual death had been told many times, imaginary details were apt to be added to it. Some of these became weird and smacked of superstitious awe.

Girard, Kansas, is about thirty-five miles almost due east of Thayer, Kansas. A family named Bender lived near that town in the early 1870's. This family consisted of the father, mother, and a daughter named Kate. The Bender family had supposedly left the vicinity of Thayer some twenty or twenty-five years before I was born; yet it was a sort of tradition in our neighborhood. I sometimes heard the old settlers discussing atrocities committed by the Benders, with almost bated breath, almost as though the Benders might be lurking near and listening to the bitter comments about themselves.

Several times there were rumors that the Benders had been recognized in some far corner of the United States. Some people believed that the Benders had not gone far away and might still be living somewhere in southeastern Kansas. Our people feared that they might take up their atrocious habits again. All of these stories, rumors, and imaginings had a tremendous effect on the mind of a timid, sensitive kid.

I imagined that every stranger I saw might be one of the Benders with blood lust in his or her heart. Many people traveled about the country in those days in covered wagons. Some of these people were said to be gypsies. Whenever I saw one of these covered wagons, I imagined that the people in it might be the Benders. If I happened to be walking down the road, as a barefoot boy, and saw one of those wagons approaching, I was apt to slip through the fence and run off across a field to avoid meeting the wagon.

The Bender story, as I remember from my early childhood, ran something like this. The three Benders lived on a farm near Thayer, Kansas. Their home was on a country road but a rather heavily traveled road for that time. It has since become a good highway and I have traveled on it. It was paralleled by a railroad which I think is a main line of the Santa Fe south from Kansas City. I do not know whether the Benders had a sign out offering meals and lodging to travelers or not, but it seems that travelers often stopped there for the night. The Bender dining room was supposed to have been divided into two parts by a curtain. The traveler would be seated at the table with his back close to the curtain. A member of the Bender family would slip up on the opposite side of the curtain from the victim and strike him on the head with a heavy object. He would be knocked unconscious. Then a trap door in the floor would be opened and the unfortunate one would be dropped into a space under the house. There he would be finished off and his valuables taken. The body was then dragged out into the garden and buried in a shallow grave.

Relatives of missing people began to investigate the disappearances. Some of them were traced to the Bender home and no farther. People began to suspect the Benders. About this time the Benders hitched their team of horses to their wagon and drove into Thayer. The main street of Thayer parallels the railroad track. The Benders hitched their team to a hitch rack and bought tickets on the railroad. They got on a train and left! No one ever seems to have seen them after that. After the team had stood hitched to the rack for a day or longer, people became more suspicious than ever and began to investigate. They went through the Bender home and studied the arrangements. They dug in the garden and located the graves of several people. This seems to be the end of the story as I recall it now. For a number of years when I was young, there would be write-ups of the Benders in the newspapers. If I remember correctly, Kate Bender was usually given the great honor of being the most bloodthirsty member of the family and the perpetrator of most of the crimes.

BEADLE REPORT OF THE BENDERS

[J. H. Beadle, author of the following account, went to the Bender farmstead about six weeks after the family's disappearance. He is identified as "Western Correspondent" for the Cincinnati *Commercial*. Reprinted from *Western Wilds, and the Men Who Redeem Them* (Cincinnati, Chicago, and Philadelphia: 1879), pp. 434–437.]

Through these counties one often sees the poor calves tied to the fence, while their bovine mammas are driven to distant ridges for the day. And, by the way, it was a calf thus tied, abandoned and dead for want of water, which first showed that the notorious Benders had fled.

Our party of four visited the Bender farm while yet the country was ringing with the story of their crimes. Taking an open hack at Cherryvale, Montgomery County, we drove seven miles north-east over as beautiful a prairie as God ever adorned or man defiled. At that distance out we descended by a gentle slope to Murderer's Vale. On the north and east rose those picturesque mounds which so romantically diversify this region; to the south and west the fertile prairie, now dotted with cultivated fields, or brilliant with rank grass and flowers, spread as far as the eye could reach; between was a slight depression of perhaps two square miles, from which a little run put out north-east, and in the center of this happy valley was the Bender farm. If the spirit of murder was there, it was certainly the loveliest form in which that dread spirit ever stood revealed. No black and blasted heath, no dark wood or lonely gorge, such as romance makes the mute accessories of horrid crime; but the billowy prairie, rising swell on swell, as if the undulating ocean, changed to firm set earth, stood fixed and motionless forever. The house had stood in the center of this vale, two miles from the nearest neighbor, and commanding a view of all approaches for that distance. But a few weeks had passed since the murders were discovered, and yet scarcely a vestige of house or stable was left. Visitors had carried them away by splinters! Even the young trees in the orchard had been dug up and removed.

The excavation beneath the house, in which the murderers had allowed their victims to bleed before burial, still bore the horrid signs. The scant rains of summer had not washed away the blood from its margin; it was half full of purple water. In the garden the graves remained just as left when the bodies were removed. Eight bodies were found there, including that of a girl eight years old, who was murdered and buried with her father. They had been buried in all sorts of positions. One man, in a round hole, lay with his head directly between his feet. A Mr. Longcor, one of the victims, lay with his little daughter between his limbs. Besides these eight, three other missing men were traced to the neighborhood, bringing the whole number of victims up to eleven. Other murders have excited the community, but none with such circumstances of barbarity as these. It appeared, from an examination of the house (the Benders kept a sort of hotel), that the victim, when seated at the table, had his back against a loose curtain which separated the room in two apartments. Behind this curtain stood the murderer, and, at a convenient moment, dealt the unsuspecting guest a deadly blow in the back of the head with a huge hammer. He fell back, the trap-door was raised, his throat was cut, and he was tumbled into the pit to lie till the last drop of gore had ebbed away. Thence he was taken at night and buried in the garden. And these fiends incarnate, after this fearful violation of the rites of hospitality and the laws of God and man, went on with their daily life—ate and drank and slept, and perhaps rejoiced and made merry, with that dreadful pool, fast filling with the blood of their victims, just beneath their feet.

The nearest neighbor was a German, named Brockman, who was roughly treated and narrowly escaped hanging by the mob when the murders were first discovered. His account of the family is curious in the extreme, though many of the details are unfit for publication. The Benders, consisting of John Bender, Sr., his son John and daughter Kate, and their mother, were from the Franco-German portion of Alsace, and spoke both languages fluently, as also the English. They had formerly lived in Illinois, but came to Kansas in 1870, and boarded some time with Brockman; then made entry on this piece of land. They were fanatical spiritualists, and Kate Bender advertised as a clairvoyant and healing medium. The young man, her brother, who distributed her hand-bills around the country, was generally regarded as a simpleton; his mother also seemed very dull, and rarely spoke. But Kate was the genius of the family. She stated, in her moments of "exaltation," that she was a "savior come again, but in female form"; and she could raise the dead, but it would be wrong to do so. She had a "familiar spirit" which directed all the movements of the family; and several persons visited and consulted her, either from curiosity or other motive. Before burial they mutilated the victims in an obscene and disgusting manner. So thoroughly was this done that when the body of Longcor was raised it was at first supposed to be that of a woman. The excised portions of none of the bodies were ever found, though the ground was thoroughly searched; and among the few neighbors who knew anything of the family's blasphemous incantations, there are dark and horrible hints as to the disposition made of these pieces. Should we accept the half that is told by the neighbors, we must conclude that this was a family in whom every natural impulse had been imbruted; that they believed themselves in league with powers to whom they offered infernal sacrifices, and murdered for mere lust of blood. It is known that, with one exception, the victims had very little money, and that their spoils did not altogether exceed $2,500. One man was known to have had but twenty-five cents.

The escape of the Benders was long a great mystery. That a family of four persons could drive to the nearest railroad station, abandon their team there, take the train and escape all the officers and detectives set upon their track, was incredible. Nevertheless, that was the report of the local officials, and the State of Kansas, apparently, made great exertions to recapture the fugitives. "Old Man Bender" became a standing joke; every old vagabond in the country was suspected, numbers were arrested, and the Utah authorities actually sent a harmless old lunatic, captured in the mountains, back to Kansas for identification. But it was noticed that Kansas officials were rather indifferent on the subject, and in due time some of the facts leaked out. There have been sensational stories about the posse overtaking the fugitives in the groves west of the Verdigris River, where a desperate fight took place, in which both the women were "accidentally killed." Without going into particulars, it is safe to say that the Bender family "ceased to breathe" soon after their fight, and that their carcasses rotted beneath the soil of the State so scandalized by their crimes.

THE BENDERS AND FATHER PONZIGLIONE

[Account from Henrietta Elma Mann, "A Brief Historical Sketch of the Settlements of Elk County" (unpublished Master's thesis, Kansas State Teachers College, Pittsburg, 1940), pp. 94–95.]

Father Paul Ponziglione of Old Osage Mission was one of the most interesting of the preachers who came to Moline, Old Boston, and Howard in the early days. He came to Kansas for the first time in 1851 and put forth untiring efforts in this section until sent by the Jesuit Order to Milwaukee, Wisconsin in August, 1889. In 1873 this ardent Jesuit had a very narrow escape from the Bender family, which was perhaps the most notorious outlaw gang in southeastern Kansas. He was on his way back to the mission from this section and was carrying a large donation of money from Catholic friends for the erection of St. Francis Church at Osage Mission. This spring evening the Father stopped and called for lodging for the night at the Bender Wayside Inn where many crimes were committed. Something about the brutal countenance of Bender and his daughter Kate, known as the Tigress, made him uneasy. He also noticed Bender place a hammer behind a curtain close to the supper table and then hold a private conversation with his daughter. Intuition warned him to leave and as his ponies were nervous and would not eat he made an excuse that he wished to look after the team. Then he hurriedly hitched them to the buggy and made his escape before his absence was discovered. A few weeks later the murder of a Dr. York led to the discovery of the Bender crimes and the finding of seven bodies buried in the garden. The good Father continued his missionary work in this part of Kansas for many years.

THE LEGEND OF DRUM CREEK

[Narrated in 1954, by Betty Brandenburg, Independence, Kansas. According to the informant, this story was told to new-comers to town. The battle referred to may be the action of May, 1863, in which Osage Indians killed eighteen Confederates. A historical marker commemorating this event stands near Independence on Highway 160. However, the legend could have arisen during the late '60's when many white settlers were occupying land which rightfully belonged to the Osage. The Drum Creek Treaty was signed in 1870.

Placing curses on families, persons, rivers, and the like is common in folklore, as are prophecies of death at a certain time or period.]

During the early days of the settlement of Kansas, there was a battle fought on Drum Creek near Independence, Kansas, with a tribe of Indians. The Battle of Drum Creek was a bloody affair in which most of the Indians lost their lives. To pay for the loss of his tribesmen, the chief of the tribe decreed that from that time forth the waters of the nearby treacherous Verdigris River would take the life of *one white child* each year. So far as I know, the decree is still in effect and being carried out. The details I do not remember, but I am sure they are available.

AN ETIOLOGICAL LEGEND

The Legend of Famora

[This legend was found among the letters and notes in the desk of Reverend Bishop Duncan who served at the Methodist mission on the Marais des Cygnes. In 1849 an apple orchard was planted at the mission; just below it was a spring which ran down toward the river and formed a large pond. The pond was once covered with the leaves of the nelumbo (water chinguapin) plant. The Indians made bread from the delicious nuts of the plant, first removing the poisonous green embryos. Reprinted from Mary E. Jackson, *Topeka Pen and Camera Sketches* (Topeka: G. W. Crane and Company, 1890), pp. 163–164.]

In the spring of 1849 I was setting out trees when one of the Indian maids who was attending school came and watched me at work. As I placed a tall, nicely-shaped tree in the earth, she said, "Don't you call on Famora to bless your tree, so it will be of some use to the world?" "No," said I, "there is but one God, and He doeth all things well."

"Do you have a god to take care of your harvest and fruits, Wyona?" I asked. "Yes, Famora is our goddess of the vegetable world or kingdom," answered Wyona. "Tell me about Famora," I said.

"Famora was the beautiful daughter of Womoka, our chief, who came from the north and drove the Pandories (the mound builders) from this land. Large fields of yunkapins and Indian corn waved in the breeze, but my people did not know which to eat of. They found food prepared, but dared not touch any of it, lest it should be poisoned. The wild deer and rabbits were scarce, and the poor warriors were hungry. Womoka tried to persuade someone to try the grain growing in the fields, but none were brave enough to taste a morsel of any food prepared. Are we going to starve? asked Womoka. No, father, I will save my people, said Famora. I will see what is good. In vain did they try to keep her from making an attempt to eat the ripe nuts and corn. Gathering a small quantity of each, she roasted it by the fire. When taken out of the fire, she knelt down by the repast to be eaten, and asked the Great Spirit to keep her from the evils and bad spirits of other hunting grounds if she should die; and if she lived, asked to be goddess over all green and ripe fruits and grain. The warriors stood with their faces covered, and the tomahawks at their feet. Famora closed her prayer, took up the brown, crisp corn, and ate of it, and then of the nuts of the yunkapin, and soon she felt better. The next day she was crowned Famora, keeper of all we have to eat and the flowers in all the vegetable kingdom.

"Her lover was not a handsome brave, and had many faults, but she loved him dearly, yet would not consent to be his bride. He followed her as she went out among the trees and flowers. One day she gathered some yunkapins, and ate them without roasting them, having previously taken out the green embryo. Famora started up and sped away like a deer. Omeka, her lover, tried to follow her, but she was far away before he had fairly started. He gathered large handfuls of the nuts, and supposing it was the green germ that she had eaten, he hulled and ate them, and then turned to follow Famora; but, alas, he fell to the earth a corpse. Famora returned and wept over him, but he had gone to the hunting grounds of his fathers. She broke off some boughs of a shrub that grew near, and covered the lifeless form of Omeka. Just as she was placing the last bough, and while holding it in her hand to break off a rough twig, she saw Omeka's father approaching. She knew she, too, must die; she could not defend herself against this warrior. In a moment the bush in her hand was transformed into a bow, the twig into an arrow, and with unerring aim the arrow had pierced the heart of the old Indian; he lay dead beside his son. The blood from his wound sank into the earth, and rose in the wood of a sycamore tree, and the wood of that tree has since been red. Omeka was very white, so the branches of this tree were also white. Famora caused it to grow near streams of water, giving the forest a gloomy appearance along the rivers and streams."

"Wyona, is this all true?"

"Yes, as true as our legends and fairies can be. We have forgotten most of them. But we never forget Famora, the prettiest queen this land ever knew, and the shrub she held in her hand, and which was changed into an arrow, is called to-day Indian arrow wood, and, looking closely, you can see the prints of her pretty hand upon the bow."

BELIEFS, SUPERSTITIONS, AND SAYINGS

WILLIAM E. KOCH
Kansas State University

Because of the wide variety of their themes and the diversity of their functions in daily life, folk beliefs, superstitions, and sayings are interesting to collect and study, and at one time or another have been the concern of many folklorists. Usage of these terms, however, is far from uniform since no precise definition has been agreed upon. The word *superstition* may have a broad connotation and include much of what we ordinarily think of as folk beliefs and the like, or its meaning may be limited to out-of-the-ordinary and perhaps peculiar practices. Unquestionably for many people the word has a derogatory connotation. Moreover, beliefs and superstitions are sometimes cast as proverbs—"Cold hands mean a warm heart"—and classified as such, thus adding another complicating factor.

Although many superstitions lack a rational foundation and are inconsistent with the laws of science, many are true or contain elements of truth appreciated by the sincere student. But it must be recognized that people often adhere to beliefs not because their truthfulness has been demonstrated but from force of tradition. If, for example, a man believes that tight corn shucks presage a cold winter, very likely he holds to this idea because his father did, not because of any independent investigation he has made.

The idea that a minor event is the cause or "sign" of a greater one is the underlying principle in a considerable number of superstitions: "If a bird flies into the house, there will be a death in the family soon," for example, or "Sleep on a piece of wedding

73

cake and you will dream of the one you will marry." Superstitions of this kind mean much to some people, who find them of help in understanding life and nature. They are the laws of "do" and "don't" which keep one from harm and provide rules of conduct. To other people, of course, superstitions mean nothing despite their having been passed on from generation to generation. But regardless of the significance of superstition to the individual, well-educated people are likely to be as familiar with this type of folklore as average persons.

There is no doubt that some superstitions are the last remnants of primitive or pagan practices whose original meaning has long been forgotten. An example of sympathetic magic that still has wide currency is item 130, listed below ("Get some hair of the dog that bit you, for luck") ; it derives from the very early belief that like would cure like. The fact that people even today associate changes of weather with the phases of the moon suggests the antiquity of some of our weather lore.

In rural Kansas especially, as one would expect, weather lore retains strong vitality. People take changes in the weather in their stride, having been previously alerted by signs and omens which have no connection with the U. S. Government Weather Bureau forecasts. A favorite weather prophecy is the old rhyme:

> When the wind is in the south,
> The bait will fly in the fish's mouth;
> When the wind is in the east,
> It's neither good for man nor beast;
> When the wind is in the west,
> 'Tis of all the winds the best.

The 266 items in this study were gathered from Kansans within the last few years and are part of a collection of materials of this kind from each of the state's 105 counties. The larger collection shows that new superstitions (for example, item 58 below) are still being born. Since the classification presented here is a loose one, some inconsistencies may be noted. For example, items under *Luck* which have to do with marriage might also be listed under *Marriage*.

All the contributors to the following collection are descendants of Kansas pioneers. Mrs. Lula Ferguson is the most direct

link to the first settlers who came west into the territory and
lived through the hardships of early days; her mother, Mrs.
Tilda Cole of Bazine, Kansas, came by covered wagon to Ness
County in the '70's.

A numbered list of contributors appears at the end of the
study. Corresponding numbers in parentheses after each superstition identify the person or persons from whom the item was
collected.

ANIMALS

1. A turtle won't let go until it thunders (1; 6).
2. If you kill the first snake you see in the spring, you will
   conquer all of your enemies that year (1).
3. It is thought by some people that if one strikes a joint snake,
   he will break in two and then if he is left alone, the two
   parts will come back together and the whole snake will go
   on his way. The truth is, only the tail can be broken off
   so easily. It will not join back on the snake but the snake
   will grow a new tail in time. This is a protective measure
   to help escape his enemies if they seize him by the tail (1).
4. The hoop snake is said to have a sting on the end of its
   tail that can kill a human being. The snake is said to take
   its tail in its mouth and roll like a hoop. It is thought to
   travel faster in this way than a fast horse can run. However,
   it can only travel in a straight line and if a person sees one
   coming, he may be able to dodge it. If the snake runs into
   a green tree, his sting will be so deeply imbedded in the
   tree that he cannot get away but the tree will die as a result of the sting (1).
5. Black snakes will suck cows—the cow must be lying
   down (1).
6. If you kill a snake, its tail will wiggle until the sun goes
   down (1; 2; 6).
7. Fish are supposed to bite better in rainy weather (5).
8. Horsetail hairs will turn into worms if left in water a few
   days (2).
9. Drop a horsehair in a tub of water, it will turn into a
   snake (4).

10. A bird in the house is an ill omen (2).
11. When a cat washes its face, it means company is coming (2).
12. A rooster crowing near the door means that company is coming (2).
13. Animals can speak at midnight on Christmas (4).
14. If you kill a toad, the cows will give bloody milk (1).

HUSBANDRY

15. If you can make plants grow you have a green thumb (7).
16. When oak leaves are the size of squirrel ears, it's time to plant corn (6).
17. Plant potatoes in the dark of the moon for a good crop (2).
18. Plant potatoes according to the moon (5).
19. Plant your potatoes on Good Friday (2).
20. Potatoes should be planted on St. Pat's day (4).
21. If a cow will not eat, she has lost her cud. The treatment is to ram an old, sour dishrag down the cow's throat. That will provide her with something to chew on until she can make a new cud (1).
22. If a cow is unthrifty, she has wolf-in-the-tail. The cure is to split the skin on the tail and rub salt and pepper in the raw wound (1).

WEATHER

23. A ring around the moon brings rain tomorrow (1; 5; 7).
24. Flies get thick around house doors before a rain (2).
25. If you hear a yellow-billed cuckoo calling, it is a sign of rain in the near future. Consequently, these birds are often called rain crows (1).
26. Bones ache means rain (5).
27. Rain on Easter means it's going to rain for seven Sundays in a row (2).
28. If cattle or horses run and play in the evening, it will rain soon (1; 2).
29. If you kill a snake and fasten it so it will remain belly side up, it will rain in a few days (1).
30. The moon on its side means rain, for all the water spills out (4).

31. Storm clouds moving against the wind means rain (2).
32. Itching corns on your toes means it will rain or that there is going to be a change in the weather (2).
33. When dogs chew on grass it means it is going to rain (2).
34. If it rains before seven, it will be clear before eleven (2; 3).
35. If it rains while the sun is shining it will rain tomorrow (2; 6).
36.   Evening red and morning gray,
  Speeds the traveler on his way.
  Evening gray and morning red
  Brings down showers on his head (4).
37.   Sun down red and sun up gray
  Will send the traveler on his way
  But sun down gray and sun up red
  Will send down rain upon his head (6).
38. The kind of weather during the first twelve days of the new year indicates what the weather will be like for the year (2).
39. The number of snowfalls during any winter is determined by the day of the month on which the first snowfall comes. For example, if the first snowfall comes on the tenth of December, there will be ten snowfalls during the winter (1; 7).
40.   Rainbow at night, sailor's delight—
  Rainbow in the morning, sailor's
   warning (1; 2; 3; 5).
41. The number of stars in the ring around the moon denotes the number of days until the weather changes (1; 7).
42. One can predict the severity of the weather by goose's wishbone (4).
43. A circle around the moon means stormy weather (2; 3; 4).
44. Sundogs mean cold weather is coming (3).
45. Dust whirlwinds mean it is going to be dry (2).
46. When the locusts sing it's a sign of dry weather (7).
47. Heavy fur on animals means cold weather (7).
48. Heavy corn shucks mean a cold winter (1; 2).
49. If groundhog sees his shadow on February 2, there'll be six more weeks of cold weather (2; 4; 5).

50. If March comes in like a lion, it goes out like a lamb (4; 5).
51. If smoke hovers near the ground, it is going to snow (2).
52. When water pipes sweat, the weather is going to change (2).
53. "I'd rather see the devil than a January robin" (3).
54. Before a cold snap, pigs scurry around and make warm nests with straw or hay (2).
55. Bad thunder will kill goslings in the shell (2).
56. A tornado never hits the junction of two rivers (4; 7).
57. Lightning never strikes twice in the same place (2).

WISHES

58. Honk the car horn three times when going under a bridge or overpass and make a wish (7).
59. Make a wish on the wishbone of a chicken (7).
60. Always make a wish when putting a ring on a person (2).
61. Make a wish on the first star you see at night (7).
62. After wishing on a star—don't look at it again (4; 5).
63. Wish on each falling star (5; 2; 7).
64. If a person is eating a wedge-shaped piece of pie and cuts the point of the wedge off and saves it to eat after the rest of the piece is eaten, he can make a wish and the wish will come true (1).
65. If you anxiously wish something to turn out well, cross your thumbs (4).
66. If you don't blow out all the candles on a birthday cake, all the remaining ones represent years until the wish comes true (5).
67. Wish on a load of hay, then turn away. If you don't see it again your wish will come true (6).
68. If a person having a birthday blows out all the cake candles, all wishes made on candles will come true (2; 4).
69. Your wish will come true if you get the peak of the wishbone when two people pull the bone apart (4).
70. At the dinner table, if you pass a dish to a person who is passing one to you, make a wish (4).

COURTSHIP AND MARRIAGE

71. Stub your toe—kiss your thumb, and you'll see your sweet-heart before nine o'clock (5).

72.   New moon, true moon, come unto me,
          Tell me who my true love shall be
          Right of me—sure to be
          Left of me—soon to be
          Back of me—never to be (4).

73. When I was a kid on the farm, there was a girl in our neighborhood who was in love with two boys. Both had proposed to her. One of the boys, Sam, lived east of her house. The other boy lived west of her house. She did not know which one of the two she really wanted to marry. To decide the matter, she took a broom out to the road in front of her house and stood it up on its brush end and let loose of it. It fell over toward Sam's house and the girl ran back to the house shouting, "I'll take Sam," and she married him (1).

74. A gift of red roses is a declaration of love (4).

75. Count seeds of apples and count corresponding letters of alphabet (that is, 3 = C) to find the initial of your future spouse (4).

76. Peel apple without breaking the peel; whirl it three times around your shoulder and drop it on the ground. Peel will form initial of future spouse (4).

77. Name corners of piece of pie with names of opposite sex—last one eaten will be name of one you love (4).

78. Counting daisy leaves—he loves me, he loves me not—and the count will tell the story (4).

79. Find occupation of future spouse by counting buttons—rich man, poor man, beggar man, thief, doctor, lawyer, merchant, chief.

80. Never give a person a sharp-pointed or sharp-sided wedding gift. It will cut your friendship (2; 4).

81.   Change the name and not the letter,
          Change for worse and not for better;

        Change the name and letter too,
        Change for good and never rue (4).

82. If you serve three times as a bridesmaid, you'll never marry (2).

83.   Married in blue, always true;
        Married in green, ashamed to be seen;
        Married in red, wish yourself dead;
        Married in yellow, ashamed of the fellow (2).

84. Married in black, wish yourself back (2).

85. Married in green, ashamed to be seen (7).

86. It is bad luck for the bride to take part in the wedding rehearsal (4).

87. It's bad luck for the bride to see the groom on their wedding day before the wedding (2; 7).

88. Friday is a bad wedding day; Wednesday is best (5).

89. If the wedding day is a nice, fair day, the couple will have a happy wedded life. If the day is stormy, their wedded life will be stormy (1; 2).

90. Bride should wear something old, something borrowed, and something blue (2; 3; 5).

91. The one who catches the bride's bouquet at a wedding will be the next one married (2; 4; 7).

92. Throw rice on the bride and groom to help bring good luck (2).

93. Sleep on a piece of wedding cake—third night you will dream of your future husband (4).

HOUSEHOLD

94. If while you are washing dishes you drop a spoon, it is a sign that a woman is coming to see you. The direction from which the visitor will come is indicated by the direction of the fallen spoon (1).

95. If a fork falls to the floor, a gentleman will call (1; 2).

96. If a knife falls to the floor, a woman is coming (2).

97. If you drop a dishrag while washing dishes, it is a sign that company is coming (1; 2).

98. If you drop a dishtowel, you'll have company (5).

99. If you step on a hole, you'll break the sugar bowl (7).

100. Sing before breakfast, cry before supper (4; 5).

101. Sing at the table and you'll cry before sunset (2).

102. Don't take cats with you when you move (2).

103. Thunder causes milk to sour sooner than ordinary (2; 4).

104. If you begin a sewing job on Friday, you will not finish it (2).

105. To find a green measuring worm on your dress means you will get a new dress (2).

BIRTH AND INFANCY

106. If a pregnant woman looks at a deformed person, her baby may be marked if she doesn't think of her child (3).

107. If a pregnant woman is frightened badly, the child will have a birthmark (2; 5; 7).

108. If a pregnant woman is frightened by some animal, the child will look like that animal (1).

109. A pregnant woman can mark her baby by things she sees when under great emotion (4).

110. Put your first baby tooth pulled under your pillow at night, next morning money will be there instead (4).

111. A baby born with a caul will be a genius or have psychic powers (4).

112. A child born after the father's death has healing powers (4).

113. Bald-headed babies are supposed to have curly hair (5).

114. More geniuses and insane are supposed to be born in the fall (5).

115. If you let baby clothes freeze, the baby will have colic (3).

116. Give a newborn baby, or one just very young, a penny. If it clutches it tightly, it will be wealthy (3).

117. Cats will suck a baby's breath (3).

118. A baby should be carried upstairs before downstairs (7).

119. Children have worms if they pick their noses (2).

120. If a child has one of its temporary teeth pulled and never

touches its tongue to the place where the tooth came out, a gold tooth will come in there (1).

DEATH

121. A bird flying into a house foretells death (4).
122. If shingles circle the body, one will die (4).
123. Dogs wailing at night means someone has died (2).
124. A howling dog means death (4).
125. If a person is ill and a dog howls outside the house, that person will not recover (1).
126. If fruit trees bear blossoms out of their regular season, it is a sign of the approaching death of some member of the community (1).
127. If a picture falls from the wall, it is omen of death (2).
128. Some of the miners in the north of England used to believe that the uncanny voices of migrating wild geese that they heard coming out of the night were the baying of what they called Gabriel's hounds. These imaginary beings were thought to be the souls of children who had died without receiving the rite of baptism. It was thought that these unfortunates were condemned to wander through space until the Judgment Day. Furthermore, their presence was believed to foretell the approaching death of some member of the community (1).
129. Sailors have always thought that their ship was almost sure to be wrecked if they have a corpse on board. Consequently, when Lord Packenham was killed in the Battle of New Orleans during the War of 1812, his body was hidden in a cask of rum to be shipped back to England. The alcohol in the rum was supposed to embalm it. The sailors found the cask and bored a hole in it to drain out the rum. When they could not get more rum by that method, they broke the cask open to get the rest of the rum and found His Lordship doubled up inside. There is said to be a poor grade of whiskey made in the Mississippi delta country that is called Packenham whiskey as a result of this incident (1).

LUCK

130. Get some of the hair of the dog that bit you for luck (6).

131. A stray black cat comes to stay at your house—good luck (4).

132. Crickets chirping around the house in the evening mean good luck (2).

133. Good luck to see a bluebird (2; 5).

134. Keep a lucky penny in your pocket book—you'll always have money (4).

135. See a pin, pick it up, all the day you'll have good luck (4; 7).

136. See a penny, pick it up, all the day you'll have good luck (4; 7).

137. Penny in right shoe for good luck (5).

138. Pick up stray hairpins for good luck (2).

139. Carrying the left-hand foot of a rabbit brings good luck (2; 4).

140. If you have poor luck at cards get up and walk around your chair three times or sit on a handkerchief for good luck (4).

141. Find a four-leaf clover and you'll have good luck (4; 7).

142. Find a red ear of corn—good luck (4).

143.   A horseshoe hung both ends up—good luck.
         With ends down all luck runs out (4).

144. See new moon over right shoulder—good luck (4).

145. If you spill salt, throw some over your left shoulder for good luck (1; 2; 4; 5; 7).

146. For good luck at weddings—wear something old, something new, something borrowed, something blue (4).

147. Carrying the bride over the doorstep is good luck (4).

148. Born with a caul is supposed to be lucky (5).

149. To work on Sunday means bad luck (2).

150. See three black crows—bad luck (4).

151. It is bad luck to haul dead chickens away (1).

152. Never bend a mule's ear, bad luck (8).

153. To kill a spider is bad luck. "The spider is the devil's wife" (4).

154. It is bad luck to kill cats (2).
155. A black cat across a path—bad luck (2; 3; 4).
156. Bad luck to kill a setting hen (5).
157. It's bad luck for a bird to fly in the house (7).
158. It's bad luck to change a wedding date (2).
159. Married in black—means bad luck (4).
160. It is bad luck for the bride and groom to see each other earlier in the day of the wedding ceremony (4).
161. It is bad luck for the engaged girl to cut the knots on ribbons of wedding presents (4).
162. It is bad luck to cut a baby's fingernails before it is a year old (2).
163. Wear newly bought clothing before washing; otherwise bad luck will come (2).
164. It's bad luck to light three things on one match (4).
165. It's bad luck to whistle in a theater (4).
166. It is bad luck to start a trip on Friday (4).
167. If you borrow salt, never return it or bad luck will follow (4).
168. A two-dollar bill is bad luck (4).
169. When moving, never take your old brooms with you—bad luck (2).
170. Walk under a ladder and you will have bad luck (2; 4).
171. Bad luck to open an umbrella in house or put hat on head (2; 5).
172. Break a mirror means seven years of bad luck (4; 5).
173. Breaking a shoestring in the morning means bad luck all day (2).
174. Friday the 13th is unlucky day (4).
175. Sweeping the house after dark brings bad luck (2).
176. If you talk about the falling star, you'll have bad luck (7).
177. Never look at the new moon over your left shoulder; it is bad luck (3; 4).
178. If you go home to get a forgotten item, always sit down before leaving the house again or bad luck will come (4).
179. Find a five-leaf clover means bad luck (4; 5; 7).
180. It is bad luck to come in one door and leave by another (2).
181. Putting on a dress backward by mistake will bring bad luck (2).

182. Wearing an opal, if not your birthstone—bad luck (4).

183. To avoid bad luck, oldest daughter of the house should burn the Christmas tree by New Year's (4).

184. A double rainbow is good luck (4).

185. On New Year's, one must be kissed on the stroke of midnight for luck during the year (4).

CURES AND ILLNESS

186. If you have chronic pains in your stomach, it may be a sign that you are liver-grown, which is supposed to mean that your liver is stuck down. The cure is to get down on the floor on your hands and knees and crawl under the dining table. First crawl through from east to west and then from north to south, forming a cross. You will probably laugh enough at this undignified procedure to shake your liver loose (1).

187. Rub goose grease on the chest to help clear up a bad cold (2).

188. Ringworms can be cured by rubbing them with green walnuts (2).

189. Drink nine swallows of water without taking a breath to get rid of the hiccups (7).

190. To cure hiccups, try to scare the person badly (2).

191. Hot toddy cures a cold (5).

192. Feed a fever and starve a cold (5).

193. Wear a band of copper wire around the wrist or ankle to cure rheumatism (2).

194. A buckeye carried in the pocket will prevent certain types of diseases (1).

195. To prevent rheumatism, carry buckeyes in your pocket (2; 3).

196. Carrying a horse chestnut in your pocket is good for rheumatism (7).

197. A small potato carried in a pocket will prevent rheumatism (7).

198. To drive pimples away, eat molasses and sulphur (2).

199. When you sneeze, you must say some version of words, "your health" to avoid illness (4).

200. A cobweb over a wound will stop bleeding (2; 4).
201. Put a coin under the lip to cure a nosebleed (2).
202. Hold a cold knife to your neck to help stop a nosebleed (2).
203. A lead shot suspended around the neck by a string will prevent nosebleed (1).
204. If you don't rub warts they'll go away (7).
205. To get rid of a wart, tie a string around it and leave the string on (2).
206. To cure a wart, bury an old dishrag at night (2).
207. If you handle toads you will get warts (1; 2; 3).
208. Drink sassafras tea as a tonic and to clear up the blood (2).
209. Place tobacco poultice on a festered sore (2).
210. To cure a ringworm, put a penny soaked in vinegar on it (2).
211. Place an onion poultice to help clear up a boil (2).
212. Mix melted lard and turpentine and then rub on the chest to help clear up a cold (2).

DREAMS

213. Your dreams will come true if you tell them before breakfast (3).
214. It's bad luck to have fruit trees bloom twice a year (2).
215. It's bad luck to dream of snakes (2).
216. To dream of a death means a wedding soon (2; 5).
217. A dream of teeth falling out means death soon to you or someone close to you (7).
218. If you dream of falling and land, you'll die (7).
219. Dreaming of high places that you are struggling to climb is a sign of a frustrated effort (7).
220. Bad luck will come if you dream of muddy water (2).

PEOPLE

221.   Sneeze on Monday—sneeze for danger
Sneeze on Tuesday—kiss a stranger
Sneeze on Wednesday—get a letter
Sneeze on Thursday—something better

Sneeze on Friday—sneeze for sorrow
Sneeze on Saturday—joy, tomorrow (4).

222. Red-haired people are hot-tempered (3).
223. Cold hands mean a warm heart (2).
224. Preacher's children are always ornery (3).
225. Weak chin means a weak character (5).
226. Small eyes mean a shifty character (5).
227. There will be a quarrel if you spill salt (2).
228. If company comes on Monday, it means company all week (2).
229. If you hand salt to another at a table, it means you will quarrel with the person (4).
230. If your ear itches, someone is talking about you (4).
231. If your ear itches, it is a sign that someone is gossiping about you (2; 1).
232. If your nose itches, it is a sign that you will have company (1).
233. If your nose itches, someone is thinking about you (7).
234. If your nose itches, you will kiss a stranger (or a fool), be in danger, or someone is coming (4).
235. An itching hand means you will get some money soon (2).
236. If fingers are crossed when telling a lie, the lie doesn't count (4).
237. If a conversation stops suddenly, it will be either twenty minutes before or after the hour at that time (4).

MISCELLANEOUS

238. You can catch a bird if you put salt on its tail (7).
239. To locate a lost article, spit in the palm of your left hand and slap the spittle with the first finger of your right hand. The greater part of the spittle will fly in the direction of the lost article. By repeating this process as you progress toward the object, you can eventually find it (1).
240. An old maid always knows how to raise children (3).

SAYINGS, PROVERBIAL AND OTHERWISE

241. Handsome is as handsome does (3).
242.   Beauty is only skin deep,

Ugly is to the bone;
Beauty lasts only a day,
Ugly holds its own (3).

243.   You never can tell
The depth of the well
By the length of the
Handle of the pump (3).

244. You never can tell by the looks of a frog how far he can jump (3).

245. Still water runs deep (3).

246. He doesn't know enough to come in out of the rain (3).

247. People who live in glass houses shouldn't throw stones (3).

248. Should the pot call the kettle black? (3).

249. What's sauce for the goose is sauce for the gander (3).

250. You can lead a horse to water but you can't make him drink (6).

251. It's an ill wind that blows no good (6).

252. A chain is no stronger than its weakest link (6).

253. Not all houses are homes (6).

254. You can build a house but you have to make a home (6).

255. Gasoline and whiskey usually mix with blood on the highway (6).

256. Gasoline and whiskey don't mix (6).

257. The grass is always greener on the other side of the fence (6).

258. You pay for what you get (6).

259. Quiet water runs deep (6).

260. An apple a day keeps the doctor away (7).

261. When the sun's in the west, lazy folks work the best (7).

262. A whistling girl and a crowing hen, always come to some bad end (1; 2).

263. If two people say the same thing at the same time, they should join their little fingers and say, "Needles and pins, needles and pins, when a man marries his troubles begin" (2).

264. Step on a crack, break your mother's back; step on a hole, break your mother's sugar bowl (5).

265. Forty-nine pounds is witches' weight (4).

266. An idle brain is the devil's workshop (3).

Contributors

1. Mr. Percy L. DePuy, age 65. Born and reared in Crawford County; first 21 years of life on farm; college graduate; retired teacher and game reserve manager. 2. Mrs. Lula Ferguson, age 75. Born and reared in Ness County; lived over 50 years on farm or ranch; homemaker and pioneer. 3. Mrs. Virginia Griswold, age 36. Born and reared in Marshall County; 22 years on farm; college graduate; homemaker and school teacher. 4. Mrs. Jane Rockwell Koefod, age 40. Born and reared in Geary County; college graduate; teacher and homemaker. 5. Miss Amelie King, age 21. Born and reared in Sedgwick County; college student. 6. Mr. Don P. Porter, age 24. Born and reared in Neosho County; college student. 7. Miss Marilyn Walton, age 21. Born and reared in Sedgwick County; college student.

PROVERBS AND RIDDLES

William E. Koch
Kansas State University

Proverbs and riddles are treated together in this study for the sake of convenience. Most folklorists consider them distinct genres of oral culture; however, they share certain characteristics. Both are among the oldest expressions of formulated thought. Both are classified under the broader heading of "folk wisdom" because they are distillations of accumulated folk experience and observation handed down from one generation to the next. Both show far less variation in·their wording than do other forms of folklore in the process of oral transmission; in fact, the ways in which proverbs and riddles are expressed are nearly invariable.

One explanation of this surprising verbal stability may be simply that they do not survive unless stated in a form which the mind finds easy to grasp and retain whole and unaltered. At any rate, their functions and purposes do account at least in part for the fact that proverbs and riddles seldom vary in phrasing. *Proverbial maxims,* for example, are intended to stay in the mind as guides to conduct; therefore, they are memorized word for word. *Wellerisms*—a type of proverb containing a quotation and its explanation—usually depend on puns and lose their force when incorrectly quoted. If a *riddle* is not stated exactly, either the answer is given away, or else a clue disappears and the riddle becomes incomprehensible. And finally, by their very nature proverbs and riddles are among the briefest forms of folklore, thus among the most easily remembered.

Although difficult to define satisfactorily, folk proverbs comprise a sizable segment of the wisdom, the humor, and perhaps the philosophy of a people. The so-called *true proverb*, which is expressed in a complete sentence, epitomizes tersely and strikingly a recognized truth or a shrewd observation on life. Epigrammatic condensations of experience, they often suggest a course of action or express a passing judgment. Many proverbs are metaphors, usually on a quite simple level. Most of them, as has been noted, remain in oral tradition in a rigidly fixed form; and since man has used proverbs from the earliest times, many are couched in archaic language.

The *proverbial phrase* and the *proverbial comparison* are closely related to the true proverb, but are not complete sentences in themselves. Many collectors or compilers, however, make no distinction between them and the so-called true proverb. Examples of the proverbial phrase are "behind the eight ball" and "putting the cart before the horse." A proverbial comparison is such an expression as "like a bump on a log" or "as mean as dirt."

According to Archer Taylor, a fascinating type of proverb, the Wellerism, goes back to Latin and Greek literature.[1] It takes its name, however, from Sam Weller, the delightful character in Dickens' *Pickwick Papers* who frequently used the form. "Everyone to his own taste, as my grandmother said as she ate the cinders" and "There is nothing so refreshing as sleep, said the servant girl as she drank the eggcupful of laudanum" are characteristic examples.

The origin of proverbs is so obscure that any attempt to ascribe one to a particular person is, to say the least, risky. Through the ages proverbs have been used both by the folk and by scholars, and through the ages people without written laws have relied on proverbs to settle disputes. In folklore, proverbs appear in ballads and folktales; in literature at certain periods they have been completely accepted and very popular, at other times considered poor form. Collections of proverbs served as textbooks in the Middle Ages and Renaissance; in eighteenth-century France entire plays sometimes were built around a proverb, which the audience was led to guess by the actions dramatized.

[1] Archer Taylor, *The Proverb* (Cambridge: Harvard University Press, 1931), p. 203.

Almost everyone appreciates proverbs. While it is difficult to generalize on their vitality in America today, a little analysis will make it evident to any person that his own speech contains proverbs and proverbial sayings. That many proverbs are current among younger as well as older people is evident from state and regional collections.

The number of proverbs and proverbial sayings is so overwhelming that probably there will never be a complete collection for reference purposes. Now that the pure "book study" of the older proverb compilations has almost exhausted itself, new studies are under way to distinguish between the proverbial lore that has actually lived on in oral tradition and that which is a reflection of modern life.

PROVERBS

[The average age of the contributors was twenty to twenty-nine years, although six were over fifty. All twenty-six contributors were residents of Riley County, Kansas; eleven were born outside the state. Thirteen had been reared on a farm or ranch.

Although most of the sixty-five proverbs presented here are commonplace or conventional, twenty-five of them do not appear in *The Frank C. Brown Collection of North Carolina Folklore*.[2] Alphabetical order seemed the most convenient system of classification. Each proverb is placed under the first important noun or, if there is no important noun, under the first important verb. The numbers in parentheses refer to the contributors listed at the end of this section.]

Action. Actions speak louder than words (25).*
All. All's well that ends well (25).*
Bed. Early to bed and early to rise, makes a man healthy, wealthy, and wise (21).*
Bird. 1. A bird in the hand is worth two in the bush (16).*
  2. The early bird gets the first worm (6).*

[2] Proverbs marked with an asterisk (*) appear in *The Frank C. Brown Collection of North Carolina Folklore* (Durham: Duke University Press, 1952), I. This work supplies annotative references to standard sources containing data on the proverb indicated.

Blood. Blood is thicker than water (2) .*

Body. The larger the body, the bigger the heart (9) .*

Bridge. Don't cross your bridges before you come to them (20) .*

Cat. When the cat's away the mice will play (23) .*

Chain. A chain is only as strong as its weakest link (25) .

Chicken. Don't count your chickens before they are hatched (4; 16) .*

Cooks. Too many cooks spoil the broth (13) .*

Dog. 1. A barking dog seldom bites (23; 7) .* 2. You can't teach an old dog new tricks (25) .*

Fish. 1. Even a fish wouldn't get caught if he kept his mouth shut (5) . 2. Fish and visitors stink after three days (16) .

Flies. You can catch more flies with honey than you can with vinegar (25) .*

Fool. 1. There's no fool like an old fool (7; 17; 25) .* 2. A fool and his gold are soon parted (4) .* 3. A fool and his money are soon parted (4) .* 4. Fools rush in where angels fear to tread (25) .

Fox. The sleeping fox catches no poultry (26) .*

Haste. The more haste, the less speed (11) .*

Hen. A setting hen never grows fat (19) .*

Horse. 1. You can lead a horse to water, but you can't make him drink (25) .* 2. Don't change horses in midstream (20) .* 3. You'll never see it on a galloping horse (12) .

Job. A job started is a job half done (2) .

Kicked. I've been kicked by the same horse (18) .

Laugh. 1. He who laughs last, laughs best (1) .* 2. He who laughs last, laughs hardest (14) .*

Life. Life begins at forty (11) .

Man. 1. A wise man changes his mind; a fool never does (11) . 2. A wise man has wise children (4) . 3. Wise men learn by others' harms; fools scarcely by their own (11) .

Minute. A minute wasted is a minute lost forever (4) .

Mud. Mud thrown is ground lost (20) .

Name. If you have the name, you might as well have the game (11) .

Nickel. Don't take any wooden nickels (15) .

Offense. A good offense is the best defense (11).

Penny. 1. A penny saved is a penny earned (11; 20; 27).* 2. Penny wise and pound foolish (11; 10; 19).* 3. Take care of the pennies and the dollars will take care of themselves (11).*

People. People who live in glass houses should not throw rocks (1).

Please. He who tries to please everybody, pleases nobody (23).

Politics. Politics makes strange bedfellows (11).

Pot. A watched pot never boils (11).*

Pride. Pride goeth before a fall (25).

Pull. It is easier to pull down than to build up (10).

Rod. Spare the rod and spoil the child (8; 11).*

Sauce. Sauce for the goose is sauce for the gander (23).*

Show. The show must go on (11).

Slip. Many a slip, 'tween the tongue (cup) and the lip (2).*

Stink. The more you stir a stink, the louder it smells (10).

Stitch. A stitch in time saves nine (12; 16; 22).*

Stone. A rolling stone gathers no moss (19).*

Stream. A dry stream carries no water (7).

Tomorrow. Never put off till tomorrow what you can do today (4; 26).*

Waste. 1. Waste not and you'll want not (4; 24).* 2. Willful waste makes woeful want (3).*

Well. A dry well pumps no water (7).

Whistle. Whistling girls and crowing hens always come to some bad ends (25).*

Wishes. If wishes were horses, beggars might ride (26).*

Woman. A wise woman never outsmarts her husband (16).

Work. All work and no play makes Jack a dull boy (4).*

Contributors

1. Gary Arnold 2. Mrs. George Barclay 3. Mrs. Robert Barclay 4. Larry Bolch 5. Gordon Bradshaw 6. Judy Burgess 7. Wayne Coffey 8. Gwen Conrad 9. Dixie Des Jardines 10. John Franks 11. Howard T. Hill 12. Irma Smith Hill 13. Janet Hoyt 14. Elizabeth Isom 15. James K. Isom 16. Norman Johnson 17. William McCormick 18. George McCord 19. Shirley McKeen 20. Charles Meyer 21. Joan Morrison

22. Alice Mosier **23.** Walt Mosier **24.** Louella Nelson
25. Mrs. Pat Sawyer **26.** Marjorie Schmedeman **27.** Dave Worley

WELLERISMS

[Of the forty contributors about three-fourths were students at Kansas State University during the spring semester, 1958. All except four were residents of the state. It is obvious that most of the following Wellerisms are of modern origin.

I have been unable to find a firmly established or standard method for classifying Wellerisms. The arrangement here is an experimental one; it has proved convenient on a small scale and might lend itself satisfactorily to a larger collection. The practice of emphasizing the identity of the speaker, however, is standard.[3] The numbers in parentheses refer to the names of contributors listed at the end of the section.]

INSECTS

(Bug) "I won't have guts enough to do that again," said the bug as he hit the windshield (37).

(Firefly) 1. "Delighted no end," said (*var.* cried) the firefly as he backed into the fan (*var.* electric fan) (17; 28; 20). 2. "I'm de-lighted," said the firefly as he accidentally backed into the fan (8).

(Flea) "Raise the drawbridge," cried the flea, as he rode down the river in his matchstick canoe (36).

(Fly) "I spec so," said the fly, as he flew away from the garbage (18).

(Termite) "Beat you, Daddy; I ate the bar," said the young termite to his father as they met in the local pub (8).

FISH

(Octopus) 1. "Let's walk hand in hand in hand in hand," said the boy octopus to his girl friend (12). 2. "I'm entangled in your love," said the octopus to his girl friend as she hugged him (9).

---

[3] Most of these Wellerisms appeared previously in William E. Koch, "Wellerisms from Kansas," *Western Folklore*, XVIII (1959), 180, and "More Wellerisms from Kansas," *Western Folklore*, XIX (1960), 196.

HOUSEHOLD

(Ceiling)   "I'll meet you at the corner," said the ceiling to the wall (1).

(Calendar)   "I see ahead," said the calendar (32).

ANIMALS

(Bear)   "My tale is told," said the little bear as he sat on ice (14).

(Cat)   "I feel strained," said the cat as he ran through a screen door (5).

(Chimpanzee)   "So long," said the chimp, sliding off the giraffe's neck (38).

(Cow)   "I'm getting that run-down feeling," said the cow as the freight train bore down on her (5).

(Dog)   1. "Ruff," cried the dog as he sat on the cactus (36). 2. "Rough, rough," said the dog as she sat on sandpaper (19).

(Monkey)   1. "I'll be a monkey's uncle," said the monkey as his sister had a baby (11). 2. "Neat, but not gaudy," said the monkey when (*var.* as) he painted his tail blue (7; 33; 35; 22; 29). 3. "This is the end of my tale," said the monkey as he backed into the fan (31) (*var.* lawnmower) (4). 4. "All's well that ends well," said the monkey when the lawnmower ran over his tail (21; 29; 33). 5. "So what," said the monkey as the sewing machine ran over his tail (13).

(Toad)   "Many masters," said the toad when the harrow turned him over (34).

PEOPLE

(Blind Man)   1. "I see," said the blind man as he picked up his hammer and saw (23; 20; 5; 17; 10; 25; 28). 2. "I see," said the blind man to his deaf daughter as he picked up his hammer and saw (8). 3. "I see," said the blind man as he bumped into the light pole (26) (*var.* tree) (28). 4. "I see," said the blind man as he told his deaf daughter to stick her wooden leg out the window to see if it was raining (30). 5. "I see," said the blind man to his deaf wife as he climbed a cherry tree to get an apple for his lame uncle (15).

(Man)   1. "You make me sick," said the man to the germ (7).
2. "Now where is that revolving door, door, door," said the man
as he slipped on the ice while going into the store (36). 3. "I've
got it all over you," boasted the old man as he sneezed (2).
4. "Oh, I feel run down," said the man who got hit by a truck
(24). 5. "This is easy," said the man falling off the log (27).

(Woman, Lady)   1. "Every little bit helps," said the lady as she
spit in the ocean (4). 2. "Everyone to their own taste," said
the woman as she kissed the cow (40). 3. "Disaster," cried
the pilot as the woman backed into the plane propellor (39).

(Boy)   "Sunday is the strongest day of the week," said the boy as
he faced six week days (6).

(Criminal)   1. "You give me a pain in the neck," said the
doomed man at the guillotine to the executioner (5).
2. "Guess I'll hang around awhile," said the prisoner from the
gallows (12).

(Occupational)   1. "Pitch," shouted the baseball player as he
stepped on the newly poured blacktop highway (13). 2. "A
little behind in my work," said the butcher as he backed into
the meat grinder (20; 16; 3; 37). 3. "We'll be all right now,"
said the doctor, "if we don't run out of patients" (14).
4. "Now is the time to see my pigs," said the farmer with a sty
in his eye (6).

Kansas Contributors and County of Residence

1. John Barry, Riley 2. Gene Berghaus, Riley 3. Bob Braden,
Miami 4. Sonie Brown, Riley 5. Walter Burns, Clay 6. Merel
Butler, Cloud 7. Kay Chappell, Riley 8. Paul L. Clark, Ellis
9. Bruce Cleveland, Cloud 10. Marcia Diamond, Leavenworth
11. Peggy Farrar, Shawnee 12. Jerome P. Farrell, Riley 13. Pat
Farrow, Leavenworth 14. Dorothy Fox, Cowley 15. Jane Fulton,
Riley 16. Leo Gardner, Riley 17. Sonja Hanson, Sedgwick
18. Kathleen Harden, Marion 19. John Hepburn, Riley
20. Robert M. Hepburn, Riley 21. David Hinderliter, Sedgwick
22. Sue Johnson, Sedgwick 23. Warren Keegan, Geary 24. Win-
die Killian, Geary 25. Carol Klecan, Jackson 26. Walter Murphy, Jackson 27. Glenda Reed, Rice 28. Marcia Ross, Nemaha
29. Dick Scrogin, Stafford 30. Jane Seitz, Riley 31. Donna
Turner, Sedgwick 32. Glenn Wagner, Riley 33. Diane Wat-

son, Sedgwick   **34.** Carole Wilmore, Shawnee   **35.** Dixie Wingate, Riley   **36.** Roberta Wray, Norton

Out-of-State Contributors

37. Mary L. Deewall, Okla.   **38.** James D. Heath, Ill.   **39.** Allan Liebler, New York   **40.** Karren Smith, Texas

RIDDLES

Riddles—verbal puzzles, often couched in confusing, metaphorical language—have excited and fascinated man since earliest times. Some of the oldest recorded are in Babylonian school texts; they were used in developing talent for primary association and comparison. Other uses and functions are revealed in ancient religious works, classical literature, and narrative folk-literature; for instance, enigma contests were popular at Greek and Roman feasts. When the Queen of Sheba heard of the fame of Solomon she came and tested him with riddles. During the Renaissance and Reformation the folk riddle offered a comparatively safe vehicle for hinting at the resentment of the poor and unlearned against the rich and lettered.

Of the various types of riddles, perhaps the most interesting is the *true riddle.* This is a thought-provoking question which asks for a solution; it says one thing and means another. According to riddle scholars, a true riddle consists of two parts—a vague general description and a specific detail which seems to conflict with it. The conflict between what is suggested in general terms and what is specifically stated arouses our curiosity. The answer resolves the conflict and appeases our curiosity. For example:

> As I was going through the garden gap
> Whom should I meet but Dick Red Cap; (a man?)
> A stick in his hand and a stone in his throat; (?)
> If you answer my riddle, I'll give you a groat.

When we guess the answer (Dick Red Cap is a cherry), we solve the conflict (why would a man have a stone in his throat?). The first idea is only metaphorically true (we assume that Dick Red Cap is a man); the contradictory assertion is literally true (a cherry has a stone in it—and a stick, the stem). The familiar "Humpty Dumpty" is another good example:

> Humpty Dumpty sat on a wall
> Humpty Dumpty had a great fall
> All the King's horses and all the King's men
> Couldn't put Humpty together again.

True riddles are usually longer and more complex in imagery than other types of riddles.

The *conundrum* is a simpler and more trifling riddle, often containing a pun or a play on words. For example:

When is a door not a door? (When it's ajar.)

Why is a man's bald head like heaven? (Because there is no parting there.)

The *sham riddle* is not really intended to be answered, either because only those with a very special previous knowledge of the subject could possibly know the answer, or because it is intended only as a joke—the questioner is teasing his audience and intends to give the answer himself. There are several types of sham riddles, among them the so-called "neck-saver" and "foolish question." In the latter, the question may seem legitimate, but the answer is an absurdity. For example:

> Railroad crossing, look out for the cars;
> Can you spell that without any r's?
> *Answer*—T-H-A-T.
>   or
> A man went away on Sunday, stayed a week and
> came back on the same Sunday. How was that?
> *Answer*—His horse was named Sunday.

The following is an example of a "neck-saver" current in the United States:

> Love I sit, Love I stand,
> Love I hold in my right hand,
> Love I see in yonder tree,
> I see Love, but he don't see me.

Answer—A man had a dog named Love. He killed the dog, sat on some of it, stood on some of it, had blood on his hand, and a piece of it was in the tree.

The custom of posing riddles, either as a pastime or for a serious purpose, seems almost to have disappeared from American folk tradition, but a knowledge of riddles has not. At least not quite, since riddle collections appear frequently in current folklore periodicals. The twenty-five riddles included here were collected in 1957 at Kansas State College, Manhattan, Kansas, from a class of nine students. The students were merely asked to write down the riddles they knew; they were unaware that they were about to study them. The results were surprising and are presented to demonstrate in a small way that riddles are alive today in oral tradition.

[The numbers after the answers to the riddles refer to the names of contributors, listed at the end of this section. Arrangement follows that of Volume I, *The Frank C. Brown Collection of North Carolina Folklore*. Riddles which also appear in *North Carolina Folklore* are noted by cross reference.]

COMPARISONS TO LIVING CREATURES

1. What has legs but cannot walk? (Table) 4.
2. What has eyes but cannot see? (Potato) 4.
3. What walks on four legs in the morning, two at noon, and three at night? (Man) 1.
   Cf. Brown, No. 5.
4. What runs all over the sink but has no legs? (Water) 6.
5. What goes all over the United States but doesn't move? (Roads) 1.
6. What runs all over the yard, comes up to the door, but never comes in? (Path) 1.
   Cf. Brown, No. 9c.

COMPARISONS TO A PERSON

7.   Old Mother Twichit has but one eye
            And a long tail which she lets fly;
            Every time she goes through a gap
            A bit of her tail she leaves in a trap.
            (Needle and thread) 5.
8.   Little Nancy Etticoat in her short petticoat
            The longer she stands, the shorter she grows.

(Candle) 2.
Cf. Brown, No. 40.

COMPARISONS TO A THING

9.   Down in the field stands a green house;
            Inside the green house there is a white house,
            Inside the white house there is a red house,
            Inside the red house there are a lot of little
              negroes swimming.
            (Watermelon) 2.
            Cf. Brown, No. 56b. Var.

ENUMERATION OF COMPARISONS

10.   Round as an apple, deep as a cup;
                All the King's horses can't pull it up.
                (A well) 2.
                Cf. Brown, No. 68.
11.   As deep as the ocean, as full as a cup;
                All the King's horses can not pull it up.
                (A well) 3.
                Cf. Brown, Nos. 71–73. Vars.
12.   Round as a biscuit, busy as a bee;
                What in the world can this thing be?
                (Watch) 5.
                Cf. Brown, Nos. 67–73. Vars.

DESCRIPTION OF THE PARTS OF AN OBJECT

13.   What is round at both ends and high in the middle?
        (Ohio) 3.
        Cf. Brown, No. 80.

DESCRIPTION IN TERMS OF COLORS

14.   What is black and white and red all over?
            (Newspaper) 5; 8; 9; 6.
            Cf. Brown, No. 85.

DESCRIPTION IN TERMS OF A SCENE

15.   Upon the hill there is a mill,
            Around the mill there is a walk;

Under the walk there is a key—name it.
(Milwaukee) 2; 5.

ARITHMETICAL PUZZLES

16.   As I was walking to St. Ives,
            I met a man with seven wives.
            Each wife had seven kids,
            Each kid had seven kites,
            How many were going to St. Ives?
            (One, only me) 5.
            Cf. Brown, No. 123, Var.
17. How long is a string?
        (Twice the distance from the middle to one end) 8.

SPELLING AND LETTER RIDDLES

18.   Railroad crossing, look out for the cars.
            Can you spell that without any R's?
            (That) 5.
            Cf. Brown, No. 133. Var. it.
19.   Nebuchadnezzar, King of the Jews,
            Spell it with two letters,
            And I'll give you my shoes.
            (It) 5.
            Cf. Brown, No. 132c. Var.

"WHAT?" RIDDLES

20. What does a negro have that will kill a cow?
        (Black leg) 8.
21. What goes 'round in button?
        (Buttin) 5.
22. What is the longest word in the English language?
        (Smiles, it's a mile between *s* and *s*) 3.

"WHO?" RIDDLES

23. If a man and woman are walking down the street and the
        man's hat blows off, who should go get it?
        (The woman, because women always go first) 9.

CATCHES

24. If a train going south, then west, switches to the north—
which way will the smoke blow?
(The way the wind is blowing) 7.

25. How far can you go into the forest?
(Half way) 8.

Names of Contributors with County Residence and Ancestry

1. William Cox, age 22, Butler County (German-English-Irish) 2. Mrs. Virginia Griswold, age 43, Marshall County (Scotch-Irish) 3. Carole Holmquist, age 21, Reno County (Swedish) 4. Barbara Kethcart, age 20, Mitchell County (Scotch-Irish and French-Canadian) 5. Mrs. Margaret Lederer, age 27, Dickinson County (German and Welsh-Irish) 6. Dorothy Lindquist, age 30, Marshall County (English and Swedish) 7. William McCormick, age 23, Riley County (Scotch-Irish) 8. Don B. Porter, age 24, Neosho County (German-English-French-Dutch) 9. Lee Ann Riggs, age 21, Jackson County (Welsh-English)

DIALECT

CHARLES BURGESS
Kansas State College of Pittsburg

Over the past seventy years, beginning with W. H. Carruth's contributions in the 1890's, there have been many studies of the language used in Kansas. Some were based on observation, others on newspapers or other printed sources; some were broadly general, others focused on a particular type of vocabulary; but despite difference in method, all reported usages which the authors considered nonstandard. Since the present study of such locutions is based on a score of earlier books and articles as well as on my own observations, I begin by listing the works to which I shall refer.[1] The abbreviations used hereafter are given at the left.

Be   Bell, Ruth Elizabeth. "Some Contributions to the Study of Kansas Vocabulary." Unpublished Master's thesis, University of Kansas, 1929.

Bu   Burnham, Josephine M. "Some Observations of Middle-western Speech," *Dialect Notes*, V (1926), 391–396.

Ca I   Carruth, W. H. "Dialect Word List," *Kansas University Quarterly*, I (1892–3), 95–100.

Ca II   Carruth, W. H. "Dialect Word List II," *Kansas University Quarterly*, I (1892–3), 133–142.

[1] Other works of special value to those interested in Kansas speech:

Burnham, Josephine M. "Three Hard-worked Suffixes," *American Speech*, II (1927), 244–246.

Carruth, W. H. "The Language Used to Domesticate Animals," *Dialect Notes*, I (1892), 263–268.

Pingry, Carl, and Vance Randolph. "Kansas University Slang," *American Speech*, III (1928), 218–221.

Ruppenthal, J. C. "Jottings from Kansas," *Dialect Notes*, V (1923), 245.

Ruppenthal, J. C., and G. D. Chase. "Russian Words in Kansas," *Dialect Notes*, IV (1914), 161–162.

Fr Froom, Esther P. "The Diction of the Newton *Kansan* from August 22, 1872, to August 14, 1873." Unpublished Master's thesis, University of Kansas, 1936.

Ha Hammond, Geraldine Elizabeth. "A Study of the Diction of the Lawrence *Republican,* May 28 to August 13, 1857." Unpublished Master's thesis, University of Kansas, 1932.

Po Pound, Louise. "Intentional Mispronunciations in the Central West," *Dialect Notes,* V (1922), 133–138.

Ra I Randolph, Vance. "Wet Words in Kansas," *American Speech,* IV (1929), 385–389.

Ra II Randolph, Vance, and George P. Wilson. *Down in the Holler: A Gallery of Ozark Folk Speech.* Norman: University of Oklahoma Press, 1953.

Ru I Ruppenthal, J. C. "A Word List from Kansas," *Dialect Notes,* IV (1914), 101–114.

Ru II Ruppenthal, J. C. "A Word List from Kansas (II)," *Dialect Notes,* IV (1914), 319–331.

Sa I Sackett, Samuel J. "A Kansas Glossary" (a four-page list compiled from works by Kansas authors 1890–1920). Typescript in the Fort Hays Kansas State College Library.

Sa II Sackett, Samuel J. "An Expression I Hear Often Any More," *Word Study,* December, 1957, p. 4.

We Wentworth, Harold. *American Dialect Dictionary.* New York: Thomas Y. Crowell, 1944.

Wy Wyatt, P. J. "I'm Not Selling Anything." Unpublished Master's thesis, Indiana University, 1957. Typescript in the Indiana University Library; microfilm copy in the University of Kansas Library; photocopy in the Fort Hays Kansas State College Library.

When these studies are compared with similar compilations made in other regions of the United States, it becomes immediately apparent that few, if any, of the words and expressions included are peculiar to Kansas. Kansans themselves do not feel that they have any distinctive language traits; so far as they are concerned, they just talk natural. And in truth it is not always easy to recognize a Kansan by listening to him talk. All the sounds and cadences of the upper Middle West may be heard in the speech of some residents of the state; but there are those whose language is so similar to that of the Ozarks that it might be mountain speech, and there are others whose language belongs to the Southwest. Moreover, people who come from the same section of the state do not necessarily talk alike. From the very beginning of its settlement, Kansas was crisscrossed with different language groups, one result being that even today there are localities where speech habits are at variance with those of neighboring communities. Nevertheless, although few originated in the state or are unique to it, there are characteristic words, expressions, and usages, some of them dating back to territorial days, that are widely current in Kansas and that are not often found in written American English.

Place-names and some of the vocabulary used in territorial days in Kansas reflect the early settlers' contact with the races and nationalities which were there before them—the Indians, French, and Spanish. The name of the state itself comes from that of an Indian tribe, the Kansa. Many towns, counties, and rivers bear names associated with the native tribes—Wichita, Pawnee Rock, Osage City, Comanche County, the Kaw River, the Republican River (named for the Pitahauerat or Republican Pawnee), etc. Place-names in the state also derive from the names of tribes which migrated or were moved to Kansas as their hunting grounds farther east became settled by white men —Ottawa, Lenape, Pottawatomie County, Wyandotte County, Shawnee County, Wabaunsee County (named for a chief of the Pottawatomi tribe), etc. Some ordinary words also come from Indian languages. While most of these, like *moccasin* and *hominy,* probably entered Kansas with immigrants from the older states, at least one Indian word may have been added to the English vocabulary in Kansas: in Osage County the Sac word for wigwam, *wic-i-up,* was said to be in common use among whites (*Ca II,* 142).

Words borrowed from the French traders who were active in eastern Kansas at an early time include *chute,* which meant a bypass in a river or side channel (*Be,* 132), and *bois d'arc* (literally, "bow wood"), pronounced *bodark,* which became a common name for the Osage orange or hedge tree (*Be,* 23). Although more Spanish words were taken over than French, probably most of them entered Kansas speech from the cattle-raising states to the south and southwest rather than from direct contact with Spanish-speaking people. *Savvy* (*Ca II*, 141) from *saber*, "to know"; *lariat* or *lariette* (*Be*, 71) from *la reata*, "the rope"; *calaboose* (*Fr*, 32) from *calabozo*, "jail"; *vamoose*, from *vamos*, "we go"; and *ranch*, from *rancho*, "farm"—these are but a few of the words of Spanish origin in common use in Kansas today. In addition there are English expressions which may be translations of Spanish idiom. For example, in 1893 Professor Carruth of the University of Kansas reported the use of the adjective *skin-full*, meaning "drunk" (*Ca II*, 142). Similarly the Spanish adjective *borracho*, meaning "drunk," is related to the colloquial noun *borracha*, meaning "wine skin," and conveys something of the same connotation as the adjective reported by Professor Carruth. This resemblance may, however, be owing to no more than coincidence.

The great majority of the words and expressions cited in the sources on which this study is based were brought from the older states and are of English origin. Some of these usages are no longer current in standard English. I remember hearing one woman in Pittsburg describe a coverlid (coverlet); she told how the wool had been dyed with indigo (blue), with hedge chips (orange-yellow), and with walnut hulls and chamber lye (brown). *Chamber lye* is a euphemistic term for urine. Shakespeare has one of his characters use this expression, saying, ". . . your Chamber-lye breeds Fleas" (*I King Henry IV*, II, i, 23). *Fice* and *feisty* are other words with a long history.

Another survival from early usage is archaic preterites. For example, sometimes Kansans use the past participle, as in "I done it" (*Bu*, 396) or "I run home after the bacon." *Taken* is substituted for *took* (*Bu*, 396). Sometimes a form completely nonstandard is used, as *drug* for *dragged* (*Bu*, 397); *ailted* for *ailed*, as in "What ailted him?" (*Ru I*, 102); or *attacted* for *attacked* (*Bu*, 395).

Other nonstandard usages are heard in Kansas. *Anymore*, *hardly*, and *scarcely* are used otherwise than in general American speech; *anymore* is heard in Kansas in affirmative as well as in negative statements (*Sa II*, 4), and *hardly* and *scarcely* find their way into negative statements as well as affirmative (*Bu*, 394). Thus we might have a sentence like: "I'm so busy anymore

I don't hardly have a chance to say hello." *That* serves for *so* in such expressions as "He's that sick he can't speak" (*Ca II*, 142). *Want* does double duty on occasion: in expressions like "He wants in" or "The dog wants out" it means not just *wants* but *wants to be* or *wants to come* or *wants to go* (*Bu*, 395; *Ca II*, 142).

There are other and more imaginative divergencies. Louise Pound has written of some of the deliberate mispronunciations of words in the central West (*Po*, 133). We may regard as examples such terms as *Sandy Kitty* used playfully for *Kansas City* (*Ru III*, 246); *diffe bitterence* for *bit of difference* (*Ru III*, 245); *pettibockers*, a combination of *petticoat* and *knickerbockers*, used as the name of a loose undergarment for girls (*Ru III*, 245); and *diangling*, a combination of *diagonal* and *angle*, used in such a sentence as "He went diangling across the field" (*Ru I*, 105).

This kind of fiddling with words is not the only linguistic activity of the Kansas folk imagination. Kansas speech is rich in metaphors, original as well as traditional. Expressions like the following seem typical:

> *There must be a bug under the chip* (*Ru I*, 104): There's something which doesn't appear on the surface.
> *Go up the spout* (*Wy*, 173): Get excited.
> *The old woman's plucking her geese* (*Wy*, 173): It's snowing.
> *A toad on a tussock* (*Ca I*, 100): Dead, lifeless.
> *As big a fool as Thompson's colt* (*Ru II*, 330): Wholly without judgment.
> *He couldn't cut mustard:* He can't quite do anything; he's not very clever.
> *I couldn't carry a tune if it was tied up in a sack* (*Wy*, 174): I can't sing.
> *Beat the devil around the stump* (*Ru I*, 103): To accomplish one's purpose while saving one's conscience by indirection. "Calling these doings parties instead of dances is just beating the devil around the stump."
> *To give the mitten* (*Sa I*, 2): To terminate an engagement, to "give the cold shoulder" to "give the brush-off." Girls at one time used to knit miniature mittens to give their boy

friends as a means of informing them that the romance was officially over. Vance Randolph reports a similar custom in the Ozarks: *"Sack:* v. t. to refuse, to dismiss. Will Sharp (Springfield, Mo., *News,* May 31, 1941) says that girls used to knit a tiny sack and send it to a boy, as a sign that they wanted no more of his attentions" *(Ra II,* 280).

It would make a dog puke: An emphatic expression used to describe something particularly disagreeable. I heard a woman who has spent the last eighty years in the south-eastern part of the state use this expression most effectively. She said of her daughter's cooking, "She gaums up messes as ud puke a dog." This statement also makes use of two other terms, the meanings of which are ambiguous in Kansas usage. *Gaum* means "to soil" or "to gum" as well as "to put together" or "to mix." A *mess* may be "a quantity of food for a meal" (as in "a mess of greens") or "a hodgepodge," "a disagreeable mixture." The last few words of the quotation, however, set unmistakably the direction of the old lady's thought.

A KANSAS GLOSSARY

This glossary will consist chiefly of a selection of words from the articles and theses listed on pages 123–125. Expressions which have previously been mentioned are not included. The criterion by which the items have been chosen was purely subjective; I have picked words which appealed to me as unusual, colorful, or characteristic. The glossary is divided into two sections: first, words which are no longer in common use, so far as I have been able to determine; and second, words for whose currency I can vouch. In the second section I have indicated where the terms have been previously reported, but I have not hesitated to modify the definitions when required by usage as I found it.

SECTION 1

Breaker (Be, 25) n. A breaking plow, as contrasted with a stir-ring plow; a plow for breaking the prairie for the first time.

Bull whacker (Be, 25) n. The driver of a team of oxen in the freighting business.

Calamity-ites (*Ca II,* 138) n. Opposition name for members of the People's party.

Carpet sack (*Be,* 41) n. A carpetbag (cf. *Ha,* 28).

Coracle (*Be,* 47) n. A boat made by stretching hides over a framework of poles. (Also called a *bouco.*)

County seat war (*Be,* 49) n. A sharp rivalry between two towns of a county to obtain the distinction of having the county court and other county offices located there.

Dodger (*Ha,* 44) n. A kind of corn bread.

Doggery (*Ha,* 44) n. A low drinking saloon.

Exoduster (*Be,* 56) n. An ex-slave who came to Kansas in the great exodus from the South in 1879. [This term was again applied to those who left the "dust bowl" in the '30's.]

Grasshoppers, the (*Be,* 61) n. Several years in the 1870's remembered on account of the destruction of crops by swarms of grasshoppers. [The term *grasshopper years* was perhaps more common.]

Hair flowers n. Strands of human hair twisted and tied so as to represent flowers. [*Hair wreaths* were made of hair flowers and often used, framed, as wall decorations.]

Jayhawk (*Be,* 68) v. To go on a marauding expedition.

Jayhawker (*Be,* 68) n. Applied first to guerilla fighters in the free state struggle and now applied to all Kansans.

Literary (*Ru I,* 325) n. "A kind of literary society or club; a gathering of persons, esp. in rural districts at the schoolhouse, nearly always in winter, and in the evening, where a program is presented, such as reciting or declaiming poetry or prose selections, reading selections, engaging in dialogues (committed to memory); debating propositions, reading original papers, essays, etc. Sometimes contests in spelling are included and even burlesque trials."

Lo (*Sa I,* 3) n. An Indian, from Pope's line in the "Essay on Man," "Lo, the poor Indian." [This unlikely word appears in Margaret Hill McCarter's novel, *Widening Waters*. It was evidently not uncommon. It is also used by Joseph G. McCoy in his *Historic Sketches of the Cattle Trade*, Kansas City, 1874. *Poor Lo* and *Mr. Lo* are variations.]

Mule-skinner (*Be,* 77) n. The driver of a team of mules.

Paper town n. A town projected but not inhabited. "It's not simply a paper town" (*Ha,* 116).

Polly-fox (*Ru I,* 111) v. To quibble or equivocate. "Judge Stewart calls the lawyers down when they polly-fox in a case."

Quill-wheel (*Ca I,* 98) n. A rattletrap wagon.

Seraphine (*Be,* 89) n. A musical instrument, a small organ.

Sod house (*Be,* 96) n. A house built of sods.

Timber claim (*Be,* 105) n. A claim taken on condition of planting a certain acreage of trees. Also called *tree claim.*

SECTION 2

Angle (*Be,* 14) n. A diagonal road from one section line road to another.

Bealing (*Ru I,* 103) n. Boil, gathering. "The baby's got bealings about his back."

Beggar's lice (*Be,* 161) n. The name of a weed having seed which clings to clothing.

Big bug (*Ca II,* 137; *Fr,* 13) n. A prominent person, a "big shot."

Black jack (*Be,* 161) n. A kind of scrubby oak found generally in northeastern Kansas and occasionally in other parts of the state.

Blinky (*Be,* 201) adj. Applied to milk that is just beginning to sour.

Blue john (*Be,* 201–202) n. Milk which has had every particle of butterfat removed. [*Blinky blue john* in southeast Kansas.]

Blues (*Fr,* 16) n. Low spirits. "Those nervous people . . . getting the blues over the weather. . . ."

Bogus (*Be,* 128) adj. Spurious, sham.

Bottom (*Be,* 128) n. The low-lying land along a creek or river; including both that subject to inundation, and that farther removed. [*Bottoms,* plural.]

Branch (*Be,* 130) n. A stream. Branch-water is distinguished from well-water.

Browse (*Ha,* 23) n. Whatever feed cattle find. Grass, leaves, any vegetation. "Part of the stock lived upon browse."

Bushwhack (*Ru I,* 104) v. To borrow with intent to return. "Somebody bushwhacked my plow." [*To bushwhack* sometimes means to steal.]

Butter and eggs (*Be,* 167) n. A plant, Linaria vulgaris, having flowers shaped somewhat like those of the snapdragon in two shades of yellow. Well known in Kansas.

Cagey, cajy (*Ru II,* 321) adj. Having sexual desire. "The stallion is quite cajy after seeing a mare go by."

Cahoots (*Ca II,* 138) n. Collusion, partnership.

Camps n. Small communities, once mining towns, in Crawford and Cherokee counties.

Caterwampus (*Ru I,* 104) adv. Awry; not straight. "He had the covers on all caterwampus." "He came caterwampus across the street."

Chimly n. Chimney. [A woman remembers that as a child in Pittsburg she learned that "children who said chimly came from homes that weren't so nice."]

Chuck (*Be,* 207) v. To put a wedge under a wagon wheel to keep the wagon from rolling.

Clabber cheese (*Be,* 208) n. Sometimes used for cheese made from clabber, commonly called cottage cheese.

Coddy (*Ca I,* 96) adj. Unconventional or out of fashion. [Of a woman who wore a long evening dress to go shopping in the afternoon, another woman says, "They always were a little coddy."]

Commit (*Wy,* 173) v. Commit to memory.

Cool (*Ca II,* 138) adj. Complete, unqualified. "A cool thousand."

Count ties (*Ca II,* 138) v. To walk on a railroad track.

Coverlid (*Be,* 212) n. A coverlet.

Cow town (*Be,* 50) n. A town such as Abilene on the Union Pacific or Dodge City on the Santa Fe from which were shipped the cattle from the great ranges of the west. These towns are still often called cow towns.

Cracklings (*Be,* 213) n. The residue left after the rendering of lard.

Crawl (*Ca I,* 95) v. To try to escape from embarrassing situations without admitting one's mistake. [Also, "We *wiggled* out" or "He *wrinkled* out."]

Devil's darning needle (*Be,* 173) n. A dragonfly with transparent iridescent wings. [Also called *snake doctor* and *snake feeder.*]

Dip n. Gravy. "Give me some dip on my bread too."

Dodger n. A handbill. "He stood on the corner handing out dodgers."

Draw (*Ca II*, 138; *Be*, 137) n. A depression in a field or prairie.

Feisty adj. (applied to girls). Wild—not in the sense of being "bad tempered," as sometimes the word is used in the South —saucy or overflirtatious.

Fice n. A cantankerous and nasty dog; one that's "snippy."

Fizzle out (*Ca II*, 139) v. To run out, to fail.

Fleas in one's nose (*Ru I*, 106) n. phr. Chimerical notions.

Folks (*Be*, 223) n. Commonly used for parents.

Force n. Worth; value. "He's not of much force."

Gas (*Ca II*, 139) v. and n. Unnecessary or insolent talk; as, "He's been gassing away all the evening."

Gaum (*Ru I*, 106) v. Gum. [This has a common meaning also of "mix" or "put together."]

Glass snake (*Be*, 176) n. A snake which, when struck, breaks in two as if made of glass. [It is supposed to be able to rejoin itself.]

Go-devil (*Be*, 225) n. A hay rake, sometimes called a sweep rake.

Gumbo (*Ca I*, 97; *Be*, 228) v. A peculiar, puttylike, dark soil.

Hedge (*Be*, 178) n. The common name for the Osage orange, which has been frequently used as a hedge.

Hedge chips n. Chips of wood from Osage orange. Said to produce an orange dye when boiled in water.

Hornswoggle (*Ca I*, 97) v. Discomfit. "I'll be hornswoggled if I'll do it."

Jim-jams (*Ca II*, 140) n. Delirium tremens.

Jimson powder n. A powder prepared with ginseng. [I heard a country man ask for this in a Pittsburg drugstore—for a baby with "bealings about his back."]

Little bitty (*Bu*, 394) adj. Little. "My mother's a little bitty woman."

Land office business (*Be*, 71) n. A rushing business, referring to the rush at government land offices when public land was offered for sale.

Light bread (*Be*, 239; *Ru II*, 325) n. Bread leavened with yeast. [An old man says, "Oh how I remember that country light bread and fresh churned butter."]

Morish adj. Part of the expression "morish taste," meaning "It has a taste that makes you want more." ["Has it got a morish taste?" asks a lady offering a second piece of cake.]

Newby n. A kind of light shawl. [A woman in her eighties, trying to remember the story of "Young Charlotte," says, "All she put on was her newby."]

Pie plant (*Be*, 184) n. A name for rhubarb common in southeastern Kansas.

Porched eggs (*Wy*, 173) n. Poached eggs.

Pud n. and adj. A cinch, an easy job. Applied to certain courses by students. "Take that—it's a pud."

Pull up stakes (*Be*, 86) v. phr. To change the location of one's residence.

Pussy (*We*, 485) adj. Pursy, fat, short-winded. "One of these men is old, short, and pussy." "He was real pussy" (*Ha*, 129).

Rosinweed (*Be*, 188) n. A sticky plant having bright yellow flowers. Called rosinweed because of a resinous substance exuded by the stem. [The gum was said to be gathered by children for chewing.]

Scrooch, scrooge (*Ca I*, 98) v. To cringe.

Section road n. A road on a section boundary. Usually applied to an unpaved or country road, a back road. A road is only called a section road when it isn't anything more important.

Shake (*Be*, 90) n. A rough slab about thirty-two inches long, riven from a log and used variously as a shingle or as clapboarding.

Skads (*Ca I*, 98) n. Great quantities, as, "skads of money."

Snake fence (*Be*, 93) n. A zigzag rail fence.

Squaunch-wise adj. and adv. At an angle, catter-corner, "caterwampus." [In southeast Kansas the term is *slaunch-wise*.]

Stirring plow (*Be*, 103) n. A plow with a shorter mold board than that of the breaking plow. The stirring plow is the ordinary kind of plow.

Stoga (*Ca II*, 142) n. A sort of boot, also a kind of cigar. "A handful of salt . . . and a good pair of stoga boots is about the ammunition necessary" (*Fr*, 254). [Also *stogy*.]

Whack (*Ca II*, 142) n. Gear; as, "The clock is out of whack."

White mule (*Ru I*, 114; *Ra*, 386) n. Any colorless whiskey or alcohol for drinking.

Whopper-jawed adj. Crooked, awry, askew. [Also *whomper jawed.*] "It's all whopper-jawed; windows out and blinds a-slant and porch floor coming in."

Work (*Ca II,* 142) v. Dupe; as, "we worked him for a five."

Work brickle (*Ru I,* 114) adj. phr. Ready to work.

FOLK VERSE

Part I

Mary Koch

Folk verse collected in Kansas includes children's rhymes, "made poems" of a moralistic or sentimental nature which found their way into oral tradition, autograph album verse, and "In Memoriam" verse. The beginning folklorist, discovering such poetry, usually does not recognize it as being of any worth whatever, for it is almost always crude both in content and form, obviously lacking in literary merit. But to the folklore scholar it is valuable as another in the long list of folk creations for which he is searching. Accepting the crudities and vulgarities of the verse, the sentimentality and the moralizing, he studies it—its persistence, its diffusion, its infinite variety—in order to interpret the life and culture of the people of the area.

Among the most accessible and intriguing types of folk verse are children's doggerel and jingles—skip-rope rhymes, counting-off rhymes, and fragments of poetry used for teasing, divining, tongue-twisting, and a dozen other purposes. To determine who shall be "it" or take some unwanted part in a game, children universally and from earliest times have chanted counting-out rhymes, sometimes called by the old traditional name, "rimbles." On school playgrounds, in back yards and alleys they are being recited today, with their characteristic rhythm and "full of fossil words worn smooth by much repetition." [1] It is a commonplace to folklorists that "In changed but recognizable sounds children have unconsciously preserved . . . passwords of the freemasons of the Middle Ages, Sanskrit sacred symbols, secret magic formulas, Irish death-rimes and druid exorcisms,

[1] C. F. Potter, *Standard Dictionary of Folklore, Mythology and Legend* (New York: Funk and Wagnalls, 1949), p. 254.

Bible characters and saints' names, Romany gypsy charms and patter. . . . It is certainly possible that our common 'Eenie, meenie, miny, mo' is a descendant of an ancient magic rime-charm used in druid times to choose the human victims to be ferried across the *Menai* Strait to the Isle of *Mona* to meet a horrible fate under the Golden Bough of the sacred mistletoe amid the holy oaks." [2]

Skip-rope rhymes are as common in Kansas as they are over the world, and in them, too, can be recognized words and sounds which have had other meanings for other people long ago. Tongue-twisters, teasing rhymes, and divining rhymes are all to be heard wherever children are at play.

"Grues," so named by Robert Louis Stevenson, are short poems of a gruesome nature about the terrible fate or the misadventures of a child with a penchant for trouble. They run in cycles of popularity.

> Little Willie on the track
> Didn't hear the engine's squeal.
> Now the engine's coming back
> Scraping Willie off the wheel.

Recently a similar type has appeared in prose form, the so-called Little Moron or Little Audrey stories. For example: "Mother, can I go out and play with grandpa?" "No, Audrey, you've dug him up twice already this week."

Following is a sampling of the various types of children's rhymes, all within my own memory, all found in Kansas and familiar to most of us.

CHILDREN'S RHYMES

COUNTING-OUT RHYMES

> Eenie, meenie, miny, mo
> Catch a nigger by the toe
> If he hollers, let him go
> Eenie, meenie, miny, mo
> O-U-T spells out goes she.

[2] *Ibid.*, pp. 254–255, 340.

or

> Eenie, meenie, miny, mo
> Catch a nigger by the toe
> If he hollers, make him pay
> Fifty dollars every day.

1, 2, 3, 4, 5, 6, 7
All good children go to heaven
What they do I cannot tell
All bad children go to—'way down yonder in the cornfield.

> One potato
> Two potatoes
> Three potatoes, OR
> Four potatoes
> Five potatoes
> Six potatoes, NOR.

GAME RHYMES

> Ball bouncing:
> > One, two, buckle my shoe
> > Three, four, shut the door
> > Five, six, pick up sticks
> > Seven, eight, lay them straight
> > Nine, ten, big fat hen
> > Eleven, twelve, dig and delve
> > Thirteen, fourteen, maids a-courting
> > Fifteen, sixteen, maids in the kitchen
> > Seventeen, eighteen, maids a-waiting
> > Nineteen, twenty, my plate's empty.

> To start a race:
> > One for the money
> > Two for the show
> > Three to get ready
> > And four to GO.

> For a pantomime guessing game:
> > Here we come.
> > Where you from?
> > New Orleans.
> > What's your trade?

Lemonade.
Show me some if you're not afraid.

TEASING RHYMES

Johnny's mad and I'm glad
And I know what will please him
A bottle of wine to make him shine
And Mary Jones to squeeze him.

or

Johnny's mad and I'm glad
And I know what will please him
A bottle of ink to make him stink
And three little niggers to tease him.

Doctor, doctor, can you tell
What will make poor Willie well?
He is sick and sure to die
That will make poor Mary cry.

Cry, baby, cry
Stick your finger in your eye
Tell your mother it wasn't I.

I see London (Paris)
I see France
I see somebody's underpants.

Teacher, teacher, I declare
I see somebody's underwear.

Shame, shame, double shame,
Everybody knows your name.

DIVINATION RHYMES

Rich man, poor man, beggar man, thief,
Doctor, lawyer, merchant, chief,
Tinker, tailor, soldier, sailor.

CHARMS

Starlight, Star bright
First star I see tonight

I wish I may, I wish I might
Have the wish I wish tonight.

When a lady-bug lights on you:
Lady-bug, lady-bug, fly away home
Your house is on fire, your children all gone
All but one, her name is Ann
And she crept under the pudding pan.

See a pin and pick it up
All the day you'll have good luck
See a pin and let it lay
You'll have bad luck all the day.

Step on a crack
You'll break your mother's back
Step on a hole
You'll break your mother's sugar bowl.

"SMART-ALECK" RHYMES

What's your name?
Puddin' shane
Ask me again and I'll tell you the same.

What's your name?
Puddin' pie
Ask me again and I'll make you cry.

What's your name?
Tom Brown
Ask me again and I'll knock you down.

RECITATIONS

Mother, mother, mother, pin a rose on me
Two little boys are after me
One is blind and the other can't see
Mother, mother, mother, pin a rose on me.

Lemonade
Made in the shade

Stirred with a spade
By an old maid.

I scream, you scream,
We all scream for ice cream.

Catches, sells

There's an old dead horse in the road.
I one it
You two it
I three it
You four it
I five it
You six it
I seven it
You *ate* it.

Derisive rhymes

No more pencils
No more books
No more teacher's
Dirty looks.

Finger rhymes

This little pig went to market
This little pig stayed home
This little pig ate roast beef
This little pig had none
This little pig said "Wee, wee, wee" all the way home.

This is the church
This is the steeple
Open the door
And out come the people.

Tickling rhymes

Eye winker
Tom tinker
Nose dropper
Mouth eater
Chin chopper
Gully, gully, gully. (tickling under chin)

TONGUE TWISTERS

> Peter Piper picked a peck of pickled peppers
> A peck of pickled peppers Peter Piper picked
> If Peter Piper picked a peck of pickled peppers
> Where is the peck of pickled peppers Peter
>   Piper picked?

FRIENDSHIP VERSE

> If you love me like I love you
> No knife can cut our love in two.

MISCELLANEOUS VERSE

> Open your mouth and shut your eyes
> And I'll give you something to make you wise.

> Good night
> Sleep tight
> Don't let the bedbugs bite.

> April fool is coming on
> And you're the biggest fool in town.

> April fool is past
> And you're the biggest fool at last.

ALBUM VERSE

The memory books and autograph albums of our childhood are filled with folk verses, some of them coming unchanged through three or four generations. The following are all taken from an autograph album which belonged to George Washington Franklin, pioneer bachelor who lived near Fort Scott, Kansas. Spelling and punctuation are as in the originals.

> 1882
> > May blessing attend you
> > Both early and late
> > And heaven assist you
> > In choosing a mate

1885

  May your life be long and happy
  May your sorrows be but few
  May you find a home in heaven
  When your earthely task gets through

1886

  Fall in the sea, fall from the deck
  Fall downstairs and break your neck
  Fall from the stary heavens above
  But never neaver fall in love

  Intelligence and coutresy not always are combined
  Often in a wooden house a golden room is found.

  Do thy duty that is best
  Leave unto thy Lord the rest

1887

  May all thy days and all thy hours
    The sunshine and the flowers
  The heat and cold the wind and rain
    Bring blessings to you in their train

1890

  Remember well and bare in mind
  A tender friend is hard to find
  But when you find one kind and true
  Never change the old one for the new.

1891

  When on this page
  You chance to look
  Just think of me
  And close this book.

  When you are old
  And cannot see
  Put on your specks
  And think of me.

  Remember me when far away
  And only half awake

Remember me on your wedding day
And send me a slice of cake.

When this porley writin page you see
Lett it be a token of love to thee.

1895
When you drink your coffee
When you drink your tea
And when you put the sugar in
Put in a lump for me.

No date:
May you live happy
And live a long life
Make a good husband
And get a good wife.

FOLK VERSE

Part II

CHARLES BURGESS
Kansas State College of Pittsburg

The following collection includes representative examples of the several types of Kansas folk verse: children's rhymes, "made poems," autograph album verse, and "In Memoriam" verse.

CHILDREN'S RHYMES

HUCKLEJEE BREAD

[More than forty-five years ago Judge J. C. Ruppenthal of Russell, Kansas, recorded the following rhyme in *Dialect Notes,* IV (1914), 108. Children sitting with hands clasped over the knees rock forward and backward at the huckles, or hips, and say it in singsong.]

> My father and mother
> Are sick in bed,
> And I must learn how
> To make hucklejee bread,
>
> Then up with your feet
> And down with your head,
> And that is the way
> To make hucklejee bread.

HEARTS LIKE DOORS

[Collected from Mrs. L. A. Coverston of Pittsburg, Kansas, by Charles Burgess, 1 April 1958. Mrs. Coverston learned the verse as a child in Illinois more than eighty years ago.]

Hearts like doors will open with ease
To very little keys
And they are these—
"I thank you, sir," and "If you please."

THE DEVIL SENDS THE EVIL WINDS

[Collected from Roscoe Boyd of Page City, Kansas, by his daughter Norma Boyd, April, 1957.]

The devil sends the evil winds
To raise the skirts up high;
But heaven's just and sends the dust
That closes the bad man's eye.

THE LORDS OF CREATION

[Collected from Maria Isabelle Walker, age 97, of Blue Mound, Kansas, by Nellie Stump and Ernestine Rowley of Blue Mound, 22 September 1958. Miss Walker learned the poem from an aunt in 1878 or 1880. She thinks it may have been in a songbook brought from Scotland. Miss Walker's family was from Pennsylvania and came to Kansas in 1855.]

The lords of creation, men, they call
And they think they rule the whole world,
But they are much mistaken after all
For they're under the women's control.
Now ever since the world began
It has always been that way,
For did not Adam, the very first man
The very first woman obey.

JINGLES FOR CHILDREN

[Collected from Mrs. Berenece Bradley of Blue Mound, Kansas, by Nellie Stump, 11 October 1958. Mrs. Bradley learned the rhymes from her mother, who came from Illinois in a covered wagon.]

Churn butter churn
Come butter come
Let little *Mary* have
Some-some-some.
(Any child's name can be used.)

Shoe old horsie—
Shoe old mare—
Let the little coltie
Go bare-bare-bare.

Little red bird in the tree,
Sing a song for me.
Sing about the roses
On the garden wall.
Sing about the birds
In the treetop tall.
Sing little red bird to me,
Sing about the birds,
Swinging in the tree.

"MADE POEMS"

A Message from the Grave

[Collected from Nellie Sparks, formerly of Iola, Kansas, by Lavone Brown of Asbury, Missouri, 9 October 1958. Miss Sparks bought the poem in leaflet form for ten cents about fifty years ago, probably in Iola or Oswego. She spoke it at several literary meetings.]

1. Come, listen to me, my comrades,
    'Tis the truth I am going to tell.
   It's the fate of a fair young maiden,
    Who in an Eastern town did dwell.
2. Her face was fair and comely,
    Her eyes were an azure blue,
   She was what men call handsome,
    And as pure as the morning dew.
3. Her parents indulged her every whim
    Her heart was as light as a bird.
   And to know her was to love her,
    But of wickedness she never heard.
4. A cloud came over this dear young life,
    A cloud, so black so drear,
   And it left her a wreck on the shores of Time,
    Where many have gone before.

5. She met, she loved, not wisely,
    But, you know the rest, too well.
  And she was left alone in her sorrow,
    To drift on the road toward Hell.

6. One night, when all were sleeping,
    She noiselessly left her room,
  And crept silently out of the window,
    Passed out in the darkness and gloom.

7. Her absence from the fireside
    Cast a gloom o'er the entire home,
  But, the mother dreamed not 'twas her own neglect
    Which caused her dear daughter to roam.

8. Like the rose, when plucked from mother Earth
    Will wither and fade and decay
  This daughter so fair, with flaxen hair,
    Crossed the River of Death one sad day.

9. But, from the time she left her home that night
    Till found a corpse on a busy street,
  Her life was as pure as a sunbeam,
    Tho her first step she could not retreat.

10. As she lay at the morgue, to be gazed upon,
    By many who passed that way,
  They dreamed not that she who lay cold in death,
    Was as pure as the new-mown hay.

11. In her purse was found a letter.
    "This was written by myself," she said,
  "And I want it read at my inquest,
    When you determine the cause of my death.

12. "I am the daughter of well-to-do parents,
    Who granted my every whim,
  But they warned me not of temptation,
    And my sorrow is full, to the brim.

13. "I prefer, not to live as a sinner,
    Before the law and sinful men,
  I will go before Christ, my Saviour.
    I know he will take me in.

14. "Because, He it was who said to the woman,
    Far back in the days of yore,
  'Neither do I condemn thee,
    Go, and sin no more.'

15. "But, a message to many other girls,
    I wish to leave before I go.

It is this: Beware, my sister,
    One false step is full of woe.
16. "I have lived, not the life of a sinner,
    But I cannot undo the past,
And tho I repent and oft-times relent,
    By man I am judged till the last.
17. "So I bid adieu to this cold, cold world,
    Soon I'll rest beneath six feet of earth.
I send a last good-bye to my mother,
    And I regret the day of my birth."
18. They laid her to rest one afternoon,
    In a far away Western State,
And these words were placed on her tombstone,
    I trust they will not be too late:
19. "The one who lies here was once full of cheer,
    And as pure as the morning dew.
Tho she fell 'neath the hand of the tempter,
    Those who can throw stones, are but few.
20. "Altho she lived not nineteen summers,
    May that noble life not be in vain.
May the lesson thus taught by her sacrifice,
    Save many from temptation and sin."

WINE IN THE CUP

[Collected from Mrs. Annie Roney Casebolt of Chanute, Kansas, by Mrs. C. L. Childers, 14 October 1958. Mrs. Casebolt was born in Wilson County, Kansas; her father was from Cork County, Ireland, and her mother from New York City. Mrs. Casebolt's father taught her this example of "temperance verse" when she was fourteen.]

Dark is the night and the eyes of the father
Sadly peer through the fast-falling gloom,
And his heart fills with dread as the form of his darling
Staggers home from the cursed saloon.

'Tis wine in the cup and its bowl's subtle glitter
And its foam like the rest of the wave
Drawing men on its tide where they float like a bubble
On its foam to a winebibber's grave.

Dark is the night and the poor dying mother
Sorely grieves as the long moments drag
As the poor helpless form of her child she does cover,
With its poor scanty clothing of rags.

'Tis wine in the cup and its bowl's subtle glitter
And its foam like the crest of the wave
Drawing one's precious wife with a child on her bosom
On its foam to a wine pauper's grave.

LITTLE BLOSSOM

[Collected from Mary M. (Brihart) Moore of Howard, Kansas, by Lucile Anderson of Chanute. Mrs. Moore heard an older sister recite "Little Blossom" on a prohibition program in 1888. One can well imagine the effect of this piece, recited by a little girl, on a temperance audience of the '80's.]

Oh dear! I's so tired and lonesome,
I wonder why Mama don't come.
She told me to shut up my pretty blue eyes
And 'fore I waked up she'd be home.

She said she was going to see Grandma,
Who lives by the river so bright.
I 'spect my Mama's fallen in there
Perhaps she won't come home tonight.

I 'dess I's afraid to stay up here
Without any fire or light;
But Dod's lighted his lamps up in heaven.
I can see them all twinkly and bright.

I 'dess I'll go down and meet Papa.
I know he has stopped at the store.
A great pretty store full of bottles.
I wish he wouldn't go there no more.

Sometimes he's so sick when he comes in
He stumbles and falls at the stair,
And once when he comed in the parlor
He kicked at my poor little chair.

And Mama was all scared and frightened
And hugged me up close to her breast,
And called me her poor little Blossom
And—but I 'dess I's forgotted the rest.

But I loves him and 'dess I'll do find him.
Perhaps he will tum with me soon
Den it won't be dark and lonesome
Waiting for Mama to tum.

Out in the night went the baby,
The dear little Blossom so fair
With eyes that were clear as the blue sky
With halo of golden brown hair.

Out in the night went the baby
Though her little heart beating with fright
'Til at last she had reached the Gin Palace
All brilliant with music and light.

Her tiny hand pushed the door open
Though her touch was as light as a breath
And her little feet entered the portal
That leads but to ruin and death.

Away down the long floor she pattered,
Her pretty blue eyes open wide
'Til she spied, in the corner, her Papa
And her tiny feet paused at his side.

"Oh Papa!" she cried as she reached him
And her voice rippled out sweet and clear.
"I fought if I'd come I should find you.
And now I's so glad I is here.

"The lights are so pretty, dear Papa,
And I fink that the music's so sweet
But I 'dess it's most suppertime, Papa,
For Blossom wants something to eat."

A moment the bleared eyes gazed wildly,
Down into the face sweet and fair,

And then—as a demon possessed him
He grasped at the back of the chair.

A moment, a second, 'twas over
The work of the fiend was complete
And the poor little innocent Blossom
Lay broken and crushed at his feet.

Then quick as a light came his reason
And showed him the deed he had done.
With a groan that a demon might pity
He knelt by the quivering one.

He pressed the pale lips to his bosom
He lifted the fair golden head.
One moment the baby's lips quivered
And poor little Blossom was dead.

Then the law in its majesty seized him
And exacted just penalty—death—
For only a fiend or a madman
Would deprive such a baby of breath.

But the man who sold him the poison
And made him the ruins of hell
Must not be less respected
Because he has license to sell.

God pity men, women, and children,
Who are crushed by this juggernaut rum.
May press, pulpit, platform, united
Fight strong 'til deliverance come.

Invitation to a Wedding

[Collected from Laurence Weigel of Hays, Kansas, by S. J. Sackett, 5 May 1958. According to Mr. Weigel the piece is used traditionally among the so-called German-Russians of Ellis County. Dr. Hans Beerman of Kansas State College of Pittsburg has supplied a translation.]

Wir kommen nicht hergeritten,
Wir kommen sicher geschritten;

Braut und Braeutigam, sie lassen Euch bitten,
Sie lassen Euch laden insgemein,
Ihr sollt auch Hochzeitsgaeste sein,
Zehn Gaens—die muessen dran,
Neunzehn Huehner und der alte Hahn,
Die sind gefuettert und so fett,
Wie ein altes Wagenbrett,
Dann kommt auch gleich die Kathrin Woes,
Und kocht auch gleich die dicken Kloess;
Sie kocht sie nach Belieben,
Und kocht auch gleich die roten Rueben.
Potz Blitz! Was faellt mir ein!
Ich hab' ja vergessen den Branntwein,
Wenn Ihr uns unser Stoecklein ziert,
So sagen wir auch wo Ihr hin-gehoert.

We do not come on horseback
We come staidly on foot
Bride and bridegroom, they ask you
To be invited all together
You shall also be wedding guests
Ten geese—they have to end in the pot
Nineteen chickens and the old rooster,
They have been fed to be as fat
As an old chopping block
Then Kathrin Woes comes right away
And cooks the fat dumplings
She cooks according to her own way
And cooks the red beets right away
Heavens . . . what am I thinking about?
I have forgotten the brandy . . . .
If you will grace our premises
We will tell you where you belong.

AUTOGRAPH ALBUM VERSE

[Whether or not these verses, found in autograph albums, are examples of folk verse is sometimes difficult to decide. The origins of the verses are seldom known. There is both written and oral transmission; mutations appear continually. The following verses are collected from an album belonging to Mrs. Laura Day of Blue Mound, Kansas. The album dates from 1891.]

When the golden sun is setting
And your mind from care is free
Won't you sometimes think of me.

When rocks and hills divide us
And you no more I see
Remember it was Dennis
That wrote these lines for you.

When hills and plains depart us,
And my face you cannot see
But when the sun is setting
Will you not stop to think of me.

Don't be a coward
Don't be afraid
And for Heaven's sake
Don't die an old maid.

As waves and ripples
follow ships at sea
May God's Blessings follow
thee.

These are verses from her husband's book.

When the golden
Sun is sinking and your
Mind from care is free and
Of absent ones your thinking
Will you sometimes think
Of me.

When the golden sun is setting and
Your mind from care is free
When you are thinking of the
Absent will you some times
Think of me.

Remember me and
My old woman,
Around the fire and
It a boomen.

[Collected from an album in the possession of Miss Laura Neiswanger of Lawrence, Kansas. The album belonged to Maggie Mohler of Osborne, Kansas; the inscriptions go back to the 1880's.]

Life is a chase—'tis a hurry
And race, with tumbles here and there!
Your footing keep sure
And your life keep pure
Nor fear to do and dare.

Life is before you,
Improve its golden moments,
Act from principle, never despair.
May success attend you.

May you remain through life the same
Unchanged in all except your name.

When the golden sun is setting,
And your heart from all care is free,
When o'er a thousand things you are thinking
Will you sometimes think of me.

[Collected from an autograph book belonging to Anna Duncan of Ness County, Kansas, by Esta Lou Riley of Dodge City. The entries are dated 1897 to 1899.]

When you are old and cannot see
Put on your specks and think of me.

As shure as comes your wedding day,
A broom to you I'll send
In sunshine use the brushy part
In storm the other end.

Here is one leaf reserved for me
From all thy sweet memorials free
But could I thus within your mind
One little vacant corner find
Where no impression yet is seen
Where no memorial yet has been
Oh, it should be my sweetest care
To write my name for ever there.

[Collected from an autograph book belonging to Elsie Conway of Dunlap, Lyon County, Kansas, by Esta Lou Riley of Dodge City.]

> The fox loves the valley
>   The deer loves the hill
> The boys love the girls and
>   I guess they always will.
>
> I dip my pen into the ink
> And grasp your album tight
> But for my life I cannot think
> One single word to write.

IN MEMORIAM

[Another type of Kansas folk verse is that composed for "In Memoriam" notices. I am told that the verses are read avidly, and that people often copy lines which they find particularly touching. When the anniversary of a family death approaches, the admired pieces are assembled and the notice inserted in the newspaper. The following appeared in the Pittsburg, Kansas, *Sun,* 25 March–9 April 1959.]

> We do not need a special day,
> To bring you to our minds,
> The days we do not think of you,
> Are very hard to find.
>
> She will never be forgotten,
> Though on earth she is no more,
> In memory she will always be with us,
> As she always was before.
>
> For all of us you did your best,
> Until the angels took you home to rest,
> In silence you suffered,
> With patience you bore,
> Until God called you home to suffer
>   no more.
>
> It doesn't take a special day,
>   To think dear dad of you,

You're thought of in "a special way"
  So often all year through.

In our hearts he will live forever,
Time may pass and bring its changes,
Fresh with every coming year.
But his memory will be cherished,
In the hearts that hold him dear.

Sixteen years have passed, and Father
We still miss you as before,
But we'll see you some glad morning,
On that bright celestial shore.

FOLKSONGS AND BALLADS

Part I

HENRY H. MALONE
University of Wichita

After the opening of Santa Fé to trade with the United States in 1821, Americans in quest of wealth and adventure traveled westward across Kansas in ever-increasing numbers. At first the smooth, rolling Kansas plains attracted only a few of these fortune-seekers, but in the '50's the tide of western migration left a number of settlers in its wake. Leavenworth and other Oregon Trail stations became hubs of permanent settlement, and by 1855, six years after the California gold rush, Kansas had a population of about 8,000. In 1859 another epidemic of "gold fever" sent covered wagons flaunting "Pikes Peak or Bust" signs across the flower-studded Flint Hills and velvety buffalo grass; of those that returned east, their signs reading "We Busted," a good many stopped in Kansas and stayed there. There was a new influx in the '60's, after the Civil War, when veterans of both the Union and Confederate armies took up land under the provisions of the Homestead Act, and the same decade saw the beginning of the cattle drives from Texas to Abilene and other shipping points. Cowboys and their herds poured into Kansas during the brief heyday of the "Long Drive"; before it was ended some of the cowpokes had filed on claims or joined the ranks of the nesters.

The story of the state's settlement has been told in many history books, but even without history books we still would know a good deal about the settlement period from its songs. A love of song was one thing held in common by the people who thronged into Kansas in those years—the migrants and the men and women who settled there. Travelers sang by their campfires as the darkness closed in around them; they recalled the old songs of the homelands they had left behind, and they made up new songs as they moved along into a new country toward a new life. Cowboys sang on the trail and through the lonely nights to soothe their resting herds; settlers sang songs of hope and courage to hearten themselves for the tasks ahead.

Many of the traditional English and Scottish ballads, frequently referred to as the Child ballads,[1] have been collected in Kansas. The Irish introduced melodies from their home island and many in the American idiom as well. Other national groups, such as the German, Swedish, Welsh, and Mexican settlers, also contributed numerous songs, but—unfortunately for the purposes of this study—their songs have been preserved only in their native tongues. Some of the most popular songs came from the Negroes of the state; by 1888 they made up about three per cent of its population. As to the emotional content of the Kansas repertoire, although there are many serious songs, the predominant mood of folksongs as a whole seems to run to the humorous, perhaps reflecting the optimism of the settlers.

Folksongs are, by definition, songs which are transmitted orally from one person to another—in other words, learned by hearing someone else sing them—and which live in the memories of people rather than on the pages of published books. In some circumstances, a folksong can also be a popular song: for example, millions of people learned "Home on the Range" from newspapers, magazines, and songbooks, but there are others for whom it is a folksong because it was learned and preserved in the way that is the distinguishing characteristic of folklore. The version presented in this study belongs to the latter category.

Although the folksong exists in an oral tradition, the folklorist does not limit himself to songs that he can collect from living informants; if he did so, he would deprive himself of songs now

[1] The term "Child ballad" refers to one of the 305 items in Francis J. Child, *The English and Scottish Popular Ballads* (Boston: Houghton Mifflin Co., 1882–1898).

forgotten or of earlier versions of songs. He also looks for those songs written down in manuscript or printed in books which derive from the oral tradition. Before collecting such songs he applies the test of variant versions: the existence of variants demonstrates that the song has gone through the process of transmission by word of mouth. In this study we have included two versions of "The Lane County Bachelor," both from manuscripts. More than enough variants of this song have been collected and published to prove its folk quality.

A *ballad* is a folksong that tells a story, usually in extremely condensed fashion. Because this separate term exists to describe narrative folksongs, some folklorists have reserved the term *folksong* for songs which do not tell a story but express an emotion, which may be serious or humorous.

The following fifteen songs were selected to represent some elements of the Kansas tradition. All have been learned and transmitted orally, all were collected in the state, and, so far as can be ascertained, six of the songs were composed within its boundaries. Ten songs were collected on tape from individuals who had learned the songs orally from someone else; the other five were contributed in manuscript versions. Of this latter group, three were written down by people who had learned them orally; one was taken down in shorthand from an informant who had learned it orally; and one derives from early manuscripts. "Home on the Range," "Kansas Land," "The Lane County Bachelor," and "Charles Guiteau" were among the most popular songs of the frontier and have often been included in folksong collections; printed versions of "The Kansas Jayhawker Song" and "The Dewey-Berry Song" have had local circulation. We have been unable to find that the nine other songs have ever been published before.

HOME ON THE RANGE

[Collected from Mrs. A. B. Hungerford, Wichita, Kansas, 3 November 1957. In the 1870's the informant's mother, Mrs. Nette H. Stafford, lived on a ranch on the Solomon River and heard "Home on the Range" sung in its original version by its creators. Mrs. Hungerford helped secure the passage of House

Bill No. 198, the 1947 act of the Kansas legislature which declared "Home on the Range" the official Kansas state song. According to this bill, the words were written by Dr. Brewster Higley, a pioneer Kansas physician, and the music composed by his friend Dan Kelly, a local druggist.[2] The song appeared first as a poem, "My Western Home," in the *Smith County Pioneer* in 1873, and later was set to music by Kelly.

In the second verse, "banks of the Beaver" refers to Beaver Creek in Kansas, and the "gale of the Solomon vale" to the Solomon River Valley. Versions of the song are given in almost every American folksong collection.]

Oh, give me a home where the buffalo roam,
Where the deer and the antelope play,
Where seldom is heard a discouraging word
And the sky is not clouded all day.

A home, a home where the deer and the antelope play,
Where seldom is heard a discouraging word
And the sky is not clouded all day.

Oh, give me the gale of the Solomon vale,
Where life streams with buoyancy flow,
On the banks of the Beaver, where seldom if ever
Any poisonous herbage doth grow.

Oh, give me the land where the bright diamond sand
Throws its light from the glittering stream,
Where glideth along the graceful white swan,
Like a maid in a heavenly dream.

I love the wild flowers in this bright land of ours;
I love too the wild curlew's scream,
The bluffs and white rocks and antelope flocks
That graze on the hillsides so green.

[2] Authorship of "Home on the Range" was established when the song became the subject of a copyright suit; the report of Samuel Moanfeldt, investigator for Music Publishers Protective Association, dated May, 1935, as well as other information on the song's history, appears in Kirke Mechem, "Home on the Range," *Kansas Historical Quarterly*, XVII (1949), 313–339, reprinted in *Heritage of Kansas*, II (1958), 11–34.

How often at night, when the heavens are bright
With the light of the glittering stars,
Have I stood here amazed and asked as I gazed
If their glory exceeds this of ours.

The air is so pure, the breezes so free,
The zephyrs so balmy and light,
I would not exchange my home here to range
Forever in azure so bright.

KANSAS JAYHAWKER SONG

[Collected from Fairy Walker Lane, Wichita, Kansas by S. J. Sackett, 1957. Mrs. Lane said the song was popular in 1898 in Melvern, Kansas. It is sung to the tune of "There'll Be a Hot Time in the Old Town Tonight."]

I'm a Jayhawker girl from a Jayhawker state,
I wear Jayhawker flowers with Jayhawker grace;
I sing Jayhawker songs, with a Jayhawker voice,
And the Jayhawker state is my own free choice.

Don't you hear the voices from the West?
The bells they ring the song that we love best;
They tell of life on that free and happy plain,
There will be a hot time in the old town tonight,
    Jayhawker!
Hear it! hear it! So strong and so clear,
The bells they ring and the wild prairies sing;
For the Jayhawker girls and the Jayhawker boys
All find a warm heart in the old home tonight.

I'm a Jayhawker boy from the Jayhawker state,
I wear a Jayhawker hat on a Jayhawker pate;
I ride a Jayhawker horse in a Jayhawker way,
In the Jayhawker state, I am bound for to stay.

Oh, the Jayhawker's skies, and the Jayhawker's days,
Are the Jayhawker's pride, and the Jayhawker's praise;
For the Jayhawker knows that the Jayhawker's rains
Fill the Jayhawker's barns with the Jayhawker's grains.

So the Jayhawker sows, and the Jayhawker reaps,
And the Jayhawker sings, and the Jayhawker sleeps;
While the Jayhawker's cows, and the Jayhawker's shoats,
Grow into Jayhawker gold, and the Jayhawker notes.

Neither Jayhawker winds, nor Jayhawker drought
Stops the Jayhawker's heart, nor the Jayhawker's mouth;
For the Jayhawker's faith is always first rate,
He has Jayhawker's pride in his Jayhawker State!

KANSAS LAND

[Collected from Ray Webster of Lincoln, Kansas, by William E.
Koch, 1958. A parody of "Beulah Land," it is sung to a tune
similar to "Maryland, My Maryland," or "Tannenbaum, O Tannenbaum." It occurs elsewhere as "Nebraska Land," "Dakota
Land," and "Idaho Land." See John A. Lomax and Alan Lomax,
Cowboy Songs (New York: The Macmillan Co., 1948), pp.
410–411. It was especially popular during the hard times of early
statehood.]

I've reached the land of corn and beans,
At first the crop looked fine and green,
But the grasshoppers and the drouth—
We'd better pull up and go south.

Chorus

Oh Kansas sun, hot Kansas sun,
As to the highest knoll I run,
I look away across the plains,
And wonder why it never rains.
And as I look upon my corn,
I think but little of my farm.

If we are poor, we're not to blame.
We'll go back East and sell the claim,
And if we succeed in getting tin,
We'll drive a herd of cattle in.

My hoss is poor; I cannot plow,
But I can trade it for a cow.

My wheat is thin, but let it pass,
The cow can feed on buffalo grass.

Chorus (for last verse)

Oh Kansas girls, sweet Kansas girls,
With sky-blue eyes and flaxen curls—
They sing and dance and flirt and play
And when a boy friend comes that way
They meet him at the sod house door,
Then be with him forever more.

THE DEWEY-BERRY SONG

[Collected from Elma Lee Bearly, Atwood, Kansas, by S. J. Sackett, Fall, 1956. This song relates an obviously one-sided report of a true incident. Mr. Dewey was acquitted. For a different version of the song and a more complete report of the conflict, see Bliss Isely, "Rulers of the Kansas Range," *Kansas Teacher,* May, 1958, p. 24. According to William E. Koch, the tune is similar to that of an old song called "I'll Be All Smiles Tonight."]

Transcribed by Elma Lee Bearly

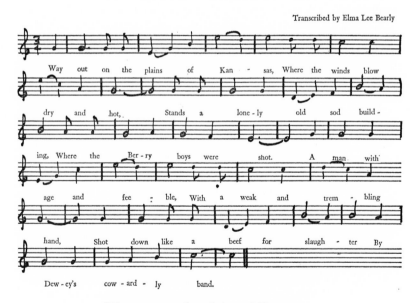

Way out on the plains of Kansas,
Where the winds blow dry and hot,

Stands a lonely old sod building
Where the Berry boys were shot.
A man with age and feeble
With a weak and trembling hand
Shot down like a beef for slaughter
By Dewey's cowardly band.

Two men in the pride of manhood,
And a man with silvery hair
Were cruelly murdered that bright day
By the outlaw millionaire.
Must wives be changed to widows
In the space of fleeting breath?
And children be made orphans?
And men be shot to death?

Oh, grand and free America
In the land where lives the brave,
Is this the glorious country
Our fathers died to save?
It is hard to think it true
In the land we love so well,
It is hard for us to believe
That men will their honor sell.

But I would think the murderers—
Although they may be free—
Those quiet, deathly faces
In troubled dreams would see.
That aged and furrowed brow,
That blood-stained hair so gray—
I'd think that Chauncey Dewey
Would see them night and day.

Can it be there is no terror
For the murderer's blood-stained hand?
Are there no courts of justice
In this glorious Christian land?
The jury has cleared the savages;
The court its verdict has given;
But they will find when done with this life
They cannot buy the courts of heaven.

THE LANE COUNTY BACHELOR

[Sung to the tune of "The Irish Washerwoman," with a different chorus for each stanza, this song was very popular among the pioneers. Certainly it was not a song that took their minds off their troubles; there is almost more truth than fiction in its humor. Two versions are presented here; for interesting variants see Vance Randolph, *Ozark Folksongs* (Columbia: The State Historical Society of Missouri, 1946–50), II, 190–191, and Carl Sandburg, *The American Songbag* (New York: Harcourt, Brace and Co., 1927), pp. 120–123.]

A: THE LANE COUNTY BACHELOR

[This version of the song was given to Forsyth Library, Fort Hays Kansas State College, by Mr. and Mrs. Ed Kepner, Dighton, Kansas, in April, 1933. According to Mr. and Mrs. Kepner, the manuscript is in the handwriting of Frank Baker, composer of the lyric.]

Frank Baker's my name and a bachelor I am,
I'm keeping old batch on an elegant plan.
You'll find me out west in the county of Lane,
I'm starving to death on a government claim.
My house it is built of the natural soil,
The walls are erected according to Hoyle.
The roof has no pitch but is level and plain,
And I always get wet when it happens to rain.

Hurrah for Lane County, the land of the free,
The home of the grasshopper, bed bug and flea.
I'll sing loud its praises and tell of its fame,
While starving to death on a government claim.

My clothes they are ragged, my language is rough,
My bread is case-hardened both solid and tough.
The dough is scattered all over the room,
And the floor it gets scared at the sight of a broom.
My dishes are scattered all over the bed,
They are covered with sorghum and Government bread.
Still I have a good time and live at my ease
On common sop-sorghum, old bacon and grease.

Then come to Lane County, here is a home for you all,
Where the winds never cease and the rains never fall,
And the sun never sets but will always remain
Till it burns you all up on a Government claim.
Till it burns you all up on a government claim.

How happy I feel when I crawl into bed,
And a rattlesnake rattles a tune at my head.
And the gay little centipede, void of all fear,
Crawls over my neck and down into my ear.
And the little bed bugs so cheerful and bright,
They keep me a-laughing two-thirds of the night.
And the gay little flea with sharp tacks in his toes,
Plays "Why don't you catch me" all over my nose.

    Hurrah for Lane County, hurrah for the west,
    Where farmers and laborers are ever at rest.
    For there's nothing to do but to sweetly remain
    And starve like a man on a Government claim.

How happy am I on my government claim,
For I've nothing to lose nor I've nothing to gain.
I've nothing to eat and I've nothing to wear,
And nothing from nothing is honest and fair.
Oh, it is here I am solid and here I will stay,
For my money is all gone and I can't get away.
There is nothing that makes a man hard and profane,
Like starving to death on a Government claim.

    Hurrah for Lane County, where blizzards arise,
    Where the winds never cease and the flea never dies.
    Come join in the chorus and sing of its fame,
    You poor hungry hoboes that's starved on the claim.

No, don't get discouraged, you poor hungry men,
For we are all here as free as a pig in a pen.
Just stick to your homestead and battle the fleas
And look to your Maker to send you a breeze.
Now all you claim holders I hope you will stay
And chew your hardtack till you are toothless and grey.
But as for myself I'll no longer remain
And starve like a dog on a Government claim.

Farewell to Lane County, farewell to the west,
I'll travel back East to the girl I love best.
I'll stop in Topeka and get me a wife,
And there shall I stay the rest of my life.

B: THE LANE COUNTY BACHELOR

[Raymond Tillotson, Shields, Kansas, found this version of the song among the papers of his father, a pioneer settler of Lane County. It was written in pencil. S. J. Sackett comments: "Three features point to its being written down from someone else's rendition, rather than copied from a text or set down from the elder Mr. Tillotson's own knowledge: the manuscript ignores line divisions; it uses abbreviations such as one might use when jotting down something someone else was giving ('Co of Lane,' 'Gov Bred') ; and the phonetic nature of the spelling occasionally betrays a word heard but not understood ('cattered,' 'Sieses') . There are also a few gaps in the song, which may indicate that the copier could not keep up with his source as the song was given orally. It is tempting to believe that the elder Mr. Tillotson may have set the song down as he heard it from the lips of Frank Baker himself."]

Frank Baker is My Name a Bachelor
I am I'm Keeping Old Bach
on an elegant plan
You'll find me out west in the
Co of Lane A' Starving to death
on a goverment clame
Huraw for Lane Co the
home of the Free the home
of the grasshopper, bed bug & Flea

My clothe they are ragged
My language is rough My
Bread is cast harden both
Solid and tough the dough is
cattered all over the room
the floor would scare at the
sight of a Broom
the dishes are scattered all
over the bed all covered with
Sorgam & Gov Bred

Then its come to Lane Co there
room for you all where
the Wind Never Sieses & rain
Never falls and Sun Never
Sets But will all ways remain
& Burn us all out on our Gov clame

How happy am I on my Gov
clame, for there is Nothing to
loose and Nothing to gain
Nothing to eat and Nothing to ware
& Nothing for Nothing is honest & fair
Huraw for Lane Co Huraw for the
west where the Farmers & labors
are ever at rest for there
is Nothing to do but swettly remain
And Starve like a man on
a goverment clame

Now all those good people
I hope they will staye &
chew there hard tack till they
Are toothless and gray
But as for My Self I'l Nolonger
remain and starve like a dog
on a gov clame
I'm going to leave the
West & travel back east to the
girl I love best I'll stop
in Topeka and get Me a
wife & there shall I stay
the rest of my life

THERE'S NO PLACE LIKE HOME

[Collected from Mrs. Bertha Parsons, Wichita, Kansas, 16 January 1959. Mrs. Parsons came to Kansas in 1882 in a covered wagon. Her parents settled in Harper County. She learned the song from her brothers quite some time before 1900. A parody of "Home Sweet Home," it is sung to the same tune.]

Did you ever get up in the middle of the night—
There's no place like home;

To hunt the paregoric, without any light—
There's no place like home;
You're sure to step on an up-turned tack,
The baby'll cry till his lungs will crack;
With your wife's cold feet in the middle of your back—
There's no place like home.

When your wife's relation come to visit you—
There's no place like home.
They bring all their clothes, and stick to you like glue—
There's no place like home.
When you have to give up the best bed you've got
And go and sleep on an old rough cot,
With your brother-in-law, who's always half shot,
There's no place like home.

THE WEAVER'S SONG

[Collected from Mrs. Bertha Parsons, Wichita, Kansas, 16 January 1959. She learned the song from her mother. Mrs. Parsons commented, "Grandfather Allen was a weaver; he had four boys and wove cloth for their suits." As she sang the chorus, Mrs. Parsons would toss her left hand to the right with the word "Whickety," and her right hand to the left with the word "whackety." She repeated the gestures with "click and clack." The word "staccato" was pronounced "stack-a-toe."]

Down by the river lives Weaver John,
And a jolly old John is he;
Maud is the name of his dear old Dame,
And a blessed old Dame is she.

Whickety, whackety; click and clack;
How the shutters do glance and ring;
Here they go; there they go; forth and back.
What a staccato song they sing.

Close by his side sits his dear old wife,
Spinning her flaxen thread.
Dear to his heart is the wheel's low hum;
It was purchased when they were wed.

Pussy is frisking about the room
With kittens, one, two, three, four;
Towser is taking his wonted nap
On the settle, behind the door.

THE PRETTY GIRL I LEFT BEHIND

[Collected from Mrs. Lois Brown, Liberal, Kansas, by S. J. Sackett, 26 July 1957. Mrs. Brown remembers it as a song her father,
a frontier minister, used to sing when she was a girl; he had
learned it from an Oklahoma cowboy. The first half of the first
stanza, unfortunately, is indistinguishable on the tape.]

Transcribed by John Chambers

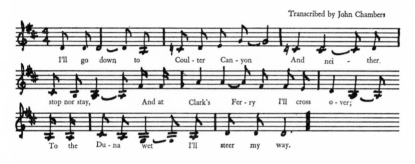

——————————————— is born to ramble
And to leave the range he's rode so long.

I'll go down to Coulter Canyon
And neither stop nor stay,
And at Clark's Ferry I'll cross over;
To the Duna wet I'll steer my way.

When I get there, another cowboy
In that there lonely camp of mine,
I'll think about my fellow cowboys
And the pretty girl I left behind.

Though her name I will not mention,
Better friends there are but few;
But the best of friends can't keep a secret.
They can keep one best they never knew.

Here's a ring; place on your finger
When far away in full gleam.
When far away and quite forgotten,
Look at this ring and think of me.

AIR YE WAKEN, MAGGIE?

[Collected from Mrs. Bertha Parsons, Wichita, Kansas, 16 January 1959. Mrs. Parsons said, "This is a scrap of an old Scottish song that Grandfather Allen brought from Ireland. Father only sang this 'once in a blue moon.' Mother only learned this much."]

Oo, mirk an' rainy is the night
An' no' a starn i' a' th' cairy.
Th' lightnin' flames athwart th' lift
An' cry o' howlets make me eerie.
Oo, air ye waken, Maggie—
Oo, air ye waken, Maggie?
Lat me in, for ooh th' win'
Gaes roarin' o'er the moorland craggy.

She oopened th' doore an' lat him in,
An' throw aside his dhrepin' plaidie;
Noo, wha' car' I for annythin'—
Noo, Maggie, sense I'm in beside ye?
Noo, sense yer waken, Maggie,
Noo, sense I'm in beside ye.
Wha' car' I for oows tha' cry
On Buertney Banks an' wa's so craggy.

OGALLEY SONG

[Collected from Charles G. Waterson, Dighton, Kansas, by Mrs. Alma D. Johnson, 26 May 1954. Ogalley probably refers to Ogallah, Kansas, once briefly a cow town; or it may refer to Ogallala, Nebraska, although the name in the song differs slightly.]

We left Nueces River in April eighty-one
With three thousand long-horned cattle, and all they knowed
    was run, oh.

We got them through the bush all right, clear up to San
    Antone,
We got some grub and headed north, as slick as any bone.

We crossed the Colorado at Austin, a big town,
And headed north until we struck the store of high renown.

The old Red River was on the prod and run from bank to
    bank,
We busted him and got across, a good horse for to thank.

The Washita was running full, but we got them all across,
And counted out on the other bank, and never had a loss.

Then we got to Dodge City on the Arkansaw,
Got a few drinks and some more grub and pulled north once
    more.

On the Smoky Hill we ran into another storm,
The boss he says this is the damnedest country I've seen since
    I was born.

THE HANCOCK BOYS

[Collected from Mrs. Ruth Miller, Dellvale, Kansas, by Alice S.
Foley, Summer, 1958. Mrs. Miller learned the song from her
mother. It took all kinds to settle the state, but the spunky Kansas girls knew how to handle them all. The name of any town
could be substituted for "Hancock."]

Transcribed by John Chambers

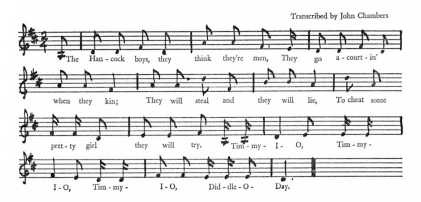

The Han-cock boys, they think they're men, They go a-court-in'
when they kin; They will steal and they will lie, To cheat some
pret-ty girl they will try. Tim-my-I-O, Tim-my-
I-O, Tim-my-I-O, Did-dle-O-Day.

The Hancock boys, they think they're men,
They go a courtin' when they kin;
They will steal and they will lie,
To cheat some pretty girl they will try.

Timmy—I—O, Timmy—I—O,
Timmy—I—O, Diddle—O—Day

They works all week in the mud and dirt
Just to buy them a holiday shirt
A rough old boot and down before
And I be blamed if anything more.

And then to an evening they will go,
They think themselves they make a show;
A double knotted handkerchief under their chin,
They look like saints choked with sin.

Now young man I suppose you're mad,
And if you are I'm very glad;
If you do not like my song,
Take your hat and budge along.

THE RAILROAD MAN

[Collected from Mrs. Sherla Bizek Furgason, Hays, Kansas, by
S. J. Sackett, Spring, 1957. Mrs. Furgason learned the song,
which became popular as the railroad tracks were pushed across
the country, from her mother. H. M. Belden, *Ballads and
Songs* (Columbia: University of Missouri Studies, Vol. IV, No. 1,
1940), p. 377, has a variant in which the girl takes the railroad
man into her parlor.]

I'll never marry a farmer,
He's always in the dirt,
But I'm going to marry a railroad man
Who wears a calico shirt.

A railroader, a railroader,
A railroader's life for me.
If ever I marry in all my life,
A railroader's wife I'll be.

Transcribed by John Chambers

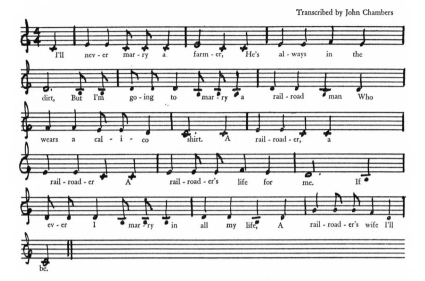

I'll nev-er mar-ry a farm-er, He's al-ways in the dirt, But I'm go-ing to mar-ry a rail-road man Who wears a cal-i-co shirt. A rail-road-er, a rail-road-er A rail-road-er's life for me. If ev-er I mar-ry in all my life, A rail-road-er's wife I'll be.

I'll never marry a printer,
He's always in the ink,
But I'm going to marry a railroader
Whose fortunes never'll sink.

He took me to his parlor
He cooled me with his fan
He whispered low in my charming ear
"Won't you marry a railroad man?"

PATANIO

[Tape recorded by Gail Burns, Emporia, Kansas, April, 1958. Mr. Burns learned the song from a schoolmate who learned it from her uncle. There is a version called "Pattonio, the Pride of the Plain" in Lomax and Lomax, pp. 356–358.]

You gaze at the picture with a wondering eye
And at the old arrow that hangs by its side.
You say, "Tell a story."—A story there's one;
With the name of Patanio, the story's begun.

I'll tell you a story that will thrill you I know
Of a horse that I owned down in New Mexico.

TUNE A—(Verse 1 only) *Expressively*   Transcribed by John Chambers

You gaze at the pic-ture with a won-der-ing eye
And at the old ar-row that hangs by its side.
You say, "Tell a sto-ry" A sto-ry there's one;
With the name of Pa - ta - ni - o the sto-ry's be-gun - n - n.

TUNE B (Verses 2-9; Verses 2 and 6 use first ending,
Verses 3-5, 7-9 use second ending)

I'll tell you a sto-ry that will thrill you I know Of a
horse that I owned down in New Mex-i-co. He was swift as an
an-te-lope and as black as a crow, And the star on his
1st Ending   2nd Ending
fore-head was as white as the snow. His plain - n - n.

TUNE C (Verse 10 only)

Of all the fine hors-es that I've 'seen draw the rein,
There is none like Pa - ta - ni - o, the pride of the plain - n - n.

He was swift as an antelope and as black as a crow,
And the star on his forehead was as white as the snow.

His hair like a lady's was glossy and fine.
He was reckless and proud, yet gentle and kind.
His neck was adorned by a long flowing mane.
They called him Patanio, the pride of the plain.

One day the captain said someone must go
For help to the border of old Mexico.
A dozen brave fellows straightway answered, "Here."
Patanio beside me, standing close and near.

Said the captain, "Your horse is the best in the land.
On the back of a mustang you have nothing to fear."
I mounted my horse and I turned his head north.
The black struck a trot and he held it all night.

When up from behind there arose a great yell,
We both knew the redskins were hot on our trail.
I rose up and jingled the bell on his reins,
Spoke his name gently and called him by name.

He answered the touch with the toss of his head;
His black body lengthened and forward we sped.
We were beating the redskins, the story was plain;
Still arrows fell around us like showers of rain.

We were beating the redskins, the story was plain,
When in my leg I felt a great pain.
Red blood rushed forth from Patanio's side,
But he never once shortened his powerful stride.

On down the trail the fort loomed ahead.
The gates were thrown open and inward we sped.
By good care of Patanio we both were soon well,
And his death long years after I'm afraid I can't tell.

Of all the fine horses that I've seen draw the rein,
There is none like Patanio, the pride of the plain.

ON THE BED GROUND IN A COW CAMP

[Collected from Andy J. Myers, Dighton, Kansas, by Alma D. Johnson, July, 1958. According to the informant, this song was "made" or "fabricated" by a man whose name on the tape

sounds as if it might be Dick Gady. The bed ground referred to
was located south of Leoti, Kansas. At the time (1882) Gady and
Myers were working for the E-K ranch "out of Garden City."]

Transcribed by John Chambers

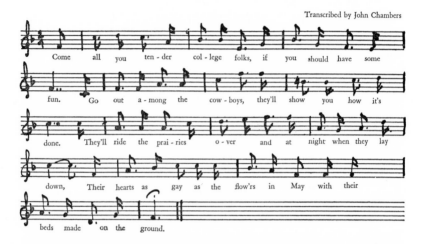

Come all you tender college folks, if you should have some fun.
Go out among the cowboys, they will show you how it's done.
They will ride the prairies over and at night when they lay
   down,
Their hearts as gay as the flowers in May with their beds made
   on the ground.

They will go to the ball and swing the girls, they are pretty
   good at that.
They will ride the bucking bronco and wear the wide brimmed
   hat,
With a California saddle, with pants stuck in their boots,
You will hear the spurs a-jingling and maybe someone shoot.

Oh, they are a little rough, I must confess at least.
They will bet on a horse race or poker seven up,
But if they win or if they lose, you will hear them squeal.
But the very next time they meet you, they'll give you a
   different deal.

Did you ever meet a cowboy, when you were hungry and dry?
And ask of him a dollar and have him deny?

No, he'll pull out his pocketbook and give you a note,
They are the very best boys to strike when you are hungry and
    broke.

CHARLES GUITEAU

[Collected from Ruth Miller of Dellvale, Kansas, by Alice S.
Foley, Summer, 1958. The ballad commemorates the assassina-
tion of President James A. Garfield by Charles Guiteau in 1881.
Mrs. Miller learned this version from her mother; other texts
may be found in Belden, pp. 412–413, and *The Frank C. Brown
Collection of North Carolina Folklore* (Durham: Duke University Press, 1952), II, 572–578.]

Transcribed by John Chambers

Come all you Christian people, come hear what I have to say,
And likewise pay attention to the few words that I say.

For the murder of James A. Garfield I am condemned to die
Upon the thirtieth day of June upon the scaffold high.

But my name is Charles Guiteau; it's a name I'll never deny.
I leave my aged parents in sorrow for to die,
But little did I think while in my youthful bloom
I'd be sent to the scaffold to meet my fatal doom.

It was on the thirtieth day of June my sister came here;
She threw her arms around my neck and wept most bitterly.
Said she: "My darling brother, today you surely die
For the murder of James A. Garfield upon that scaffold high."

It was down there at the depot I tried to make my 'scape,
But the crowd all being against me it proved to be too late.
The judge he read the sentence. The jury wrote it down:
Upon the thirtieth day of June I'm to meet my fatal doom.

But my name is Charles Guiteau, my name I'll never deny.
I leave my aged parents in sorrow for to die,
But little did I think while in my youthful bloom
I'd be taken to the scaffold to meet my fatal doom.

FOLKSONGS AND BALLADS

Part II

JOAN O'BRYANT
University of Wichita

The ten songs in the following section are chosen from the more than fifteen hundred which my students and I have collected in Kansas during the past few years. Most of my collecting was done in counties near Wichita (Sedgwick, Butler, Cowley) and near Pittsburg (Crawford, Cherokee, Labette).

Two of the songs, "Lady Margaret" and "The Golden Vanity," are Child ballads; I have also collected in Kansas eleven other Child ballads, two of them in fragmentary form. Another, "Risselty Rosselty," may be derived from a ballad in the Child collection. "The Miller and His Three Sons" and "The Gypsy Maid" are listed in G. Malcolm Laws, Jr., *American Balladry from British Broadsides* (Philadelphia: Publications of the American Folklore Society, Bibliographical and Special Series, No. 8, 1957); "Pretty Peggy O," while not listed in Laws's bibliography, also derives from a British broadside.[3] Although "The Three Rogues" is probably not a broadside ballad, it is another song of British origin.

---

[3] Broadside ballads were printed on one side of a large sheet of paper for distribution or posting. Since they were sung to well-known tunes, usually only the words were reproduced. Some broadsides were of folk origin, perhaps adapted, while others were original, journalistic ballads, a number of which later entered into oral tradition and developed the variant versions that are the mark of oral transmission. Extant broadsides date from the sixteenth to the nineteenth century.

161

"McAfee's Confession" is a journalistic ballad,[4] of the type known as a "criminal's goodnight," of American origin. Also of American derivation is "The Jealous Lover," a very common song; it belongs to a class which has not been given an official name by folklorists but which I would call "murdered girl" ballads. "Comin' Back to Kansas" apparently is local in origin and circulation; I know of no other version.

Without exception, the singers from whom I collected sang in the traditional, straightforward manner without accompaniment and sounded much like traditional singers from the Ozarks or the southern Appalachians. Most of the singers were middle-aged (although one was over eighty), and none corresponded to the popular idea of a traditional folk singer. Most lived in town, several in Wichita (a city of 250,000) ; none fit the "backwoods-barefoot-log cabin" pattern.

FAIR MARGARET AND SWEET WILLIAM
(CHILD 74)

[Collected from Mrs. Florence Martin, Pittsburg, Kansas, August, 1958. Mrs. Martin grew up near Berryville, Arkansas, where she learned the song from her mother, who called it a "real old-time love song." This ballad, which Mrs. Martin knew under the title of "Sweet William and Lady Margaret," seems to be well known in America. Child, II, 199, remarks that it was "a favorite of the stalls," which might account for its popularity. The rose-and-briar ending, which is usually considered a standard feature of the ballad, is missing in the Kansas version. For some other American texts see Belden, pp. 48–52; Randolph, I, 108–112; and *The Frank C. Brown Collection of North Carolina Folklore*, II, 79–84.]

Sweet William he rose one morning in June,
He dressed himself in blue.
Pray tell to me the love, love, love
That's between Lady Margaret and me.

---

[4] A "journalistic ballad" is one which has the same purpose as a present-day newspaper: the dissemination of news. Many of these, like the tabloid press, play up sensational events.

I know not a thing about Lady Margaret's love,
I'm sure she don't love me,

TUNE A—Verses 1, 2, 3, 4; Verses 6, 7; Verses 10-15   Transcribed by Betty Welsbacher

Sweet Wil-liam he rose one morn-ing in June. He dressed himself in blue. Pray tell to me the love, love, love That's between La-dy Mar-garet and me.

TUNE B—Verse 5

The day being gone and the night com-ing on When
all men were a-sleep, Sweet Wil-liam dreamed he saw Lady
Mar-garet Stand-ing at his bed feet.

TUNE C—Verse 8

Night be-ing gone and day com-ing on When all men
were a-wake, Sweet Wil-liam a-rose and said there was trouble in his head From the dream that he dreamed last night.

TUNE D—Verse 9

He dreamed his room was full of wild swine And his
love was swim-ming in blood.

TUNE E—Verse 16

Fold up, fold up those Ire - land sheets Made of lin - en so fine. To - day you weep over Lady Margaret's cof - fin, To - morrow you'll weep o - ver mine.

But tomorrow morning at eight o'clock
Lady Margaret my bride shall see.

Lady Margaret was standing in her own hall door
Combing her silken hair,
When she spied sweet William and his bride
As to the church drew nigh.

She threw away her ivory comb,
Back her silken hair.
Lady Margaret went into her room
Never more to return.

The day being gone and the night coming on
When all men were asleep,
Sweet William dreamed he saw Lady Margaret
Standing at his bed feet.

Saying, how do you like your bed, kind sir,
And how do you like your sheet?
And how do you like your new wedded wife,
Who is lying in your arms asleep?

Very well, very well do I like my bed,
Very well do I like my sheet.
Much better do I like that fair, pretty girl,
That is standing at my bed feet.

Night being gone and day coming on
When all men were awake,
Sweet William arose and said there was trouble in his
head
From the dream that he dreamed last night.

He dreamed his room was full of wild swine
And his love was swimming in blood.

Then he called up his merry mates all,
Called them one, two, three,
And then he asked leave of his wife
Lady Margaret to go and see.

He rode 'till he came to Lady Margaret's hall,
He rapped so loud at the ring.
There was none so ready as Lady Margaret's brother
To rise and let him in.

Is Lady Margaret out at church today,
Or is she in the hall?
Or is she in the dining room,
Among those merry ladies all?

Lady Margaret is neither at church today,
Neither in the hall.
Lady Margaret is in her cold coffin,
Laid out against the wall.

Pull down, pull down those Ireland sheets
Made of linen so fine.
Let me once kiss those clay cold lips
That so often have kissed mine.

Then he kissed her on the chin,
Then all on the cheek,
Then he kissed the clay cold lips
That so often had kissed him.

Fold up, fold up those Ireland sheets,
Made of linen so fine.
Today you weep over Lady Margaret's coffin,
Tomorrow you'll weep over mine.

THE SWEET TRINITY (THE GOLDEN VANITY)
(CHILD 286)

[Collected from Mrs. Letha Watkins, Wichita, Kansas, July, 1958. Mrs. Watkins grew up in Greenwood County, Kansas, and said her father often sang this song, which was known in her family as "The Golden Willow Tree," while he rocked her and the other children on his lap. Child prints three texts of the ballad, and most American versions appear to be closest to his Version C. The ballad seems widely known in America. See Cecil J. Sharp, *English Folk Songs from the Southern Appalachians* (London: Oxford University Press, 1932), I, 282–291; Belden, pp. 97–101; Paul G. Brewster, *Ballads and Songs of Indiana* (Bloomington: Indiana University Press, 1940), pp. 158–164; Randolph, I, 195–202; and *The Frank C. Brown Collection of North Carolina Folklore,* II, 191–195.]

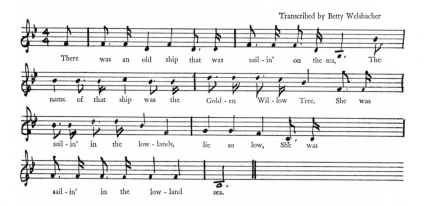

Transcribed by Betty Welsbacher

There was an old ship that was sailin' on the sea,
The name of that ship was the Golden Willow Tree.
She was sailin' in the lowlands, lie so low,
She was sailin' in the lowland sea.

There was an old ship that was sailin' on the
    sea,
The name of that ship was the Golden Willow
    Tree.
She was sailin' in the lowlands, lie so low,
She was sailin' in the lowland sea.

We hadn't been a-sailin' more than leagues two
    or three,
When we came in sight of the Turkey Roguery,
She was layin' in the lowlands, lie so low,
She was layin' in the lowland sea.

When up from below came a little cabin boy
Saying, what will you give me the ship to
    destroy?

I can sink her in the lowland, lie so low,
I can sink her in the lowland sea.

Well, says the captain, I'll give you money, I'll
  give you ease,
I've an only daughter you may marry when you
  please,
If you'll sink her in the lowland, lie so low,
If you'll sink her in the lowland sea.

So he took off his coat and in jumped he,
Swam 'til he came to the Turkey Roguery,
She was layin' in the lowland, lie so low,
She was layin' in the lowland sea.

He had a little auger that he kept for this use,
He put nine holes in the bottom of the boat,
For to sink her in the lowland, lie so low,
For to sink her in the lowland sea.

Now some with their caps and some with their
  hats
Were trying to stop up the salt-water gaps,
For they were sinking in the lowland, lie so low,
They were sinking in the lowland sea.

He said to the captain, now take me on board,
And be to me as good as your word,
For I sunk her in the lowland, lie so low,
I sunk her in the lowland sea.

Oh no, said the captain, I can't take you on
  board,
Nor be to you as good as my word,
But I can sink you in the lowland, lie so low,
I can sink you in the lowland sea.

If it weren't for the love that I have for your
  men,
I'd do to you what I did to them.
I'd sink you in the lowland, lie so low,
I'd sink you in the lowland sea.

So he turned on his back and down went he,
Waving farewell to the Golden Willow Tree.
He was sinking in the lowland, lie so low,
He was sinking in the lowland sea.

RISSELTY ROSSELTY

[Collected from Mrs. Lizzie Troup, Winfield, Kansas, May, 1958. Mrs. Troup came to Kansas from Missouri as a child and learned from her father a number of songs, including this one, which went by the name of "Nickerty Nockerty Now, Now, Now." In Mrs. Troup's version the nonsense phrase "risselty rosselty," which gives the song its standard title, has been replaced by "wisselty wosselty." A Missouri version of this song is recorded by Vance Randolph, IV, 190–193, and he refers to a version recorded in Nebraska by Louise Pound. Some folklorists consider the song a secondary version of "The Wife Wrapt in Wether's Skin" (Child 277) omitting the narrative element, which consists of the slattern's punishment: her husband would not thrash her but took her out to his wool shack, laid a sheepskin across her back, and thrashed the sheepskin.]

Transcribed by Betty Welsbacher

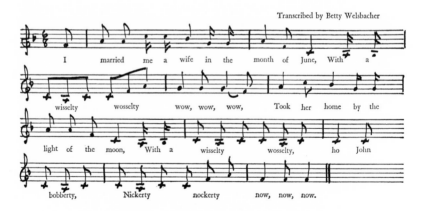

I married me a wife in the month of June,
With a wisselty wosselty wow, wow, wow,
Took her home by the light of the moon,
With a wisselty wosselty, ho John bobberty,
Nickerty nockerty now, now, now.

She swept her floor but once a month,
With a wisselty wosselty wow, wow, wow.
And every stroke it brought a grunt,
With a wisselty wosselty, ho John bobberty,
Nickerty nockerty now, now, now.

She combed her hair but once a year,
With a wisselty wosselty wow, wow, wow,
And every stroke it brought a tear,
With a wisselty wosselty, ho John bobberty,
Nickerty nockery now, now, now.

She churned her butter in dad's old boot,
With a wisselty wosselty wow, wow, wow,
Instead of a dash she wiggled her foot,
With a wisselty wosselty, ho John bobberty,
Nickerty nockerty now, now, now.

She peddled her butter all over town,
With a wisselty wosselty wow, wow, wow,
The print of her foot was on every pound,
With a wisselty wosselty, ho John bobberty,
Nickerty nockerty now, now, now.

She strained her cheese through dad's old sock,
With a wisselty wosselty wow, wow, wow,
The toe jam run down into the crock,
With a wisselty wosselty, ho John bobberty,
Nickerty nockerty now, now, now.

She went upstairs to make the bed,
With a wisselty wosselty wow, wow, wow,
She fell over the chair and bumped her head,
With a wisselty wosselty, ho John bobberty,
Nickerty nockerty now, now, now.

She went outdoors to milk the cow,
With a wisselty wosselty wow, wow, wow,
She made a mistake and milked the sow,
With a wisselty wosselty, ho John bobberty,
Nickerty nockerty now, now, now,

PRETTY PEGGY O

[Collected from Mrs. Florence Martin, Pittsburg, Kansas, August, 1958. Mrs. Martin described the song, which she called "Pretty Peggy," as her "favorite love song" because it was taught to her by her grandfather, who learned it in 1846 while he was a soldier in the Mexican War. The song is not very common in America. Sharp, II, 59–62, prints four versions of it from Kentucky and North Carolina; and Belden, p. 160, one from Missouri. In his notes Sharp refers to British versions in Grieg's *Folk-Song of the North-East,* Christie's *Traditional Ballad Airs,* Ford's *Vagabond Songs and Ballads,* and a broadside by Pitts called "Pretty Peggy of Derby."]

Transcribed by Betty Welsbacher

I'm going over the sea, Pretty Peggy O,
I'm going over the sea to die,
Where you'll never more see me,
So fare you well, Pretty Peggy O.

Our captain he was young, Pretty Peggy O,
Our captain he was young,
He was scarcely twenty-one,
And he died for the love of Peggy O.

Our captain's name was Wade, Pretty Peggy O,
Our captain's name was Wade,
And he died for a maid,
And they buried him in the Louisiana country, O.

Through the courts you shall ride, Pretty Peggy O,
Through the courts you shall ride,
With your true-love by your side,
And be as grand as any in the ivory, O.

What would your mother think, Pretty Peggy O,
What would your mother think,
For to hear the guineas chink,
And the soldiers marching around you, O?

You're a person I adore, Pretty Peggy O.
You're a person I adore,
But your calling is so low,
I'm afraid your mother would be angry, O.

She came tripping downstairs, Pretty Peggy O,
She came tripping downstairs,
Combing back her yellow hair,
To take her last fare-you-well from sweet William, O.

THE THREE ROGUES

[Collected from Mrs. Elsie Tower, Labette County, Kansas, June, 1958. Mrs. Tower learned the song as a child, but was unable to remember where she first heard it. She has lived most of her life in Labette County. "The Three Rogues" is a humorous ditty which Belden says was "originally, in England, sung of the time 'when Arthur ruled this land.'" This line was changed in America to "In good old colony times." There seems to be little variation in the American versions I have seen. For some American texts see Belden, pp. 268–270; Randolph, I, 416; and *The Frank C. Brown Collection of North Carolina Folklore,* II, 458–459.]

In good old colony times
When we lived under a king,
Three roguish chaps fell into mishaps
Because they could not sing.

The first he was a miller,
And the second he was a weaver,

Transcribed by Betty Welsbacher

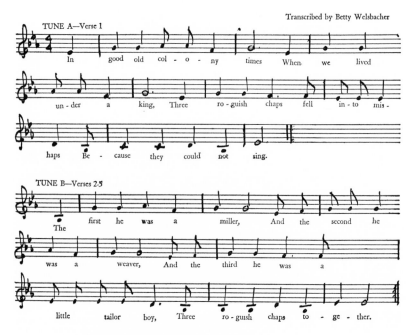

TUNE A—Verse 1

In good old col - o - ny times When we lived un - der a king, Three ro - guish chaps fell in - to mis - haps Be - cause they could not sing.

TUNE B—Verses 2-5

The first he was a miller, And the second he was a weaver, And the third he was a little tailor boy, Three ro - guish chaps to - ge - ther.

And the third he was a little tailor boy,
Three roguish chaps together.

The miller he stole corn,
The weaver he stole yarn,
And the little tailor boy stole broadcloth enough
To keep those three rogues warm.

The miller got drowned in his dam,
And the weaver got hung in his yarn,
And the sheriff clapped his hands on the little
  tailor boy
With the broadcloth under his arm.

With his broadcloth under his arm,
With his broadcloth under his arm,
And the sheriff clapped his hands on the little
  tailor boy,
With his broadcloth under his arm.

THE MILLER AND HIS THREE SONS

[Collected from Mrs. Elsie Tower, Labette County, Kansas, June, 1958. This satirical account of the dishonest miller, which Mrs. Tower knew under the title "The Miller's Sons," seems to be widely known in America and Britain. Belden says, "The earliest appearance of our ballad that I have found is a broadside in the Roxburghe and Douce collections (*Roxburghe Ballads,* VIII, 611–2) dated by Ebsworth 'c. 1730,' from which the traditional texts gathered in the last century do not greatly vary." For some American texts see Sharp, II, 221–224; Belden, pp. 244–247; Randolph, I, 359–365; and *The Frank C. Brown Collection of North Carolina Folklore,* II, 440–444.]

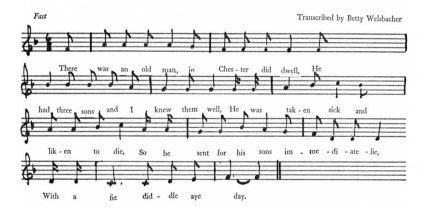

Fast   Transcribed by Betty Welsbacher

There was an old man, in Chester did dwell,
He had three sons and I knew them well,
He was taken sick and liken to die,
So he sent for his sons immediatelie,
With a fie diddle aye day.

First he called for his oldest son,
My son, my son, my race is run,
And if to you this mill I leave,
Pray tell to me what toll you'll give,
With a fie diddle aye day.

Oh father, you know my name 'tis Ralph,
And of every bushel I'll take one half,
Every bushel that I do grind,
I'll make as good living as I can find,
With a fie diddle aye day.

My son, my son, 'tis you won't do,
'Tis you won't do as I have done,
The mill to you I cannot leave,
For by such toll no man can live,
With a fie diddle aye day.

Then he called for his second son,
My son, my son, my race is run,
And if to you this mill I'll leave,
Pray tell to me what toll you'll give?
With a fie diddle aye day.

Oh father, you know my name 'tis Dick,
Out of every bushel I'll take one peck,
Every bushel that I do grind,
I'll make as good living as I can find,
With a fie diddle aye day.

My son, my son, 'tis you won't do,
'Tis you won't do as I have done,
The mill to you I cannot leave,
For by such toll no man can live,
With a fie diddle aye day.

Then he called for his youngest son,
My son, my son, my race is run,
And if to you this mill I'll leave,
Pray tell to me what toll you'll give?
With a fie diddle aye day.

Oh father, you know I'm your darling boy,
And stealing corn is all my joy,
I'll steal the corn and swear to the sack,
And box the boys when they come back,
With a fie diddle aye day.

My son, my son, 'tis you will do,
'Tis you will do as I have done,

The mill is yours, the old man cried,
And then he closed his crystal eyes,
With a fie diddle aye day.

McAFEE'S CONFESSION

[Collected from Mrs. Lizzie Troup, Winfield, Kansas, August, 1958. With the exception of two fragments printed by Sharp, II, 15–16, most of the published texts of this criminal's goodnight are quite close to the version presented here. Belden says the song "spread no doubt by print, altho the only ballad print of it that I have found is that of Missouri D." He relates the ballad to the hanging of John McAfee in Dayton, Ohio, on 28 March 1825. Mrs. Troup told me that the song was "a true song" but had no evidence to confirm it. It had been sung to her as "true." Olive Woolley Burt, *American Murder Ballads and Their Stories* (New York: Oxford University Press, 1958), p. 22, says that the ballad "is supposed to recount an actual murder that happened in West Virginia. However, I have not been able to discover any particulars of the crime." She prints a text from Portland, Oregon, which is close to the other full texts I have seen. For some other texts see Belden, pp. 317–321, and Randolph, II, 24–29.]

Transcribed by Betty Welsbacher

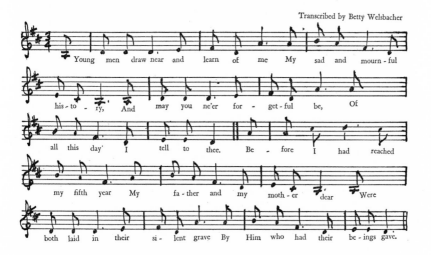

Young men draw near and learn of me My sad and mourn-ful his-to-ry, And may you ne'er for-get-ful be, Of all this day' I tell to thee. Be-fore I had reached my fifth year My fa-ther and my moth-er dear Were both laid in their si-lent grave By Him who had their be-ings gave.

Young men draw near and learn of me
My sad and mournful history,
And may you ne'er forgetful be,
Of all this day I tell to thee.

Before I had reached my fifth year
My father and my mother dear
Were both laid in their silent grave
By him who had their beings gave.

No more my mother's voice I heard,
No more my mother's love I shared.
No more was I a father's boy,
I was a helpless orphan boy.

But providence, the orphan's friend,
A kind relief did quickly send,
And snatched from want and penury
Poor little orphan McAfee.

Nine years was I most kindly reared
And oft times kind advice I heard,
But I was thoughtless, young, and gay,
And oft times broke the Sabbath day.

Then came the fatal day
When from my home I ran away.
It proved the deed that changed my life
For I took unto myself a wife.

She was kind and good to me,
As any woman need to be,
Alive would be I have no doubt
Had I not seen Miss Hettie Stout.

Well do I mind the very day
That Hettie stole my heart away
My love for her controlled my will
And it caused me my wife to kill.

Was on one pleasant summer's night,
The sky was clear, the stars shone bright,
And as my wife lay on the bed
I approached her and thus I said:

Here, wife, is medicine I brought
For you this day, which I have bought,
Take it, my dear, it will cure you
Of those wild fits, pray take it do.

She gave to me a tender look
And in her mouth the poison took,
And with her baby on the bed
Down in her last, long sleep she lay.

I, fearing that she was not dead,
My hands upon her throat I laid,
And there such deep impressions made
Her soul soon from its body fled.

O then my heart was filled with woe,
I cried, O whither shall I go?
How can I quit this awful place
This world again how can I face?

The moments now are drawing nigh
When from this earth my soul shall fly,
To meet Jehovah at the bar
And my final sentence hear.

Dear friends, I bid you all adieu
No more on earth shall I see you,
But in heaven's bright and flowery plain
I hope to meet you all again.

THE GYPSY MAID

[Collected from Mrs. A. L. Hartley, Wichita, Kansas, April, 1958. Mrs. Hartley knew the song as "The Gypsy Wedding." It comes, says Randolph, "from a ribald English song, 'The Little Gypsy Girl' (Ebsworth, *Roxburghe Ballads,* 8, 1897, p. 853)." The song does not appear to be very widely known. Another American version appears in Randolph, I, 437–439.]

My father's a gypsy
And I am a gypsy too,
My mother died and left me
Some counting for to do.

Transcribed by Betty Welsbacher

With a knapsack on my shoulder
I bid them all farewell,
I took a trip to London
Some fortunes for to tell.

As I was a-walking,
A-walking down the street
A nice, handsome lawyer
Had I chance to meet.

He loved my pretty brown cheeks,
He loved them so well,
He said, my pretty fair maid
Won't you my fortune tell?

O yes sir, O yes sir,
Hold out to me your hand,
For you have such a fortune
Far off in dixon's [distant?] land.

You've courted many fair ladies
You've put them all aside,
It's now this little gypsy girl
That is to be your bride.

He took me and led me
To a palace on yon shore,
Servants were waiting there
To open wide the door.

The wedding bells did ring,
The gypsy music played,
Now it's a celebration
For a gypsy wedding day.

THE JEALOUS LOVER

[Collected from Mrs. Irene Tingley, Wichita, Kansas, April, 1958. This is one of the best known of all folksongs in America. There are eighteen texts in the Missouri collection, and Randolph prints ten, including several fragments. Helen Hartness Flanders, *The New Green Mountain Songster* (New Haven: Yale University Press, 1939), p. 79, says, "A folk singer who does not know it ['The Jealous Lover'] is a rare exception." There are twenty-two texts and fragments in *The Frank C. Brown Collection of North Carolina Folklore*. Another version of the song from Kansas was recorded by Eugene Jemison, "Solomon Valley Ballads," Folkways FP23.]

Transcribed by Betty Welsbacher

Under the weeping willow
All silently dressed in white,
Lies the form of Nellie
All silent in her grave.

It was on one Sunday evening
When gently falls the dew,
Up to her lonely cottage
Her jealous lover drew.

O come, let us go a-wandering
Upon the meadow gay,

O come, let us go a-pondering
Upon our wedding day.

O I'm so sad and lonely
I do not care to roam,
For roaming is so weary
I pray you take me home.

Up stepped her jealous lover
And he makes one solemn vow,
Not a mortal hand can save you
In a moment you must die.

Down upon her knees before him
She gently pleads for life,
But in her snow-white bosom
He plunged a fatal knife.

He sighed not when he crushed her
To his young but cruel heart,
He sighed not when he pierced her
For he knew that they must part.

O Edward, I'll forgive you
If this be my last breath,
O Edward, I've never deceived you,
And she closed her eyes in death.

COMIN' BACK TO KANSAS

[Collected from Mrs. Clara Ballard, Butler County, Kansas,
April, 1958. Mrs. Ballard has lived in Butler County all her life
and learned the song as a girl. I have found no versions of it in
any of the collections I have examined.]

Transcribed by Betty Welsbacher

They are comin' back to Kansas,
They are crossin' on the bridge,

You can see their mover wagons
On the top of every ridge.

On the highways and the turnpikes
You can see their wagons come,
For they're comin' back to Kansas
And they're comin' on the run.

Who's a comin' back to Kansas?
Why, the migratory crowd
That left the state some months ago
With curses long and loud,

And they swore by the eternal
They would never more return
To this Kansas land infernal
Where the hot winds blast and burn.

Where the rivers run in riot
When you want it to be dry,
Where the sun so fiercely scorches
When you want a cloudy sky.

So they loaded up the children
And they whistled for the dog,
Tied a cow behind the wagon,
To the butcher sold the hog.

Hitched the ponies to the schooner,
Turned her prow toward the east,
Left this beastly state of Kansas
For a land of fat and feast.

Did they find it? No, they didn't,
Though they roamed the country o'er,
From the lakes up in the northland
To the far off ocean shore.

And they found that other sections
Had their tales of woe to sing,
So they're humpin' now for Kansas
At the breakin' forth of spring.

CUSTOMS

S. J. SACKETT
Fort Hays Kansas State College

A custom is a traditional practice or observance; a folk custom, as the name specifies, is one practiced or observed by a group of people, not merely by a family or an individual. Two common types of folk customs are illustrated by the observance of calendar festivals and of significant personal occasions: New Year's, Valentine's Day, Independence Day, Hallowe'en, Thanksgiving, and Christmas are examples of the first; christenings, weddings, and wakes of the second. A third class includes those customs which, although they may have an ancillary function, serve chiefly as the occasion for a social gathering. Thus, while the pioneer literary had an educational purpose, it was welcomed as an opportunity to meet periodically with other members of the community; and similarly today, although baby showers are held in order to give presents to the expectant mother, women are pleased at the chance to get together and visit. A fourth category of customs pertains to the ordinary way of life of a people, their manner of doing things, but no examples of this class are included here because as yet comparatively few such customs have been recorded in Kansas. Collectors have devoted their attention to the other three, probably because they are more colorful and striking.

In the past Kansas, like other pioneer states, had a number of customs now unfamiliar to us—the literary, for example, and the box social. Moreover, frontier conditions affected the way Kansas pioneers celebrated such occasions as Decoration Day and Christmas. In studying these customs we add to our understanding of frontier life.

In our own day there are still many Kansas communities composed of the descendants of European immigrants who brought with them the customs of their native lands. Some of these national groups celebrated calendar festivals which were not common in the American tradition; the Swedes, for example, celebrated Midsummer's Eve. Other newcomers adapted unfamiliar calendar festivals to their own purposes, as, for instance, the Bohemians observed Bohemian Day at Thanksgiving. National groups also had their own traditional ways of marking important occasions, such as weddings. While some of their traditional practices are still observed, the force of others has diminished as the younger generation, more completely Americanized, has lost interest in maintaining the traditions of their forebears. These customs should be recorded before they disappear.

Nowadays Kansans observe only a few customs which their fellow Americans do not. It would be tedious, therefore, to recount the manner in which the ordinary American calendar festivals are celebrated, or to describe contemporary Kansas bridal showers, weddings, and housewarmings. But there are a few Kansas communities which observe customs that, while certainly not bizarre, are a little uncommon, and thus deserve notice. In this study they are represented by three western Kansas shivarees.

PIONEER CUSTOMS

Calendar Customs

First Christmas in Kansas

[Collected from Mrs. H. A. Opdycke, Russell, Kansas, by Wilmer Strecker, 15 April 1960. Mrs. Opdycke's father came to Kansas in 1875, and the other members of the family joined him in April of the following year.]

There were no churches in Russell when we came, but they did build the Congregational Church that year. They were hoping to have it finished in time to have a observance of Christmas held, but they failed. But they did get it enclosed so they could put up a Christmas tree in the vestibule of the old church. That was my first Christmas tree, and of course one that I never could forget.

I well recall the first Christmas in Kansas—and that by the way would be my birthday—the first Christmas that I ever have any recollection of. My parents were building a house in town, but it was not completed yet, so we were living in what they called the cellar—not the basement. There were no basements in those days; they were cellars. We were living in the cellar. And I remember how it looked with that piece of carpet up at the door, to substitute for a door. But I specially remember on Christmas morning that in my stocking there was this little toy and an orange.

There was a storm in the night, and you who are familiar with Kansas blizzards know how the snow can drift in; and I remember waking in the morning and seeing the snow on the bed, but that was all lost to my memory when I saw the stocking with this little doll and the orange. You must remember that in those days an orange was really something to be coveted for the simple reason there were no refrigerator cars with which to move fruits and vegetables in those days. You could only enjoy them just for a little while, just during the season. In fact, up to the time I was twelve or fourteen, fifteen years old, an orange still was a great treat.

Decoration Day

[Collected from Mrs. H. A. Opdycke, Russell, Kansas, by Wilmer Strecker, 15 April 1960.]

I remember that we considered Decoration Day the big day of the year, next to Christmas. You might understand how that might be from the simple fact that fully seventy percent of the population of Russell at that time were the boys who had been in the Civil War. The G. A. R. (Grand Army of the Republic), the organization among the soldiers then—and our American Legion today has the same place that the G. A. R. did at that time—consequently the Decoration Day was looked forward to with keen anticipation by the children.

There was always the parade on Main Street, and we usually walked out to the edge of town, where we were put into wagons, the children, and taken to the cemetery, and there were brief exercises out there. Then in the afternoon there was always the speaking up in what was called the Opera Hall, the building now known as the Cliff Hotel, a two-story stone building, the same then as it is now. And below they had a billiard hall and livery stable. Above was the old—what we called the Opera Hall, where all entertainments of any kind were held, being the only building in the town suitable.

I recall specially one Decoration Day because my mother had made me a new white dress, and it had an embroidered yoke, and it had embroidery on the ruffles. I was very, very proud of it. But it rained that day, as it very often did on Decoration Day, and when we would march, the parade, out at the edge of town, where we were, we children, picked up and put in wagons—and I want you to know, when I say "wagon," that's what I mean; it were a lumber wagon. It was almost— In the earlier days there was no other way of transportation. I well remember it was— The lumber wagon was followed by the old spring wagon, the spring wagon by the buggy, and the buggy by the phaeton, and so on down. But in those days it was the lumber wagon was our means of transportation. And on this particular day it started— The farmer— We were all sitting in the back of his wagon, and it began to rain. And of course he had no protection whatever, only some old horse blankets that he had. And he very kindly wrapped us up as best he could. But you can all realize the result on my white dress, those wet horse blankets. So that's the day that I can never forget.

Soldiers' Reunions

[Collected from Mrs. H. A. Opdycke, Russell, Kansas, by Wilmer Strecker, 15 April 1960.]

Although I've said before that the life was drab for children, yet we had our entertainments, and among the—one of the things which we looked forward to each year was what they called the soldiers' reunion. You remember it had only been about ten years since the close of the Civil War, and this country, fully seventy percent of the people here had been soldiers, and so that was even before the G. A. R. (the Grand Army of the Republic) —before that organization was realized.

So once a year they'd have what they called the soldiers' reunion, and it would be held on the creek over south of what is now Lucas. But you must bear in mind there was no Lucas there at that time—no railroad, nothing there but the prairie. The reason for holding it there on those creeks, I suppose, was from the fact that it—there was shade provided. As I told you, there's no shade whatever at— People hadn't been here long enough yet to grow the trees to provide the shade. They had to depend on nature, and on the creeks there was the shade.

The soldiers' reunion would last a week always, and the tents were set up just as they'd be in a fort, in rows, and we'd have streets, and each family then would occupy the tent that was assigned them. During the daytime we children amused ourselves by playing games, I remember that, and then evenings they would have what they called their campfires. They had really a campfire. You must remember that that's all the light they'd have; there was no electricity, there was no gas, there was nothing but the moonlight and the lantern light. They'd string the lanterns around in the trees, I remember that, and they'd have the light from the campfires.

They would have speakers; sometimes they would have a speaker from abroad—from the state, perhaps from Topeka; or some man that had prominence in the war, something of that kind. Then the music was always furnished by nothing but the fife and drum corps; I forget what they called it. That was the music. And how stirring it was, and how we enjoyed it. And of course the war songs were very popular at that time, and in the evenings through the week, when we'd meet, well, we'd sing those old war songs; and in the later years, when they'd organized sort of a band here in Russell, if they would come over and play for the reunion, for some evening entertainment, of course that would be the highlight of the whole week's reunion. You remember there were no music in the schools, no such thing as a high school band, nor any other kind. It was just the fife and the drum, unless, as I said, if it was possible for them to come over. But you must remember it required a full day's travel to get over there, and they never thought of going and coming in a day. It was one day to go and the other day to return. So that was another one of the pleasantries of our childhood that I can never forget.

First-Footing

[Collected from Helen M. Medill, Hays, Kansas, by Bonnie Harbaugh Womichil, 11 December 1958. Mrs. Medill was born in Linn County, Kansas.]

New Year's Day custom called "first-footing," which consisted of taking a basket containing wine and fruitcake and calling on all your friends early in the morning New Year's Day and having a drink of wine and a piece of fruitcake at each house.

Log-Rolling Picnic

[Collected from Myrtle Triplett, Bogue, Kansas, by Barbara Kenyon, 28 June 1958.]

For many years the pioneers of Graham County, Kansas, held a picnic early in July in a grove about a mile west of Bogue, Kansas. They called it the Log-Rolling Picnic. It began as a sort of political rally but in later years became more of a social gathering and was sponsored by a lodge.

A Pioneer Christmas

[Collected from Mrs. H. F. McCall, Sr., Ulysses, Kansas, by Joe A. Wilcox, 20 May 1958.]

Instead of a Christmas tree, they had a Christmas arch, and the gifts were suspended from this. There were no trees in western Kansas at the time.

CELEBRATION OF AN IMPORTANT OCCASION

Quaker Weddings

[Collected from the Rev. Mr. Barnett, Haviland, Kansas, by Cherel Ballard, 19 April 1959.]

The original Quakers who came to Haviland believed in simplicity in living, in meetings, and even in weddings. The wedding service itself was quite simple, requiring only one sentence each by the bride and groom—seventy-six words in all. No minister officiated. No ring was used. There was no music or flowers. No special occasion was made for the wedding; it took place in a regular meeting. No new dress was made for the occasion.

While the ceremony itself was brief and simple, the investigation that was made before the wedding was most extensive. This included query as to whether or not the parties were in good health. If the committee did not personally know each of the parties, an investigation was made of their eligibility—whether or not either had a living mate. Divorce was not recognized.

The man must be able to provide a home and show prospects of making a living. The bride must have a "hope chest," although this could consist of barest essentials. Also the bride must know how to make a home with very little in the way of worldly goods.

The custom of the Quaker wedding service in which the bride and groom performed their own wedding vows without the aid of a minister is no longer used. But at one time it was the accepted form. No civil license was required, and the marriage was recognized by civil law as being legal. However, the certificate, which was signed by bride and groom and by all present members of the meeting, was filed with the county clerk.

The following is taken from the *Quaker Discipline* and from the *Discipline of the Kansas Yearly Meeting:*

6. A committee of two men and two women shall be appointed to attend the marriage, to see that it is properly conducted and make report to the Monthly Meeting. . . .

9. At a suitable time in the meeting the parties should stand up, and taking each other by the right hand, declare to the following effect, the man first: "In the presence of the Lord, and before these witnesses, I take thee, —— ——, to be my wife, promising with divine assistance, to be unto thee a loving and faithful husband, as long as we both shall live." The woman repeating the same, changing the name.

10. A certificate is then to be signed by the parties, the man first, the woman adopting the name of her husband; and then it is to be audibly read by some proper person. At the conclusion of the meeting it should be signed by others as witnesses.

SOCIAL GATHERINGS

Early Literaries and Sunday Schools

[Mrs. Margaret Haun Raser of Jetmore, Kansas, writes articles on life in early-day Hodgeman County for the Jetmore *Re-*

publican. On 11 April 1957, the paper printed a letter from Mrs. Ollie Holbrook Boucher, a former resident of Hodgeman County now living in Kingsbury, California, commenting on one of Mrs. Raser's articles. It drew the following reply from Mrs. Raser, 18 April 1957.]

The letter from Olive (Holbrook) Boucher in last week's *Republican* brings to my mind pleasant memories of those happy days when we both went to Literary at a country school house. As to the Literary's status in today's affairs, I will quote a little jingle that tells it pretty well:

> That old time Literary enjoyed by old and young
> No doubt is gone forever, half forgotten and unsung.
> It did not fit the tempo or the rhythm of today,
> So it went out with the bustle, the bloomer, and the stay.

The Literary was a place of recreation for all the people in the neighborhood; it gave women and girls a place to wear a pretty new dress (although a calico) or a desire to fix their hair prettily (no money for a hair do), but it gave them a wish to make themselves look their best; they were going somewhere. Maybe transform an old garment into a pretty costume with some ribbon or a bit of lace. Lonesome homekeepers could visit there, exchange news or gossip, and take part in the program; that put new energy into monotonous lives and gave them something else to think about, talk about, sing about, or write about besides the regular work routine. The whole family would go in the lumber wagon. The moonlight was wonderful; if there were no moon, the stars seemed to hang low and bright as if they had something to say. The young swains always saw that the school teachers and farmers' daughters had a way to go.

Literaries were educational; people learned to give readings, speak pieces, sing, how to use Parliamentary Law, debate, review current events, learned dramatics as in plays and dialogues. Everybody was welcome and had a chance to take part. Then there was the Newspaper. Everybody could contribute. Some took to writing poetry for the paper which was very clever. Some items were comic and displayed wit on the part of the contributors. Once Ollie and her brother Henry put on a little play. He was supposed to be grouchy and over-bearing; he put on a long false nose to help him look the part. Of course it made us all laugh. The next week a news item reported that "Mabel [his girl friend] said Henry's long nose just tickled her."

Another time Ollie and Mabel sang a duet which was very nice. So Edith Bower [mother of the editor of the Jetmore *Republican*] and I thought we would sing a duet. I had to sing the alto; it was not difficult, just ran along in natural order; we rendered it quite well and had lots of compliments. Several times we were asked to sing again. I found another duet, but it was difficult. I couldn't read the alto very well but thought I might do it. We had no instrument to start us, and Edith had to have me start her on the soprano, which I did; then I couldn't pick up the alto and made discords. I just couldn't hit the right notes. I guess the tones I emitted must have sounded like someone in distress, as after the program several persons said they were sorry I was sick. There was nothing wrong except I was trying to sing alto that was too difficult for me. Nobody asked us to sing again.

Then the Literary had mock trials. The society selected the prosecutor and the defendant and officers of the court. The jury was chosen at time of trial. Everything was intended to be carried on as in real court, except witnesses were not supposed to tell the truth; mock trials were all fiction. Literary programs for the most part promoted good morals and Christian living. Officers were elected each month so that no one group was supposed to be "running" it. All had a chance. Literaries and Sunday schools were held in school houses if there were school houses.

Mr. and Mrs. Wittrup organized the first Literary Society in that part of the county in 1886 at their own home, Wittrup P. O., SE 2–24–26.[1] Mr. Wittrup was a minister and anxious to help young people by giving them the social and educational advantages offered by the Literary. There was Literary in the old stone house on lot 21 in Jetmore about 1880 or 1881. Also Sun-

[1] Mrs. Raser refers to the method of describing the location of land authorized by Congress in 1796. The first number is that of the section; the second, of the township; and the third, of the range. Thus the location of the Wittrup home would be the southeast quarter of section 2, township 24, range 26.

day school about that time. Mrs. Forinish told me Mr. Stevens was superintendent and Bill Stevens was organist.

Elouise Holbrook said her father organized Sunday school in 1886 at Pogues Grove because there was no building. At an earlier date there was Sunday school at Purdy's on 10–24–25 in that locality. Mrs. Hunter rode a mule throughout her community extending invitations to come to her home to organize Sunday school near Point of Rocks. Hodgeman Community and Orwell both had Sunday school and Literaries. The people of Lower Sawlog and Buckner organized Sunday school, unsectarian, known as Hodgeman County Union Sabbath School, 1879, held at a sod house one mile north of J. R. Wilson's; the building was being fitted for a school room. Location about 26–22–22.

All these pioneer Sunday schools made everybody welcome. An old pioneer says denominational Sunday schools do not show the interest nor manifest the spirit as in the non-denominational, free-for-all Sunday schools of the pioneers. As the county depopulated and filled up again, Literaries and Sunday schools would come and go. There may have been other such gatherings.

Sunday school was organized at Holbrook about 1885. Their School District No. 27 was organized that year. The school house was on NE 6–24–24. In 1885 S. M. Holbrook, Sr., and his six sons settled in that community. The Sunday school was carried on the whole year, but Literary was held during winter or school months. People from Jetmore often attended gatherings there, especially Sunday school conventions which were held every three months in different school houses in the south part of the County. In 1902 they decided to have Literary at Quail Trap, four miles south, instead of Holbrook, as the center of population had drifted that way. I taught Quail Trap that year, and this was where Ollie and I attended Literary together. The Bower family lived in that district; Edith was a faithful member and friend.

The pioneers were moral giants, but civilization (or maybe it's education) has left them no place in American life. People today are losing something in not having made the acquaintance of the pioneer who had force of character that is deficient in so-called higher civilization. There was something about the handshake, the facial expression, the tone of voice and spirit of friendliness, that was different and cannot be described in words. The friendship of the pioneer was love refined. Take all the dross from love, the suffering, longing, heartaches, etc., and you have pure love, such as God and the Angels love, which we call friendship. Such is the friendship of the pioneer, and it seems to last for life, as Ollie's and mine. Edith, Mabel, and Henry, and more of the merry party, have left us to join the Angelic throng, who have a place for the pioneer.

Box Socials

[Collected from O. J. Halsted, Topeka, Kansas, by P. J. Wyatt, 16 June 1956, and included in "I'm Not Selling Anything: Some Folklore from Kansas" (unpublished Master's thesis, Indiana University, 1957), pp. 119–120. Box socials provided the opportunity both for a pleasant social occasion and to raise money for some worthy cause. At these gatherings, which usually were held at the church or the school, box lunches prepared by the women of the community were auctioned off. Since the privilege of sharing the box's content with its provider also was often included in the purchase price, there were times when the bidding was spirited: rival suitors, for example, might send the price way up. Among other kinds of socials were pie socials, strawberry socials, and ice-cream socials—the last-named an especial treat in a day when ice cream was unobtainable commercially and had to be made at home.]

H. I-uh wanted to do a little demonstration here, of what we used to put in our time at, years ago when we were young folks. They used to have box socials at these school houses, 'nd pie socials. And I wanted to just demonstrate what we used to do here.

Now-uh, we're about ready to start our box social, and-uh I think most of the folks here tonight really knows what this proceeds are going for. We need some new curtains for this schoolhouse, and we also need some new maps for these kiddies to study. So, the women and girls around the neighbood has fixed some nice boxes, and I know you boys will want to eat with you girls, so if you'll jist give me your kind attention, we're 'bout ready to start this box social.

Now, boys, here's another one. It's a dandy! Oh! Ain't that a beauty! [Here he goes into the auction calls.] Sold to that gentleman right there for a dollar seventy-five.

W. Well, now, wait a minute there! You're not gonna turn it off so soon! What—uh—after all the boxes were sold, you had maybe fifty boxes?

H. Oh, twenty-five or thirty.

W. Twenty-five or thirty? Then everybody went with their partners—

H. Yeah. Supposin' you had a box there, 'n' Bill Jones bought it. He took you, 'n' set down here in this seat and ate.

W. O. K. And that's all there was to that part of it.

H. 'Course we'd have an entertainment before the box social.

W. Oh! Before the box social!

H. Oh, yes.

W. What'd you do after?

H. We'd eat our lunch and go home.

W. No dancin' or anything like that?

H. No, no. Just go right home.

W. Yeah. Well, now, most of the fellas knew what their girl's box looked like.

H. They—lot of um did, yes.

Mrs. Rushton (Mr. Halsted's sister). That's why they'd run um up.

H. The girls would wipe their mouth, ya know, or they'd do something—fix their hair, ya know.

R. Then they'd go after them.

W. Oh! Mrs. Halsted says, "If they didn't they traded!"

H. Yeah! That's right! Now that's true, too! Yeah!

W. Well, what would happen if two fellas would start biddin' on the same girl's box?

H. It'd go awful high! And someone in the crowd, if a guy was—school teacher there, and some guy was a-goin' with 'er there, maybe half a dozen of um would throw in, ya know, an' —an' give the money to one guy to run it up on him, ya see.

W. Oh! Ya would!

H. Yeah! That was dirty.

W. Yeah, that was kinda dirty! How high would they go?

H. Oh, I don't think—back in them days, ya know, money

was scarce, 'n', you know, boys didn't get very good wages. I have known um to pay two, two-and-a-half for a box.

W. Boy! They sure wanted that supper bad, didn't they!

Comforter Tyings

[Collected from Garrah Winslow, Atwood, Kansas, by Lo-Rita Edwards, 8 January 1960.]

In the early days in Rawlins County it was the custom to hold a comforter tying. Neighbor women would gather at a friend's house to tie off several comforts (bed covers) and visit.

Pound Parties

[Collected from Mrs. Nancy T. Clark, Munden, Kansas, July, 1960. This custom still persists.]

Pound party, or pounding, the custom of taking foodstuffs to new people, especially ministers. Originally pounds of butter, lard, cakes, etc. Now canned food, etc. This was done for us in Phillips County. It has been done for us as a Methodist minister's family.

CUSTOMS OF NATIONAL GROUPS

SWEDISH CUSTOMS

Holidays in Sweden

[Collected from Mrs. Julia Norstrom, Larned, Kansas, by Helen Norstrom, her daughter-in-law, Summer, 1958. The informant's description of customs in her native Sweden gives an idea of the kind of traditions brought to Kansas by Swedish immigrants.]

Christmas. We started celebrating Christmas the night before Christmas, when we had a big feast in the evening; and then after we were through, we had reading and singing, and after that we distributed gifts. As evening went along and later on, we lit the Christmas tree and had games and dancing around the Christmas tree. We had candles on the tree. We would all celebrate up to midnight. Then at three o'clock in the morning we got up and went to early service at five o'clock. The service lasted about an hour and a half. We came back home about eight-thirty and we all had refreshments or breakfast. Then we retired to be ready for the party that evening, which lasted all night. The parties lasted all night, and we got home about five o'clock in the morning.

When we first got to the party in the evening about seven o'clock, then coffee was served and a lot of fancy cookies to go with that. Then after that was over, we would visit and probably a few games until about nine o'clock; then a smorgasbord was served.

The smorgasbord dates back to the time of the Vikings. They have the smorgasbord because the traveling and transportation were difficult. When people gathered for special occasions, they would have to remain there for several days. It was customary for each one to bring something from home. The host would supply whatever else was needed. They brought pickles and dark bread because that would keep any length of time. That is, several days—as long as the guests were staying. They brought all kinds of pickled food, dark bread, all kinds of cookies and puddings. The smorgasbord includes a dark rye bread with molasses, dark molasses. Kind of sweet bread. Then rye bread and white bread, hard tack, meatballs, lingon jam and jelly, Swedish brown beans, pressed jellied veal, potato baloney, lutfisk, Swedish meatballs, cheese tray—oh, I could go on and on.

The lingon jam was made from lingon berries. They are little red berries. They grow practically wild some places and you pick them and preserve them in water and they are shipped all over the different parts of the States for consumers. You then fix them into jam and jelly. Used mostly as a preserve today. We still can get them at Christmas time most places. At least in the big cities, larger cities.

As night went along, we would have our games and our periods of dancing, and between they would have toddies, hot toddies, four or five times during the night. At four o'clock in the morning we had a big feast and the party was then over. After the meal was over, we did some more visiting and about five o'clock we were all ready to depart.

Midsummer's Day. The evening before, we would celebrate some for some reason. We always stayed out for parties that night, too. Night before Midsummer—that would be 24 June—

there was always some activities we used to go to, usually beautiful weather and all. We also would stay out that night and dance and play games till daylight. Have refreshments. Another occasion for young folks to get out.

Easter. The night before Easter we would make up this great big bonfire. We would invite neighbors and friends, those that cared to dance, and would invite some musicians. We would dance—you would mostly dance around that fire until midnight. That fire, you could see it for miles and miles there. You would put tar in there, a barrel almost full of tar, and you can imagine it really made a big fire. We ended up about midnight because Easter day everybody got ready to go to church.

Swedish Christmas Customs

[Collected from Lydia Hven, Garfield, Kansas, by Karen Shumate, 8 April 1961.]

The Swedish custom of the *Julotta* service has been practiced for many years at the Lutheran church in Garfield, Kansas. This church service was held at 5:30 every Christmas morning. The ringing of the bells announced to people for miles around that it was time to come to the church to rejoice during this happy Christmas season. The church was decorated with pretty, glowing white candles in the windows, which served to show the people the way to the church and also served as light during this early morning hour. The Christmas trees, one on each side of the altar, were decorated with fruits—oranges, apples, cranberries, and nuts—and the small candles on each branch were shining brightly. As the group gathered, the people began singing Christmas songs, and the regular church service was then conducted in Swedish. The service seldom lasted less than one and a half hours.

Special foods were *dapp i grytan.* This is a gravy made with chunks of pork. This was poured into a big bowl and placed in the center of the table. Everyone gathered around the table and dipped their piece of bread into the bowl. This was the day before Christmas. Christmas Day foods were *lutfisk,* lingon berries, rice cooked in milk, fruit soup (made from dried apricots, prunes, and raisins), Rye Krisp, potato *karv* [sausage], and *drycka,* a drink made from hops and sugar. Christmas Eve was the time of the biggest celebration. A big meal was served. The Christmas story and a prayer was given by the father. The children were always very anxious for the father to quit praying so they could open their presents.

Swedish Wedding Custom

[Collected from Rose Erickson, Phillipsburg, Kansas, by Shirley Miller, 20 October 1957.]

At a wedding reception, when the guests tap on their water glasses, the bride and groom must stand up and kiss. After they have kissed, the guests can again tap their glasses and name the couple they wish to stand and kiss next.

Swedish Birthday Custom

[Collected from Mrs. Allen Burns, Great Bend, Kansas, by Emerson MacDonald, 1 April 1960.]

The person celebrating the birthday remained in bed until coffee was brought to them along with the birthday gifts.

Danish Christmas Baskets

[Collected from Frieda Klinzman, Agra, Kansas, by Nancy T. Clark, July, 1960.]

Make small baskets of boxes, bits of paper, lace, etc., for each member of the family at Christmas time. Christmas morning these are filled with nuts and fruit or candy.

English Customs

Easter Eggs

[Collected from Mrs. Dale Leichliter, Nickerson, Kansas, by Zula Bierly, 14 July 1960.]

Easter eggs [were] colored and placed in the children's shoes for Easter morning.

English Christmas Custom

[Collected from Leone McDougal, Copeland, Kansas, by Zula Bierly, 16 July 1960.]

The first person to shout, "Christmas gift!" on Christmas morning must be presented with a fine gift from the remaining members of the family.

IRISH CUSTOMS

St. Patrick's Day (Ulster Version)

[Collected from Mrs. Ruth Hopson, Phillipsburg, Kansas, by Mrs. Edna Hopson, 22 June 1958. Mrs. Ruth Hopson was born in Topeka, Kansas.]

On St. Patrick's Day my grandmother always gave we grand-children orange ribbons to wear. She told us, "You are Orange-men from Ulster, and you dinna wear the green."

Irish Funerals

[Collected from Maude Edwards, Atwood, Kansas, 8 January 1960, by her daughter, LoRita Edwards. Mrs. Edwards was born in Kansas City, Kansas.]

When [I] was a girl it was the custom for neighbors and friends to "sit up" with a corpse. Many nights when a young girl [I] could remember sitting with [my] mother in the room contain-ing the coffin, dimly lit by a kerosene lamp, in a ghostly, eerie atmosphere, waiting for the next sitters.

GERMAN CUSTOMS

German Christmas Custom

[Collected from Elvena Stites, Hill City, Kansas, July, 1960.]

We always left three ears of corn for Santa Claus' reindeer. The three represented the three wise men.

German Wedding Custom

[Collected from Mrs. Anna Schroer, Dresden, Kansas, by James A. Schieferecke, 3 December 1960.]

The horse and buggy race after each wedding. The bride and groom must beat everyone from the church to their home.

GERMAN-RUSSIAN CUSTOMS

New Year's

[Collected from Bernard J. Brungardt, Hays, Kansas, 21 March 1959.]

New Year's customs were a little bit different among our

people. Our people had a habit of wishing each other happy New Year each New Year's morning very early. That is, of course, winter time, and it is dark at that time, but it was not unusual I know for people to come to our door at five o'clock in the morning, and you had better be ready and you had better be up at that time of the morning. They were always using— The older boys, the teenagers, would always use a shotgun or something to be sure you knew they were coming, or that you knew they were outside the door. The small ones would have cap pistols, and they would come in and wish you a happy New Year, which in literal translation was a little bit longer than the ordinary "Wishing you a happy New Year," because in addition to a happy New Year you wished them unity and happiness in this life and life in the ever after. There was a little significance attached to that.

Everybody had to be ready with something to give to these wünschers and wishing this happy New Year. The older folks, of course—that is, the teenage boys, those which were of marriageable age—they would normally go to the place where there were girls of that age, and the girls were there with ribbons. They would attach a ribbon to the lapel of the boy who they wished a happy New Year. Or if for— Incidentally, there were several colors of ribbons; if there was a boy they particularly liked, the girl had one color of ribbon for him, and another color ribbon for the usual run of the boys. But the small children, boys and girls together, when they came to wish happy New Year, they usually got candy, nuts, and things like that, which was a carry-over from probably St. Nicholas Day, and when people in Germany used to give nuts and candy and sweets. I know that it was quite an event for us; several days before New Year's we would try to get a big box of some kind. We would be— In later years, little sacks in the grocery stores. We bought the sacks—and the local grocer knew that they had to have the sacks on hand—and we would buy the sacks, and we would fill them: so many peanuts in each; one apple in each; so many pieces of this candy and so many pieces of that candy; and usually a penny in the bottom of that. If you had a particular good friend of the family, there was a nickel or a dime. It all depended on if you were a close relative or not a close relative. If you were a godchild you might get considerably more than that.

Now that was the wünsching. It would continue, so far as the people generally were concerned, for the New Year's Day. But actually the older people would go wünsching for the next five days, until the Feast of the Three Kings—that is, the sixth of January. And the older folks, instead of getting, of course, their sweets, would just sit and visit and get their drinks of liquor, and there was always something to eat; that is, the eats were standing on the table, and if anybody would come in, well—if you wanted to eat a little something, or if you wanted to drink a little whiskey, why, they were in the mood to eat a little bit.

New Year's Wish

[Collected from Lawrence A. Weigel, Hays, Kansas, 1958. This is the verbal formula referred to above by Mr. Brungardt.]

Ich wünsche Euch ein glückseliges Neujahr, langes Leben, Gesundheit, Friede und Enigkeit, nach dem Tode die ewige Glückseligkeit.

Translated: I wish you a happy New Year, long life, health, peace and unity, and after death eternal happiness.

Holy Week

[Collected from Bernard J. Brungardt, Hays, Kansas, 21 March 1959.]

One other little custom. For those of you folks who may be going to the Catholic Church know that during Holy Week, the latter part of Holy Week, we don't ring the bells. The bells, especially in the small communities—and this is traditional in Germany—ring to call the people to church. In our community, of course, the bells rang usually at the half-hour before church time with a single bell, and then at a quarter till or ten till, depending on how big the town was or how far the people were away, why, the bells would all ring together, usually three of 'em, telling you that this was fifteen minutes before time and you'd better get on your horses to get there. Well, towards the end of Holy Week we don't have that; we have what we call "clappers." In church, for instance, instead of having our little bells to call attention to the important parts of the Mass, why, they used these wooden clappers. And in these communities they would—the servers would go around with the clappers in town, had pretty good sized ones, to do the clapping down the street instead of having the bell ring for the first time, the bell ringing for the second time.

And then as a reward for doing that service to the people, on Easter Day, usually the servers would come, and they would knock on each door with the clappers, and they would say:

> Glapper, glapper, Eier 'raus,
> Somst schlage ich dir ein Loch in 's Haus!

Which is the equivalent of "I'm rapping for eggs, and if you don't give me eggs I'll knock a hole in your house," or something like that, and they would get the eggs and sweets as a reward for that.

Weddings

[Collected from Herman J. Tholen, Hays, Kansas, 30 October 1958.]

One of the customs in the old days of the German-Russian weddings in Ellis County was that the orchestra was not hired by the bride and groom or the parents of the young couple but their services were paid for by the individuals who attended the dance. And it was done in this fashion. They would throw coins on the dulcimer, and as it went through the wires, of course, it would add to the sound, so that everybody knew that they were being paid, and the orchestra of course would steam up and play a few pieces, until the coins quit coming; they'd slack up and quit and maybe have an intermission a little bit longer than the dancers liked, and somebody'd start throwing in coins again. Of course, after they'd gotten enough fifty-cent pieces and silver dollars—they were all coins in those days instead of paper money—the orchestra of course would start up again and play a few more hochzeits or whatever they called for until the coins quit comin', and then they'd slack up again. That would go on that way, and the same orchestra would play all afternoon and till maybe two or three o'clock in the morning, as long as the dancers were willing to keep paying. There wasn't any set fee or any set time that they were hired for; they simply played as long as the dancers were willing to dance and to feed the kitty.

The auctioning off of the bride's slipper in recent years has been changed from just getting the highest individual bid that they could get from the audience, to a method of each bidder paying only the amount that he raises the bid. In other words, somebody might start off with a dollar or two dollars, and others raise him a dollar or two, and keep on going like that as long as anyone was willing to raise the bid; but each bidder paid only the amount that he raised the bid from the last previous bid. So in that way the amount realized for the slipper is much greater and not near as hard on any one particular person or guest.

Double Weddings

[Collected from Mrs. Othelia Knutson, WaKeeney, Kansas, by Egla E. Steinle Olson, 30 June 1958.]

A double wedding was one of the traditions of the German-Russian people that came to Trego County.

In many cases, my mother would make a bride's gown, and as was the custom in those days, she had to be on hand early that morning to dress the bride, and the lady that made the other bride's gown would be there to dress her bride. The veil and wreath were stitched to the bride's hair. This was "tying the bride," an honor coveted by every other woman in the community. Aside from this honor, the next in line was first cook at the wedding feast. Usually four to six cooks attended this interesting work, depending on whether it was a one- or three-day affair. Some weddings lasted three days—where guests visited, sang songs, and danced day in and day out, consuming enough food to fill a warehouse.

To many it was a day of joy and high speculation. There were fresh-killed beeves hanging in the chill granaries usually on both farmsteads, with rings of pork sausages, smoked and otherwise; plump dressed ducks and chickens lying on cloth-covered shelves in washhouses, all waiting to be brought together and cooked. I knew too there would be a wash boiler full of golden rich noodle and butter-ball soup, and enough pies and fancy *kaffeeküchen* to fill the clean scrubbed floors of both attics.

I thrilled at the bright garlands of paper roses that took days and nights to make, the fluted hearts and trailing streamers that decorated the gay bridal cortege of automobile and carriage.

Autos had no heaters then as now, nor were there tight windows to roll up and keep the weather out, so the happy couples would speed away, after the ceremony, snug under white covers, streamers and garlands flying in the wind. Some had flowers fastened to the frames and wheels of their buggies and to the harness of their horses, and they in turn would thunder after them. Soon the hooves of our horses added to the drumming on the hard frozen roadway, leading to the wedding feast.

The meal seemed to last for hours, but what did we young girls care? We sat in the gaily decorated buggies and pretended we were elegant brides.

Little tikes would trail out of the house, bringing with them slices of buttery coffee cake; still others had a high time playing fox and geese or throwing snowballs in a snowy field.

When the tables were cleared away and the fiddles and dulcimer struck up a lively tune, we older girls hied ourselves inside to watch wide-eyed and feel a mite jealous at all the crisp paper bills being pinned to the bosoms of the brides. Another feature was the selling of each bride's slipper. The bride would receive her slipper again as well as the money. This was a great time for everyone—young and old.

Wedding Dances

[Collected from Bernard J. Brungardt, Hays, Kansas, 21 March 1959.]

After church, after their marriage— In our Church, the folks [getting married] are up front in the church, and the rest, most of the people, are already out of the church, and the newly married couple would come back. For some reason or other the servers always fixed it so they could get out to the back door before the married couple could get to the back door, and servers would stand on one side of the aisle and servers on the other side with a little rope to keep them from going out until they had tipped. Quite often the best man would do the tipping to the servers, but quite often it was the bridegroom himself.

And then, of course, as long as they were in town, they would march to the home; and I say "as long as they were in town" because ordinarily they lived in town, and they went out to do their farming. When they went home, the bride would stand on one side of the door outside, and the husband would stand on the other side of the door; and, as the people—the visitors or the invited guests—would come, they would pass in between them and congratulate them as they went in.

It was customary among a good section of our people that the bride and bridegroom would not eat breakfast with the rest of the people. They would sit at the breakfast table while the rest of them would eat, but they wouldn't eat then. After the rest of them got through eating, or just before they got through eating, they would go over into maybe a neighboring small room, and they would be served in private for their meal together.

After that, why, the musicians were called out, and they would start the wedding march. They would march around the room and keep on marching around while the guests would pin their little offerings onto the bridegroom or the newly married girl. And when they didn't have any money to pin on—bills, for instance—or didn't want to put as much money into that, they would take calico. It was not unusual to see—to take a long strip of calico and wrap it around the bride, you know, as a gift to the bride.

After they had marched around and were sure that everyone had made his little donation that wanted to make a donation, of course they would start to dance. The bride and the bridegroom would dance three dances together; it was just customary, three —it had to be three, I don't know why. And that was all that the bridegroom saw of the bride for a long time, then, because after that he never danced with the bride during the day because everybody else had to have a chance to dance one dance with the bride; and by evening the poor bride was worn out. And incidentally, if you were rich enough to have a three-day wedding, why, of course the bride had to reappear the next day and probably the third day.

The musicians had to be tipped, and where the wedding was in a relatively small place, where the house wasn't too large, why, they had one man designated to pick out the people who were gonna dance, and you danced only when they asked you to dance; and if you danced when you weren't asked to dance, why, you would be taken off the floor. And then of course the musicians, who knew— They consisted of somebody to play what we now call—oh, it was the equivalent of a zither almost; dulcimer they call it now, I think, played with little mallets, little hammers; there was always a fiddler and sometimes there was a cello with that; sometimes there was a cornet. Cornets were prevalent among our people; they had those over in the old country. Sometimes they'd get lazy; they wouldn't play, and of course the obvious was that if they don't play, the best thing you could do was go ahead and tip 'em. It was not unusual for them, of course, to shove a bill underneath the strings so you could see it, so you would tip likewise and wouldn't be tipping in too small amounts.

Some Bohemian Customs

[Collected from Emil H. Zahradnik, Wilson, Kansas, 9 November 1958.]

Bohemian Day

As far back as I can remember, Thanksgiving Day was always called Cesky Den, or Bohemian Day. And this community always celebrated Thanksgiving as Cesky Den, and that was a big dance here in Wilson. And that drew a crowd at the Opera House, or what used to be the Sokol Hall and now it's called the Opera House. Originally the Z. C. B. J.[2] sponsored it, but there are several Bohemian lodges' organizations here, and they have merged, and the building now belongs to all of them jointly, and it is called the Opera House. And the management— three representatives from each one of these lodges—are the ones that sponsored these dances for a number of years now.

[2] In American, that's the Western Bohemian Fraternal Organization. There's another, C. S. A., that's the young section of the Bohemian organization, Cesko-Slovensky Amerikani; and then there's J. C. D. . . . and there's Sokol, and that is just what it says [Falcon], except that's the athletic organization that thrived here for—oh, I'd say forty or fifty years, but the lodge still exists. We are members of the lodge; I'm at present the president of the lodge.—*Informant*

They used to have plays, yes, and it usually 'd start in the afternoon or—early afternoon or early evening and then have a play in the evening and then the dance following the play— Bohemian play and then the dance following the play, and that, too— The music was furnished by the brass band, and that was quite a band for years. Mostly, I guess all, were Bohemians, and traditionally the Bohemian people seemed to specialize in brass instruments.

Q. The Thanksgiving celebration you were telling us about is kind of a harvest thing, do you think?

No, I wouldn't say it's a harvest thing, it's just— Probably Thanksgiving has been selected as the—as a day of celebration for the Czech people; possibly that might be the original, although I never heard it explained as such. . . . Of course the Czech people have quite a settlement here; they certainly made an occasion of it. However, it has kind of got to the point where people don't seem to take the interest in it that they used to. However, we will have a Thanksgiving dance again this Thanksgiving in Wilson at the Opera House. But it will not be sponsored by these Bohemian organizations that— The local orchestra here is going to have charge.

Wedding Customs

The wedding customs were much different than they are now. Quite often the wedding party was escorted to the minister or justice of the peace with a brass band; likewise, escorted back to the home or wherever they intended to celebrate the occasion. And the band then of course would furnish music for a dance, and the dance would usually start before sunset, or immediately after the wedding party arrived, and last till daybreak or sunup. And of course plenty of food and as a rule they had beer.

One thing, I don't know whether it'll be suitable for your recording here, but I remember years ago there was a little store, an inland store, just south of—about a mile or three-quarter of a mile south of Black Wolf, and they used to sell beer there. And a young man came there to buy his beer for his wedding, and the proprietor asked him, "How many kegs do you want?" And he said, "Well, I don't know. I've got about so-

and-so many coming to the wedding." And, well, the proprietor said, "Well, it just depends now how they'll drink; if they'll drink like people or if they drink like hogs. If they drink like people, why you'll need sixteen kegs, but if they drink like hogs, eight'll be enough." When he asked how come, well, he said, "A hog knows when he's got enough, but people don't."

But that was quite the custom. They did have plenty of refreshments, and true enough, quite often they'd get quite jolly, but there was—in my time I never remember any rough time of any kind. The people went there for a good time, and we had a good time.

Cakes in them days I don't believe were considered as important as other food. There was usually a big meal served, especially for the relatives; and then of course shivarees were the go always. Those that were not invited to a wedding, why, they'd gang up and shivaree the newlyweds and that again— they'd just roll out a keg of beer for 'em; if they was more of 'em, they'd roll out two kegs for 'em. And they'd roll the keg off into a convenient place and tap it and drink their beer and enjoy themselves that way, I guess.

In the early days here your dances, even your public dances, would start before dark and usually would last till sunup. And everybody had a good time; it wasn't that— We didn't get together too often in them days, and when we did, why, we really made an occasion of it.

Mrs. Zahradnik: They really believed more in dressed fowl, like geese and ducks, and the women would get those ready days before the wedding, so that there was plenty of meat and more so than elaborate cakes. And they'd feed people by the dozens; they didn't have a reception like they do now—it's just a cake and probably coffee. They had big meals, and they called that a reception. And then they'd make of course their kolaches and rolls and maybe a houska or two several days before. They didn't have the freezers like they have now, but they just had a way of keeping them as fresh as they could and served 'em at these weddings. . . .

Most of the Bohemians have the houska at Christmas time, but they did have it at weddings as well. . . .

FRENCH-CANADIAN NEW YEAR'S

[Collected from Evelyn Manny, Bogue, Kansas, by Barbara Kenyon, 28 June 1958.]

The French people have an old custom of celebrating the New Year by starting on New Year's Eve and going from house to house, eating and drinking and making merry. Many time they join the party, and they all go on to the next home. This continues all New Year's Day.

PRESENT-DAY CUSTOMS

Three Western Kansas Shivarees [3]

1. [Collected from Karen Cooper, Hoxie, Kansas, by Ward Patterson, 11 May 1959.]

After a couple get back from the honeymoon, a group comes to the house and tears it up. The groom pushes the bride down Main Street in a wheelbarrow.

2. [Collected from Robert Brand, Sharon Springs, Kansas, by Ward Patterson, 11 May 1959.]

After the wedding trip, the groom pushes the bride down Main Street in a wheelbarrow and gives away cigars and candy bars.

3. [Collected from Bob M. Oslum, Syracuse, Kansas, by Ward Patterson, 12 May 1959.]

It is the custom of the young people to get a bride and groom after they have been married a few days and have the husband push the wife down Main Street in a wheelbarrow (a distance of four blocks), with horns blowing and a lot of noise about ten or eleven at night.

---

[3] It is interesting that these three towns, with their similar but not identical customs, are not especially close together. Hoxie is the seat of Sheridan County in northwest Kansas. Sharon Springs is the seat of Wallace County, ninety-two miles southwest of Hoxie by the most direct route. Syracuse, the seat of Hamilton County, is sixty-five miles due south of Sharon Springs on State Highway 27.

DANCES AND GAMES

S. J. SACKETT
Fort Hays Kansas State College

During the last half of the nineteenth century the most common folk dance on the Kansas frontier—as elsewhere in the country—was the square dance. Typically, a dance would be held in
someone's barn; it drew young men and women for miles
around, and they would dress for the occasion as near the height
of fashion as frontier conditions and their ingenuity would
allow. A caller and a fiddler were the essentials for holding a
dance: if there were performers on other instruments among the
local talent they were warmly welcomed, but a fiddler sufficed.
Callers were in more plentiful supply than musicians and
musical instruments. Square-dance tunes were fast and lively—
they kept the dancers moving—and also tended to be intricate
since the fiddlers prided themselves on their ability to play
difficult music. "The Irish Washerwoman" was perhaps the most
frequently heard fiddle tune in Kansas; at any rate, it is the
one now most commonly found in the repertoires of early-day
fiddlers. Other popular tunes bore such names as "Soldier's
Joy," "Mississippi Sawyer," and "Devil's Dream"—this last so
tricky that even the devil could only dream of rendering it
without a mistake.

The national groups which immigrated to Kansas after the
Civil War brought with them their own dances and in some
cases their own instruments as well. The hammered dulcimer,[1]
the ancestor of the piano, came to western Kansas with the
German-Russians. Among round dances characteristic of this
group are waltzes, polkas, schottisches, and hochzeits. The hochzeit was danced chiefly at weddings (*Hochzeit*—literally "high

---

[1] The hammered dulcimer is in no way related to the plucked dulcimer of
the Appalachians; the latter is, in fact, misnamed.

time"—means *wedding*). Like the polka, it is in fast two-four time, but the step is different: you step to the side with one foot, bring the other behind it, and then hop with the first—it resembles a waltz step speeded up to take two beats in the measure instead of three. Although such dance forms as the waltz and the polka were traditional among the Bohemians and common to several other national groups, each had its own tunes which had their own distinctive national flavor.

Another kind of amusement on the frontier was the play party. The participants referred to their activities as "playing games," but actually play-party games were more like dances. Calling an activity a game implies an element of competition— the pitting of an individual or a team against another individual or individuals, another team, or the rules of the game itself. Although some play-party games, such as "The Miller Boy" and "Skip to My Lou," had a competitive element, it was unimportant. In all play-party games the really significant factors were two: young men and women were brought together, and they moved rhythmically in time to music. In comparison to the attainment of these objectives, whether "it" or his antagonist won the race around the circle in "Skip to My Lou" was of no consequence. In short—and despite the opinion of the participants—play-party games may be considered dances—in some cases, dances with trimmings borrowed from games.

The play party came into being because of the scarcity of musical instruments on the frontier and because many parents had a moral objection to dancing. It differed from the barn dance in three respects. In the first place, the play-party game was danced (or "played") to songs sung by the dancers themselves, whereas instruments provided music for the dance. It was proverbial on the frontier that "the fiddle was the devil's instrument," and when a fiddle joined in, girls who were dancing play-party games would stop short at the first note. (An informant, Pearl Cress of Plainville, Kansas, told one of my students that her mother had defined sinning to her as "somethin' that comes out of a fiddle.") Another difference between the play-party game and the dance was that the former was most commonly a round game and the dance, except among the immigrant groups, was almost always a square dance. In a few instances the same steps were used for both games and dances; the Virginia reel, for example, was danced to "Weevily Wheat." The third difference was that the play-party game employed a one-hand clasp as compared to the two-hand or waist clasp of the dance; however, again this was not invariable. There were girls on the frontier who would consent to dance if only a one-hand clasp was used; and there were a few play-party games in which the dancers utilized the two-hand clasp, or even the waist clasp.

Because the play-party songs were danced to, the words frequently recounted the instructions. Thus in "The Miller Boy" the words "The wheel turns around to gain what it will" refer to the fact that the players were marching in a circle. Similarly, the succeeding verses of "Weevily Wheat" contain instructions for the dancers. After the boy and girl skip down toward each other, they are to perform the step required by the words; if the dancers sing "Left hand to your weevily wheat," they swing each other using a left-hand clasp, or if the song calls for "Do-si round your weevily wheat," they dance around each other without clasping hands.

Many of the play-party games which were the customary entertainment of adolescents, courting couples, and young married people (before the babies came) are now played by children; but fifty years ago they were for adults only. Children had their own games, many of them still played, but many now forgotten. Before baseball was introduced, one-hole cat was very popular; T. W. Wells of Hays, who was born in Russell County in 1877, recalls playing one-hole cat as a boy. To occupy the long winter evenings there were indoor games which reveal the settlers' remarkable capacity to devise entertainment from very simple material. "Fox and Geese" (the indoor version) and "Old Mill" were two of this type. The national groups which settled in Kansas brought their own children's games as well as their national dances and songs: two examples of German-Russian children's games are included below to represent an area in which there has been little collecting.

Children in Kansas today play many of the same games as boys and girls in other parts of the United States. Children's games have less variety than formerly, and girls normally take part in games such as baseball which at one time were considered strictly boys' games. In general, children today are less prone than were their parents and grandparents to play folk games learned from their peers. Perhaps in rebellion against the "supervised play" organized by teachers, playground directors, and little-league managers, youngsters enter with extra zest into amorphous games—playing cowboy or space man or cops-and-robbers. Some folk games have survived, however, especially among girls; they play hopscotch, jump-rope, and jacks, and boys still play marbles. And such games as "Hi-Hitler" described below, which resembles an old game called "King of the Mountain," are evidence that adult regimentation has not entirely suppressed either youthful imagination and inventiveness or the old folk games.

At the present time there is no generally accepted method of collecting and recording folk dances, except perhaps by sound motion pictures. Two notation systems for recording ballet, the Benesh System and Labanotation, appeared independently at about the same time a few years ago, and it is possible that one or both might be adapted to recording folk dances. So far as I know, however, the use of either system remains only a possibility. Music for dances can be, and is, collected on tape, but it is unsatisfactory to present dance music on the printed page of a book designed for the general reader. About all that can be done in a study on dances is to present the square-dance calls, as has been done here. Games are easier to collect and record.

DANCES

WALTZ QUADRILLE

[Collected from O. J. Halsted, Topeka, Kansas, by P. J. Wyatt, 16 June 1956, and included in "I'm Not Selling Anything: Some Folklore from Kansas" (unpublished Master's thesis, Indiana University, 1957), p. 111.]

> First couple waltz center and there you divide;
> With the lady glide center, gent 'round the outside;
> Honor your partner and a-don't be afraid,
> Swing corner lady and-a waltz, promenade.

Second couple waltz center and there you divide;
With the lady glide center, gent around the outside;
Honor your partner and a-don't be afraid,
Swing corner lady and-a waltz, promenade.

SOLDIER'S JOY

[Collected from O. J. Halsted, Topeka, Kansas, by P. J. Wyatt, 16 June 1956, and included in Wyatt, "I'm Not Selling Anything: Some Folklore from Kansas," p. 131. "Soldier's Joy" was one of the most popular hoedown tunes on the frontier.]

Honor your right, and now your left,
'N' ya-all join hands, and circle left,
Break, an'-a swing, an'-a promenade back.

First couple! Balance and swing.
Lead to the right. Four hands up. Four on around.

On to the next, and-a four hand round.
Four, two, an'-a six, an'-a eight hand round.
Gents! Cut a shine!
You swing your'n, and I'll swing mine.

On to the next, and-a four hands up.
The four in the round.
Ladies! Do! And-a gents, you know,

And-a one more change
And home ya go!
Swing!
Now on the corner, if ya ain't too late.
Allemande left, and promenade eight.

BIRDIE IN THE CAGE

[Collected from Ray Simpson, Plainville, Kansas, by Judith Hegwer, Spring, 1959. Mr. Simpson explained that the birdie is the girl and the crow is the boy.]

First couple bow, first couple swing and lead right out to the center of the ring. Four joining hands and around you go, birdie in the cage they bar high. Birdie hops out and crow hops

in. Crow hops out and four hands around and on to the next
you go.

AROUND THAT COUPLE

[Collected from Ray Simpson, Plainville, Kansas, by Judith
Hegwer, Spring, 1959.]

Around that couple and take a peek. First couple bows, first
couple swings, and lead right out to the center of the ring.
Around that couple and take a peek, back to the center and
circle four. Allemande left, grand right and left, meet your
partner and swing your sweet. Promenade your lady home.

PIONEER GAMES

PLAY-PARTY GAMES

The Miller Boy

[Collected from Mrs. V. Feely, Jennings, Kansas, by Raymond
L. Stacey, Summer, 1958. "The Miller Boy" is one of the most
popular of all play-party games, and several other versions have
been found in Kansas. For variant versions of it and most of the
other play-party songs given here, see B. A. Botkin, *The American Play-Party Song* (Lincoln: University Studies, University of
Nebraska, Vol. 37, 1937), and Leah Jackson Wolford, *The Play
Party in Indiana* (Indianapolis: Indiana Historical Society Publications, Vol. 20, No. 2, 1959).]

We used to play this, and we took couples and held hands, and
one person was in the center. We all sang:

> Happy is the miller boy who lives by the mill,
> The wheel turns around to gain what it will.
> A hand in the hopper and the other in the sack,
> The ladies step forward and the gents fall back.

Then the one in the center tried to grab a partner, and the
one left out had to be ready to start when the wheel started.

Little Red Wagon Painted Blue

[Collected from Hettie Belle Crisler, Natoma, Kansas, by
Judith Hegwer, Spring, 1959. This is one of several versions of

the ubiquitous "Skip to My Lou" collected in Kansas. The customary rules for this game were that the person who was "it" —who was characterized by the others as being a "little red wagon painted blue," or perhaps a "rat in the cream jar"— skipped around the circle. He grabbed the arm of one of the girls standing in the circle with their partners, and the two of them began skipping around the circle arm in arm. If they got back to the girl's place before her erstwhile partner, who was skipping after them trying to catch them, then "it" joined the circle and the boy who had lost his partner was the new "it." Sometimes he sang, "I'll get another one, a better one than you," as one of the verses, to assuage his wounded vanity.]

Little red wagon painted blue,
Little red wagon painted blue,
Little red wagon painted blue,
Skip to my Lou, my darling.

Skip, skip, skip to my Lou,
Skip, skip, skip to my Lou,
Skip, skip, skip to my Lou,
Skip to my Lou, my darling.

Circle around two by two,
Circle around two by two,
Circle around two by two,
Skip to my Lou, my darling.

Four Play-Party Songs

[In 1957 Lola Adams Carter of Dodge City rounded up a number of the older residents of that community who used to go to the Prairie View school there and attend its functions. During the course of the evening, they sang some of the old play-party songs, and Mrs. Carter recorded them. "Down in the Holler," "Marching 'Round the Levee," "Weevily Wheat," and "Pawpaw Patch" are transcribed from that tape.]

Down in the Holler
Down in the holler
Where the pigs used to waller,
Oh there's somebody waitin' for me.

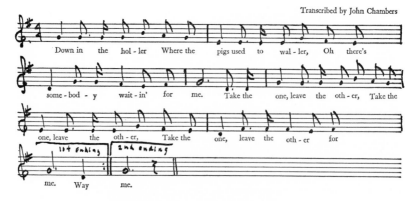

Take the one, leave the other,
Take the one, leave the other,
Take the one, leave the other for me.

Way down in the holler
Where the pigs used to waller,
Oh there's somebody waitin' for me,
Take the one, leave the other,
Take the one, leave the other,
Take the one, leave the other for me.

Marching 'Round the Levee

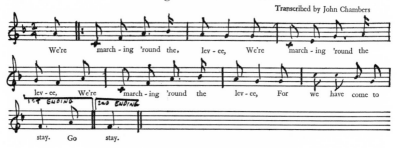

We're marching 'round the levee,
We're marching 'round the levee,
We're marching 'round the levee,
For we have come to stay.

Go forth and choose your lover,
Go forth and choose your lover,

Go forth and choose your lover,
For we have come to stay.

I measure my love to show you,
I measure my love to show you,
I measure my love to show you,
For we have come to stay.

I kneel because I love you,
I kneel because I love you,
I kneel because I love you,
For we have come to stay.

Goodbye, I hate to leave you,
Goodbye, I hate to leave you,
Goodbye, I hate to leave you,
For we have come to stay.

Weevily Wheat

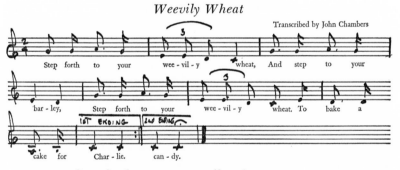

Transcribed by John Chambers

Step forth to your weevily wheat,
And step to your barley,
Step forth to your weevily wheat
To bake a cake for Charlie.

Right hand around your weevily wheat,
Right hand around your barley,
Right hand around your weevily wheat
To bake a cake for Charlie.

Left hand around your weevily wheat,
Left hand around your barley,
Left hand around your weevily wheat,
To bake a cake for Charlie.

Both hands around your weevily wheat,
And both hands around your barley,
Both hands around your weevily wheat,
To bake a cake for Charlie.

Do-si around your weevily wheat,
Do-si around your barley,
Do-si around your weevily wheat,
To bake a cake for Charlie.

Charlie is a fine young man,
Charlie is a dandy,
Charlie likes to kiss the girls
And send them sugar candy.

Pawpaw Patch

Transcribed by John Chambers

Here oh here goes pretty little Ellen,
Here oh here goes pretty little Ellen,
Here oh here goes pretty little Ellen,
Way down in Koko Bend.

Come on, boys, we'll all go and see her,
Come on, boys, we'll all go and see her,
Come on, boys, we'll all go and see her,
Way down in Koko Bend.

Here oh here goes pretty little Albert,
Here oh here goes pretty little Albert,
Here oh here goes pretty little Albert,
Way down in Koko Bend.

Come along, girls, we'll all go and see him,
Come along, girls, we'll all go and see him,

Come along, girls, we'll all go and see him,
Way down in Koko Bend.

Pickin' up pawpaw, puttin' 'em in your pocket,
Pickin' up pawpaw, puttin' 'em in your pocket,
Pickin' up pawpaw, puttin' 'em in your pocket,
Way down in Koko Bend.

OUTDOOR GAMES

Three Outdoor Games Not Associated with a National Group

[Collected from Hettie Belle Crisler, Natoma, Kansas, by Judith Hegwer, Spring, 1959.]

Three Times around the House. Someone is it. All those that are playing try to go around the house three times without the person that is "it" catching them. If someone makes it, then the person has to be "it" again. If they get caught, they have to be "it."

Star Light, Star Bright, Where Is the Old Witch Tonight? Someone is the witch. Everybody else hides their eyes, and the witch will hide. Then, when they count to ten, those that aren't "it" go out and start walking around and the witch will be hiding someplace, and she will come out. When they go out they say, "Star light, star bright, where is the old witch tonight?" and the witch will run out, and if she touches one of them they're "it," and if she can't get anyone she has to be the witch again.

Bear. It's more or less a game of tag. It's usually played in a yard where there are lots of trees. All the trees are bases, and the person that is "it" tries to catch those that are playing as they run from tree to tree. If the person that is "it" can't, he can point to someone and count to ten and they will have to leave their base. Usually he can touch someone then.

Two German-Russian Games

Usau

[Collected from John A. Dinkel, Victoria, Kansas, by Ward Patterson, Spring, 1959.]

We had a game for where we played. We had six there, and
there was maybe four, five, six boys or girls together there. We
took an old tin can, hit that kind of around a little, and we had
as many always as there was boys and girls there, and we had
sticks about three or four feet long, and we played that game we
call "usau." So we had one then, he had to stay in the center, and
whoever hit that can there and another party could get in his
hole. Each one of them had a hole around the center hole, and
each one of them had to keep his stick in there. Then the one in
the middle would hit that can there, and he'd hit that can
either way. It didn't matter which way, but he'd hit that can, and
wherever that can went to, that fellow had to hit that can, and so
it got to go someplace else. That person in the middle, when he
had a chance, he'd put his stick in this fellow's hole there, so this
boy had to go in the middle. Lot of times it took a long time
before this boy got out of the middle, but he got out off and on,
and then we had another game.

Karotgar

[Collected from John A. Dinkel, Victoria, Kansas, by Ward
Patterson, Spring, 1959.]

We took round pieces of wood. We cut them off from trees
about six inches long and about an inch and a half, two inches
thick in diameter. We had two ends, seven sticks on the west
end and seven on the east end. That was apart about twenty
steps, something like that; then there is two or four or six
players. Well, each player had a stick—we cut them from the
trees too. They was sticks about an inch or maybe little over an
inch thick, and about two and a half foot long. We made a line
around them small sticks. We set them up, laid one on the
ground, then we set up three of them with the end up on top
of that one that was lying on the ground—the back end down
on the ground. Then we laid another two on top of them and
one up in the middle. Both ends was the same. We tried to throw
them out of that ring; we throwed our sticks what we had, and
whoever had them all out first—them short pieces of wood out of
that ring—he won the game. Then we had to change. We always
had to change whenever somebody won a game. We had to go

to the circle. The parties on the east end had to go west, and the parties on the west end had to go east. We played a lot of that.

AN INDOOR GAME

Old Mill

[Collected from V. A. Kear, manager-curator of the Sod House Museum, Colby, Kansas. The instructions are not recorded in Mr. Kear's exact words.]

You take a square board, ten or twelve inches square, and mark it as shown in the diagram. This makes the playing board.

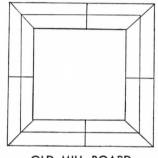

OLD MILL BOARD

Each player has nine counters. These may be buttons or beans or any small object, but each player must be able to distinguish his counters from those of the other player. The players take turns placing their counters, one at a time, on the places where the lines intersect the squares. The object is to get three in a row, either along one side of a square, along one of the lines connecting the squares, or diagonally along the sides of the squares (one on the corner of the inside square, one on the midpoint of the side of the middle square, and one on the corner of the outside square) and at the same time to prevent your opponent from doing the same thing. If all nine counters are played without either player winning, then the players take turns moving their counters, one at a time, to new positions. The new position must be connected to the old position by a line or a side of a square, and no intersection may be jumped on a move; the piece must land on the nearest intersection.

BOYS' GAMES

Hi-Hitler

[This game was observed on a vacant lot in Hays, Kansas, July, 1959. The boys treated "Hi-Hitler" as one word, as is shown by the fact that at the conclusion of the game one boy squatted down and hopped forward on the balls of his feet, his right arm raised, saying, "Look! Hi-Hitler is a bunny rabbit!" Clearly the name Hitler meant nothing to them. The oldest of the boys was ten or twelve.]

The boy who was "it" stood at one end of the vacant lot, while the others came toward him from the other side, their right arms raised in an approximation of the Nazi salute, and calling out, "Hi-Hitler!" "It" had to catch one of them before they reached the line at his end of the vacant lot. The one he caught was "it" for the next game.

Two Marble Games

[Collected from Robert Sackett, then aged nine, Hays, Kansas, Spring, 1961.]

Pot. A game played by several players. A hole is dug in the ground, and each player puts in from one to five marbles (the same number for each player). The players cast their shooters at a line to determine the order of play. They shoot at the hole in turn until at least one of them has his shooter in the hole. If there is only one shooter in the hole, its owner wins all the marbles; if there are two or more, their owners divide them, unless one calls, "No splits." In this case the marbles are left in the hole, each player adds another marble, and the game is played again. The term "pot" is also used to describe the marbles in the hole, but not the hole itself. The expression is probably borrowed from poker.

Ten-holer. A game played by several players. All begin at a line about six feet from the first hole and shoot for this hole. (See diagram of ten-holer course.) When each player gets his marble into the first hole, he begins to shoot for the second, third, fourth, and fifth, in that order. The players take turns

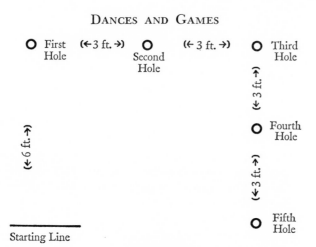

TEN-HOLER

shooting. As each player reaches the fifth hole, he turns around and retraces his path, until finally he is shooting for the starting line. The first player to shoot his marble over the starting line is the winner and wins his opponents' marbles. Informant's younger brother, John, eight years old, thought he had also heard this called "five-holer."

Girls' Games

Pigs in a Pen (Jacks)

[Collected from Mrs. Shirley Brendel, Hays, Kansas, June, 1959. This is one of the innumerable ways of playing jacks.]

You play first ones, then twos, and so forth, one at a time—in other words, you pick up all the jacks one at a time, then two at a time, and so forth. You have to put them underneath your hand; that's why it's called "Pigs in a Pen." You throw up the ball and have to catch it on the first bounce, but you have to pick up the jacks and put them underneath your hand before you catch the ball.

Jump-Rope Rhymes

Cinderella

[Collected from Judith Irby, Bogue, Kansas, by Barbara Kenyon, 29 June 1958. Miss Irby was then eleven years old.]

Cinderella, Cinderella,
Dressed in yellow,
How many times did she kiss her fellow?
One, two, three, etc.

Johnny Over the Ocean

[Collected from Mary Koch, Manhattan, Kansas, Spring, 1961.]

Johnny over the ocean,
Johnny over the sea,
Johnny broke a teacup,
Blamed it on me.
I told Ma,
Ma told Pa,
Johnny got a lickin',
Ha, ha, ha!
How many lickin's did he get?
One, two, three [etc., until the jumper misses]

Blue Bells

[Collected from Gaylene Irby, Bogue, Kansas, by Barbara Kenyon, 29 June 1958. Miss Irby was then nine years old.]

Blue bells, cockle shells,
Evy ivy overs.

One-Two

[Collected from Candy Ball of Hays, Kansas, Summer, 1959, when Miss Ball was eleven years old. This is, of course, an old and common rhyme, but it is interesting to find it still in use.]

One-two, button your shoe,
Three-four, shut the door,
Five-six, pick up sticks,
Seven-eight, lay them straight,
Nine-ten, a big fat hen.

Mother, Mother

[Collected from Sue Suran, Hays, Kansas, July, 1959. Miss Suran explained that this jump-rope rhyme is used by four girls jumping together. First one is jumping alone, then with "In comes the doctor," the second joins her, with "In comes the nurse," the third, etc. They leave off jumping in the same way.]

> Mother, mother, I am ill;
> Call the doctor from over the hill.
> In comes the doctor,
> In comes the nurse,
> In comes the lady
> With the alligator purse.
> Out goes the doctor,
> Out goes the nurse,
> Out goes the lady
> With the alligator purse.

Teddy Bear

[Collected from Cynthia Smith, a student at Fort Hays Kansas State College, July, 1959.]

> Teddy bear, teddy bear, go upstairs,
> Teddy bear, teddy bear, say your prayers,
> Teddy bear, teddy bear, turn out the light,
> Teddy bear, teddy bear, say good night.

FINGER PLAY FOR INFANTS

Jack and Jim

[Collected from Mrs. Boyd Saunders, Bogue, Kansas, by Barbara Kenyon, 28 June 1958.]

Our mother taught us a finger game called "Jack and Jim." Stick a small piece of white paper on the first finger of each hand. Put these two fingers on the edge of a table and say, "Here's Jack and Jim. Fly away, Jack; fly, Jim," and raise hands above shoulders. By changing to middle finger the birds fly away. By changing again they can come back.

RECIPES

MARJORIE SACKETT
Fort Hays Kansas State College

Folk recipes are not learned from cookbooks or other written sources. They have been handed down orally for generations: a daughter learns the recipe by watching her mother use it. One of the contributors to this collection, for example, sat down with her mother to transcribe some recipes that had never been recorded before. "Then you put in some flour," the mother said at one point. "How much flour?" "Enough flour." "Well, how much is that?" "Enough to thicken it." They then measured out the flour to determine the quantity needed to bring the mixture to the correct consistency. Most of the recipes which follow were collected in this way.

The first three are pioneer recipes, presented to show how the pioneer housewife made do with the foodstuffs she found on the prairie. Two recipes brought to Kansas by settlers from Eastern states also are included. All the rest are associated with one or another of the many national groups which have settled here—the Swedish communities at Scandia and Lindsborg, the Danish group at Denmark, the German settlements at Victoria and Schoenchen, the Bohemians at Timken and Atwood, the French-Canadian town at Damar, or one of the many other similar communities in the state.

From the 119 recipes assembled for this project we chose those which seemed most characteristic because they appeared most often; those which offered the most typical display of various kinds of food; and those which gave the widest representation to different collectors and informants. We also tried to keep the correct proportion of recipes from each national group. All the recipes, with the exception of that for dandelion wine, were collected and submitted by students at Fort Hays Kansas State College.

The reader is reminded that this is a compilation of field-collected materials, not a cookbook. A uniform style of abbreviations for measurements has been used, but otherwise the recipes are presented exactly as the informants gave them to the collectors. By cookbook standards some of these recipes are incomplete, and none should be attempted without first checking carefully to make sure that adequate instructions are given.

PIONEER RECIPES

CASSEROLE OF RABBIT

[Collected from Mrs. Caroline Pryor, Garden City, Kansas, by Mrs. Esther L. Thompson, 4 July 1958. Mrs. Pryor came to Kansas from Illinois in 1889, when she was nine years old.]

Dress a young full-grown rabbit; cut in small pieces and wash thoroughly; let soak in salt water one-half hour; pour this water off, put the rabbit in a casserole, add salt and pepper to taste, add 2 T. of butter and 1¼ c. of water; cover and cook until tender. Then the rabbit may be lifted out and 2 c. of sweet milk added; when boiling hot, thicken with 2 T. of flour worked smooth with 3 T. of cold milk. The gravy may be served in a separate dish, or all may be served together from the casserole.

CORN COB SYRUP

[Collected from Mrs. Emily Roberts, Palco, Kansas, by Marie K. Steeples, 28 June 1958.]

Boil 12 clean corn cobs (red ones add more color) about two hours in enough water to make two cupfuls when well cooked. Strain and add 4 c. of brown sugar. If you want a thick syrup, cook for at least one-half hour.

HOMINY

[Collected from Mrs. Emily Roberts, Palco, Kansas, by Marie K. Steeples, 28 June 1958.]

Choose a large iron kettle or boiler and soak ½ bushel of corn in cold water for one day.

Then cook until done having added 1 c. of lye. Drain and wash through four rinses to clean out the lye.

This was made during cold freezing weather, when the hominy could be stored without freezing in the refrigerator. Just set it outdoors. We did not have refrigerators of course in those days.

RECIPES FROM EASTERN STATES

DANDELION WINE

[Submitted by Mrs. Hilda Frye of Arnold, Kansas, 18 March 1958. Mrs. Frye commented: "The following recipe, written on tablet paper and yellow with age, was found among the recipes of Mrs. Alice Frye (Mrs. Hilda Frye's mother-in-law). It is not known whether it was brought from Virginia or whether it was given to her by a friend here in the early days. Mr. and Mrs. Frye came to Trego County in the early eighties. Leslie Frye does not remember that they ever made the Dandelion Wine, (but) dark brown stains on the recipe look as if it had been used."]

To two quarts flowers slice 4 lemons, over this pour 4 quarts of hot water, not boiling, set away 3 days, then put on the stove and boil 20 minutes. Strain and add 3 lbs. of sugar. Put in a jar, tie a cloth over it, set in a cool dark place to ferment. When you can hear it working, pour off and bottle.

QUAKER CINNAMON ROLLS

[Collected from Elma Kobler, Hays, Kansas, by Marie K. Steeples, 1 July 1958. Mrs. Kobler learned the recipe from her mother, Sibbyl Paxson, who was born in North Carolina. It is not clear when the sugar is added, probably with the egg and salt.]

1 cake yeast dissolved in	4 T. sweet cream	1 t. salt
½ c. warm water	½ c. sugar	1 egg
1½ c. milk	4 T. butter	6 c. sifted flour

Add cream to milk, stir, then scald. Cool to lukewarm in a large bowl. Add the butter melted, then the dissolved yeast. Add gradually the flour and when there is a fairly thick batter add the egg and salt. Add the rest of the flour. You may need a little more flour. This may vary, depending on the consistency of the cream and the size of the egg. There should be a light dough. Let rise until doubled in bulk. Lightly knead down. Let rise one-half hour then roll out in long roll about 6 to 8 inches wide depending whether a large or small cinnamon roll is wanted. It should be about ⅓ of an inch thick.

Spread with the following ingredients:

¼ lb. butter	3 t. cinnamon
¼ c. honey	½ c. brown sugar
¼ c. thick cream	

Spread the butter all over the surface. Butter should be soft. Mix brown sugar and cinnamon and sprinkle on. Drop bits of honey here and there. Then the cream in similar manner but do not try to spread. Roll as you would a jelly roll. Cut in slices ¾ or 1 inch thick. Let stand to rise till nice and light. Bake in a pre-heated oven for 10 minutes at 400°, then reduce the heat to 350° and bake 15 minutes longer.

IRISH RECIPE

GINGER ALE

[Collected from Mrs. John Murphy, Dighton, Kansas, by Alice Gabel, Fall, 1957. As collected, the recipe does not make clear what one does with the lemons; presumably it is the rinds only that are put in the crock.]

6 gal. water ⎫
12 lbs. sugar ⎭ Bring to boil

Add ½ lb. ginger, broken in small pieces.
Bring to boil. Let simmer 40 minutes.
10 lemons. Pare rinds very thin. Put in crock and add hot syrup mixture. When cold add 1 T. yeast and pour in a cask. Seal and let set 2 or 3 weeks.

SWEDISH RECIPES

LUTFISK

[Collected from Julia E. Norstrom, Larned, Kansas, by her daughter-in-law, Helen G. Norstrom, Summer, 1958. Mrs. Norstrom was born in Hinneryd, Smolen, Sweden.]

Drop fish pieces into salty water and keep at boiling point for about 15 minutes. Do not boil hard. Cool and pick out all bones and skin. Serve with rich cream sauce, made as follows:

¼ c. butter   ¼ c. flour

Mix well, and add 2 c. rich milk. Stir continually. Salt and pepper to taste. More butter may be added. Some like to add a little mustard to the sauce. This is optional.

(Putting the fish into a thin muslin bag when boiling is a good idea, so that the fish may be easily lifted out of water when cooked.)

KJÖTTBOLLAR

[Collected from Julia E. Norstrom, Larned, Kansas, by Helen G. Norstrom, Summer, 1958. Although the recipe is not specific on this point, ground meat is used.]

2 lbs. beef	1 egg
½ lb. pork	2 T. milk or water
About 1½ slices fresh bread, or	A pinch of sugar
4 or 5 crackers	A bit of chopped onion
Ground allspice, nutmeg,	
paprika	

Soften the meat with a little cold water. Moisten the bread before adding to the meat.

Make into small balls, roll in flour, and put in hot shortening and fry until brown.

Put on a lid (not tight) and steam a little.

LEFSE

[Collected from Mrs. Anna Nelson, La Crosse, Kansas, by Margaret Lee, Fall, 1957. Miss Lee notes that lefse is often eaten with lutfisk. The recipe does not make clear whether the sugar is added with the shortening or with the flour.]

4 c. mashed potatoes	1 t. salt
⅓ c. shortening	1 t. sugar
½ c. cream	2 c. flour

Boil potatoes, mash very fine and add cream, shortening, and salt. Beat until light and let cool. Add flour. Take piece of dough and roll as for piecrust, rolling as thin as possible. Bake on top of stove or pancake griddle until light brown, turning frequently to prevent scorching. Use moderate heat. When baked, place between clean cloths to keep from becoming dry.

PLÄTTAR

[Collected from Mrs. E. P. Lundeen, Garfield, Kansas, by Jeanie Morrow, Fall, 1957. Plättar are fried like pancakes.]

3 eggs—beat well	1 t. salt
2 c. milk	2 t. sugar
1 c. flour	

Mix. The batter will be very thin. Let stand about 1 hour.

FLAT BRØD

[Collected from Mrs. Sylvan Lee, La Crosse, Kansas, by Margaret Lee, Fall, 1957.]

2 c. white flour or	1 t. salt
equal parts graham and white	2 T. shortening

Combine ingredients. Add boiling water to make a stiff dough, stirring continuously. Cool. Roll out thin on a board sprinkled with corn meal. Bake on top of stove, turning so as to brown evenly; finish drying in oven for crisp flatbread.

DANISH RECIPES

AEBLESKIVER

[Collected from Mrs. Clara Ruby, Lincoln, Kansas, by Leola Shaffer, 8 July 1958. Mrs. Ruby was born on a farm near Denmark, Kansas; her parents, Mr. and Mrs. Jens Nielsen, were both Danish immigrants. Apparently this dish is cooked on top of the stove.]

2 c. buttermilk	2 c. flour	3 eggs
1 t. baking powder	½ t. salt	1 t. soda
	3 t. sugar	

Beat egg yolks, add sugar, salt, and milk; then soda and baking powder which has been sifted with the flour. Last add the stiffly beaten egg whites. Cook until bubbly, turn carefully, using ice pick or two-tong fork, finish cooking on other side. Serve with sugar, syrup, or jelly.

(These require a special cooking pan. It is an iron pan similar to muffin pan. Each cup would be about half full of the dough.)

FRUIT SAGO SOUP

[Collected from Mrs. Clara Ruby, Lincoln, Kansas, by Leola Shaffer. Mrs. Ruby comments, "The following is a special dish for a mother with a newborn baby." When the cinnamon is added is not clear, but very likely it is put in with the raisins and prunes.]

2 qt. water	½ c. raisins, cooked	1 c. prunes,
½ c. sago, or minute	1 cinnamon stick,	cooked
tapioca	optional	½ c. fruit juice
	½ c. sugar	

Stir sago into boiling water; add raisins and prunes. Boil slowly until sago is clear. Add fruit juice and sugar. If preferred more juice and sugar may be added. Serves eight.

GERMAN RECIPES

PFEFFERNÜSSE

[Collected from Mrs. D. P. Steinle, now of Ontario, California, but originally from Dorrance, Kansas, by her daughter, Mrs. Egla E. Steinle Olson, 30 June 1958.]

2 c. dark syrup or molasses	2 c. sugar	2 c. lard
½ t. black pepper	1 c. black coffee	1 t. salt
½ t. nutmeg	1 t. soda	½ t. cloves
½ t. ginger	1 t. baking powder	1 T. anise seed

Mix together and add flour to make a stiff dough. Roll into long rolls—diameter about 1 inch—and cut with a sharp knife about ½ inch widths. Bake in a 325° oven for about 10–12 minutes. These last indefinitely.

(This recipe is an old German recipe that was brought to America with our earliest pioneers. No Christmas is complete without them.)

KREBBEL

[Collected from Leola Scheideman, Great Bend, Kansas, by Helen G. Norstrom, Summer, 1958.]

Beat 4 eggs well, then add:

½ c. sugar	1 c. sweet milk	½ t. lemon
4 T. melted	½ t. salt	flavoring (optional)
shortening	Flour enough to make	
1 t. vanilla	a rather stiff dough	

Roll out thin and cut in strips about 2″ × 5″. Then cut a slit lengthwise down the center of each strip leaving about an inch on each end, stretch, and twist into different shapes and bake in deep hot grease.

KRAUT BERUCK

[Collected from Mrs. Kathryn Nuss, Great Bend, Kansas, by Eunice Folds, 8 July 1958.]

Melt some butter in a skillet. Cut in some onions and simmer for a while. Cut cabbage real fine and add to the onions. Cover with a lid and steam until done. Fry some hamburger in small pieces; after this is done, mix with the cabbage, roll out bread dough, cut in square pieces, spoon cabbage in and pinch dough together. Let rise ½ hour and bake.

(A package of ready-mix yeast bread was used.)

ZELTS KÜCHEN

[Collected from Mrs. D. P. Steinle, formerly of Dorrance, Kansas, by Mrs. Egla E. Steinle Olson, 30 June 1958. The "riffles" are a topping made by crumbling the ingredients together with the fingers. The water may be warmed before adding it to the melted sugar.]

Filling:

2 c. sugar	½ c. flour ⎫	(Thickening for filling)
2 c. water	⅔ c. water ⎭	Mix to a smooth consistency.
⅛ lb. butter	1 c. flour ⎫	
¼ t. cinnamon	½ c. butter or ⎪	Make "riffles" out of this.
1 t. vanilla	shortening ⎬	
	2 T. sugar ⎭	

Melt 2 c. sugar in a skillet so that it has a medium brown color; add the 2 c. of water. (The sugar will harden after the water is added.) Cook this until hardened sugar has melted and is of a thin syrupy consistency. Add ⅛ lb. butter. Then add the above flour and water mixture slowly (for thickening) to the syrupy consistency and stir well. Add the vanilla and cinnamon. Be sure this mixture is cooled.

Use a rich bread dough. Roll out ½ inch thick and put it into a 10 × 14 inch pan (shallow—1¼ inch or so deep). Be sure dough is well pressed into corners and along edges of pan. Let this rise for about a half hour. After the dough in the pan has risen, use a fork and puncture the dough here and there. Pour the filling over the bread dough, then crumble the "riffles" over the top of the filling.

Bake in a preheated hot oven (350°) for several minutes and turn oven to about 300°. Takes about 30 minutes to bake the küche.

(Grease the pan before bread dough is put into the pan.)

SCHMIERKÄSE PIE

[Collected from Katie Rudman, Bogue, Kansas, by Barbara Kenyon, 7 July 1958. Mrs. Rudman learned the recipe from her mother, Mrs. Magdalena Eichman.]

Make a single crust pie. Fill with the following:

Using milk and eggs make a custard base. If eggs were not available it could be thickened with flour. Sweetening could be sugar, but the old-timers used sorghum, which gave it a different flavor. To the custard add a cup of cottage cheese and ½ c. raisins (ground). Season with nutmeg and bake in a slow oven until custard is done or when cut with a silver knife the knife comes out clean.

ROKE GRÜTZE

[Collected from Mrs. Lottie Furst, Norton, Kansas, by Alice Foley, Summer, 1958. Mrs. Furst was born in Nürnberg, Germany.]

Juice of strawberries, raspberries, currents, blackberries, etc. Sugar for 3 c. of mixed fruit juice. Bring to a boil, add about ½ c. sugar and 4 T. cornstarch dissolved in cold water. Bring to a boil again, until above gets as fairly thick white sauce and gets firm as gelatin after setting.

AUSTRIAN RECIPE

STOLLEN

[Collected from Mrs. Edward Batchman, Ellinwood, Kansas, by Geraldine Fosdick, Fall, 1957. Mrs. Batchman commented that this was a Christmas dish. The melted butter and sugar are presumably put on top of the dough just before baking.]

1 c. milk
½ c. granulated sugar
½ t. salt
1 pkg. active dry yeast
¼ c. warm (not hot) water
5 c. sifted all-purpose flour
½ c. canned diced citron
½ c. finely cut-up candied
  cherries

Grated rind of 1 lemon (may
  be added)
1 c. seedless raisins
1 c. slivered, blanched
  almonds
2 eggs, well beaten
¾ c. soft butter or margarine
1 T. anise seed, crushed
¼ c. melted butter or
  margarine
2 T. sugar

In large saucepan, scald milk; add ½ c. sugar, salt; cool till lukewarm. Meanwhile, sprinkle yeast onto water in small bowl; stir until dissolved. Add to lukewarm milk, with 1 c. flour; with egg beater, beat to remove lumps. Cover with clean towel, let rise in warm place (about 85° F.) about 1½ hours, or until doubled in bulk.

Now stir in citron, cherries, almonds, lemon rind, raisins, eggs, soft butter, crushed anise seed, then 3 c. flour. On lightly floured surface, knead 1 c. flour into dough until dough is smooth and elastic. Let rise till doubled in bulk. Knead into lengthwise strips about 2″ in diameter. Place in greased pan and intertwine or braid three strips together. May be decorated with blanched almonds and candied cherries.

Let rise till doubled in bulk. Bake at 350° F. Bake from 50 to 60 minutes or until golden.

HUNGARIAN RECIPE

STERATZ

[Collected from Mrs. Edna Blankenburg, Oakley, Kansas, by her daughter, Judith Blankenburg, 27 June 1958. Mrs. Blankenburg's maternal grandmother came from Gols, Hungary; her mother, however, was born in Herndon, Kansas, as was Mrs. Blankenburg herself. Mrs. Blankenburg comments that steratz is a one-dish meal, needing only dessert and drink to complete it.]

4 eggs	2–2½ c. milk
½ t. salt (scant)	Flour

Beat eggs well; add salt, milk, enough flour to make batter as thick as waffle batter. Mix well.

Prepare hot skillet with 2 heaping tablespoons shortening melted in it. Pour in batter. When a light crust has formed on the batter, turn batter with continuous chopping motion until none of the batter sticks to pan. Sprinkle with 2–3 T. granulated sugar over batter. It should be a golden color, depending on the eggs. Serves 4.

It may be eaten with canned fruit and syrup over it as a sauce or with piccalilli, depending on the diner's taste.

BOHEMIAN RECIPES

KOLACKY [1]

[Collected from Mrs. Lewis Talsky, Ellsworth, Kansas, by Frank and Lewis McAtee, Fall, 1957.]

½ c. sugar
⅔ c. butter or part butter, part oleo or lard (Crisco makes the dough nicer)

1 t. salt
1 c. cold water

Bring to boiling point. Crumble 1 cake yeast (or use the dry yeast; 2 cakes of yeast makes rising faster) in large bowl. Add ¼ c. lukewarm water; soak awhile. When hot mixture is cool, add to yeast. Then add 1 c. mashed potatoes, 2 eggs, well beaten. Add 2 c. flour, beat 3 minutes, add flour until soft dough forms (6 or 7 c. flour—I never measure mine). Let rise until double, punch down. Put in refrigerator. Cover with wax paper and tight lid, last a week. Then when ready to make kolaches, make small buns, put on greased pans, and set in warm place to raise. When double in size, punch down the center and fill with filling such as prunes, apricots, or poppy seed.

This recipe does not have to be put in refrigerator. It can be used when made or you use part of it and refrigerate the other part.

TAZENA STRUDLE S JABLKY

[Collected from Mrs. Maurine Ehrlich, Atwood, Kansas, by Donald Chandler, 29 June 1957. Mrs. Ehrlich's mother, Anna Haflina Shimmick, was born in Kanin, Czechoslovakia.]

Melt a piece of butter the size of a large walnut in a cup of lukewarm water. Beat in one egg, a fourth of a cup of sugar and pinch of salt. Sift a quart of flour on the bread board, make a well in the center, pour into it the foregoing, and knead the dough thoroughly, beating it with a rolling pin. Cover with a hot bowl and let it stand one hour. In the meantime peel and slice thin eight apples. Pick over and clean half a pound of raisins and fry bread crumbs in butter. Now spread a white cloth on the table, [place dough on cloth and spread until] almost transparent (it must not tear or break). Two can do this much better than

[1] *Kolacky* is the proper Bohemian plural, but the dessert is usually referred to by its Anglicized name, "kolaches."

one. Then sprinkle with bread crumbs, then cover with the apples, sprinkle with raisins, sugar, cinnamon, and melted butter over the dough. Lift the cloth at one side and thus roll the strudel up like a jelly roll. Butter a baking pan, turn the strudel into it carefully, rub it over with butter and bake slowly one hour. Rub with butter after it begins to bake, and when it is half done, pour over it a cup of milk or cream. When done, cut in slices, dust each thickly with powdered sugar and serve.

RIDKE DOMACI KVASNICE

[Collected from Mrs. Maurine Ehrlich, Atwood, Kansas, by Donald Chandler, 29 June 1957.]

Boil six peeled potatoes in a gallon of water, in the evening. Strain, saving the water, mash the potatoes, and press them through a sieve. When the potatoes are cool, pour over them the water in which they have been boiled, add one piece of dry yeast or one piece of compressed yeast, dissolved in tepid water, or one cup of liquid yeast, a cup of sugar, half a cup of salt. Mix and let it stand until morning. In the morning pour off a pint of this yeast for future use and use the remainder for making bread. This starter is used instead of the regular sponge; that is, you may set the dough with it in the morning when you want to bake. Put a pint of the starter in a mason jar and keep in a cool place for future use. It will keep two weeks. When ready to bake bread the next time, boil potatoes and proceed as directed, adding the starter instead of yeast. If you do not make enough bread to use a gallon of water, use less potatoes, etc.

FRENCH-CANADIAN RECIPES

BLOOD PUDDING

[Collected from Mrs. Evelyn Manny, Bogue, Kansas, by Barbara Kenyon, 28 June 1958. Mrs. Manny's mother, Mrs. Mary Francoeur Saindon-Ribordy, was born in Kankakee, Ill., of parents who had suffered the dispersal of the Acadians described in Longfellow's *Evangeline*.]

When a hog has been stuck for butchering, catch the blood in a clean pan, stirring in salt while blood is running in the pan to keep it from curdling. Strain through a cloth.

For each quart of blood used add 1 pint of milk. To this add

1 c. fresh fat which has been ground. Season with 1 medium-sized ground or chopped onion, 1 level teaspoon of cinnamon and ½ t. of cloves.

Bake in oven till done. (About like a custard but is eaten as a main-course food.)

PEA SOUP

[Collected from Mrs. Emily Roberts, Palco, Kansas, by Marie K. Steeples, 28 June 1958.]

Soak a quart of dried peas in water to cover, overnight. Next morning cook slowly with pork soup bone. Salt to taste. For a variation a little thickening was added.

APPENDIX: MOTIF
ANALYSES

Folktales

Windy Fate of a Kansas Tenderfoot
X924. Lie: remarkably thin person.
X1611. Lies about the wind.

Harnessing the Wind
F963. Extraordinary behavior of wind.
X1611.1. Lies about big wind.

Tall Cyclone Stories
X1611.1. Lies about big wind (cyclone, tornado).
X1740. Absurd disregard of natural laws.

It's Hard to Believe
F790. Extraordinary sky and weather phenomena.
X1640. Lies about dry weather.

Changeableness of Kansas Weather
X1606.2. Lies about quick change in weather from warm to cold.
X1623. Lies about freezing.

Ground Squirrel Digs Hole in Dust Storm
X1611.1. Lies about big wind.

The Buckskin Clothes That Shrank
X1750. Absurd disregard of the nature of objects.

The Sand Hill Dodger
X1381. Lie: the side-hill beast. Animal with two short legs on one side for convenience in living on hillsides. It can walk around the hill in only one direction.

The Hoop Snake
X1321.3.1. Lie: hoop snake. Snake takes its tail in its mouth and rolls like a hoop toward its victim.

Shooting Blackbirds
X1471. Lies about large trees.
X1250. Lies about birds.

Quick Wit
X1012. Lie: person displays remarkable ingenuity or resourcefulness.
X1720. Absurd disregard of anatomy.

Two in One
X1122.2. Lie: person shoots many animals with one shot.

All the Geese That Resulted from One Shot
X1122.2. Lie: person shoots many animals with one shot.
X1124.3.1. Gunshot splits limb and catches feet of birds. Type 1890.
X1156. Lie: other unusual methods of catching fish.
X1241. Lies about horses.

A Fish Story
X1154. Lie: unusual catch by fisherman.

A Kansas Legend
X1411.2. Lies about large pumpkins.
X1401.1. Lie: animals live inside great vegetable, feeding from it.
X1455.1. Lies about cornstalks.

Intelligent Insects
X1411.2. Lies about large pumpkins.
X1282. Lies about bees.

Great Wheat Country
D1652.1.3.3. Inexhaustible wheat.

Tall Sunflowers
X1740. Absurd disregard of natural laws.

Big Straw Stack
X1800. Miscellaneous lies and exaggerations.

Grasshoppers Starved to Death
X1288. Lies about grasshoppers.

The Cat He Couldn't Kill
X1211. Lies about cats.
X1720. Absurd disregard of anatomy.

Chickens Get Ready to Be Moved
B469.5.1. Helpful chickens.

Never Out of Rattlesnake Oil
U110. Appearances deceive.

Saving the Family's Money
K2130. Troublemakers.
K1892. Deception by hiding.

Counting the Indians
X1700. Lies: logical absurdities.

Corn Rows
X934. Lie: remarkable spitter.
X1560. Lies about cities.

Sweet Revenge
X1800. Miscellaneous lies and exaggerations.

He Goot Horse
K134.5. Owner trades a blind horse. He gives a description that
   is literally correct.

Justice Joyce
J1170. Clever judicial decisions.

Hanging the Jury
M1. Senseless judicial decisions.

For Mechanical Purposes
X1780. Absurdity based on the nature of the object.

The Flying Jayhawk
X1250. Lies about birds.

Fighting a Grizzly
X972. Lie: remarkable fighter.
X1221. Lies about bears.
X1130. Lie: hunter's unusual experiences.

Zavolana Smrt (Death Is Called)
C11. The Old Man and Death. Weary old man wishes for death. When Death appears at the summons he asks for help with the load.

The Girl Who Was Scared to Death
N384.2. Death in the graveyard; person's clothing is caught; the person thinks something awful is holding him; he dies of fright.

The Little Glassman
D2062.1. Heart removed by magic.
F281. Fairy replaces man's heart with heart of glass.
K175. Three wishes.

PAUL A. GATSCHET
St. Joseph's Military Academy

Legends

Takaluma, the Phantom Indian
D1840. Magic invulnerability.
E235.4.5. Return from dead to punish theft of skull.

A Phantom Train on the Kansas Pacific
E535.4. Phantom railway train.

The Midnight Harvester
E363. Ghost returns to aid living.

The Runaway Tractor
F960. Extraordinary nature phenomena (lightning).

The Haunted Stone House
K1888. Illusory light.

Old Joe's Ghost
K1887. Illusory sounds.
K1800. Deception by disguise or illusion.
X460. Humor concerning professions (constable).

The Sheriff's Clay Pipe
X460. Humor concerning professions (sheriff).

The Legend of Marais des Cygnes
D161.1. Transformation to swans.
D670. Magic flight.

Legends of Waconda Springs
T81.6. Girl kills self after lover's death.
T92.11. Rivals contesting for same girl.

The Bender Legend
K959. Fatal deception, treacherous murder.

The Legend of Drum Creek
M341.3.3. Prophecy, drowning in a particular stream.

The Legend of Famora
N332. Accidental poisoning.

William E. Koch
Kansas State University

KANSAS FOLKLORE IN PRINT: A BIBLIOGRAPHY

In general, the choice of items for the bibliography was based on two criteria: whether the article dealt primarily with folklore of Kansas, and whether it appeared in a book, a magazine, or a thesis. Items which meet both standards appear in Part I. Part II consists of entries in which folklore appears in some quantity but is only accidental or secondary in the author's purpose.

I

Bingham, Mabel. "The Legend of Waconda," *The Aerend,* Spring, 1933, p. 125.

Bissell, W. O. "Folk-Lore, Phillipsburg," *Phillips County Post,* Souvenir Edition, July 12, 1906. (Two local stories.)

Coburn, F. D. "Some Kansas Facts and Fictions," *Report of the Kansas Commission Trans-Mississippi and International Exposition.* Topeka: 1878.

Cory, Charles E. *Place Names of Bourbon County, Kansas.* Ft. Scott, Kan.: Whiteside Publishing Co., 1928. (Names and name origins of streams, towns, townships, ghost towns, etc.)

Davenport, Gertrude C. "Folk-Cures from Kansas," *Journal of American Folklore,* XI (1898), 129–132. (Forty-four cures collected in Douglas and Coffey counties.)

Devoe, Carrie. *Legends of the Kaw: The Folklore of the Indians of the Kansas River Valley.* Kansas City, Mo.: Franklin Hudson Publishing Co., 1904.

Dinkel, Phyllis A. "Old Marriage Customs in Herzog (Victoria), Kansas," *Western Folklore,* XIX (1960), 99–105.

Green, Charles R. *Tales and Traditions of the Marais des Cygnes Valley.* Olathe, Kan.: Author, 1914.

Gritten, Mary L. "Folklore as a Motivation in Class and Community," *Bulletin of the Kansas Association of Teachers of English,* April, 1957, pp. 1–3.

Harrington, J. P. "American Indian Place Names," *Nature,* CXLII (1938), 960.

Hay, R. "Kaw and Kansas: A Monograph on the Name of the State," *Kansas State Historical Society Transactions,* IX (1906), 521–526.

Hull, Myra E. "Cowboy Ballads," *Kansas Historical Quarterly,* VIII (1939), 35–60. (Fifteen songs with words and music, including several variants.)

―――. "Kansas Play-Party Songs," *Kansas Historical Quarterly,* VII (1938), 258–286. (Twenty-four songs with words, twelve with music.)

Koch, William, and Mary Koch. "Beat the Drum Slowly, Boys," *Kansas Magazine,* 1956, pp. 8–12. (Discussion of the bad men and balladry, with reference to killers in Kansas.)

―――. "More Wellerisms from Kansas," *Western Folklore,* XIX (1960), 196.

―――. "Opportunities in Kansas Folklore," *Bulletin of the Kansas Association of Teachers of English,* February, 1956, 9–11.

―――. "Wellerisms from Kansas," *Western Folklore,* XVIII (1959), 180.

―――. "Kansas History and Folksong," *Heritage of Kansas,* V (May, 1961), 3–32.

―――. *Teaching Folklore in the Schools: A Symposium.* Manhattan, Kan.: The Castle-Patrick Publishing Co., 1961 (for Kansas Folklore Society).

Lathrop, Amy. "Pioneer Recipes from Western Kansas," *Western Folklore,* XX (1961), 1–22.

Lippert, Dale. "Cowboy Lingo (Horse Talk)," *The Aerend,* Summer, 1936, pp. 157–159. (Examples of slang terms regarding horses.)

McMullen, Mildred L. "The Prairie Sings: Northwest Kansas Folksongs." Unpublished Master's thesis, University of Kansas, 1946. (Collected chiefly in Norton County.)

Mechem, Kirke. "Home on the Range," *Kansas Historical Quarterly,* XVII (1949), 313–339. (Discusses facts and fictions about the state song.)

———. "The Mythical Jayhawk," *Kansas Historical Quarterly,* XIII (1944), 3–15. (An entertaining and informative article on the origin and development of the state bird.)

O'Leary, H. D. "Slang in Kansas," *Nation,* XCIV (1912), 462.

Pingry, Carl, and Vance Randolph. "Kansas University Slang," *American Speech,* III (1928), 218–221.

Porter, Kenneth W. "Kansas Song," *Journal of American Folklore,* LX (1947), 299–301. (Text only of a frontier ballad.)

———. "Some Central Kansas Wellerisms," *Midwest Folklore,* VIII (1958), 158–160.

Randolph, Vance. "Wet Words in Kansas," *American Speech,* IV (1929), 385–389.

Ruppenthal, J. C. "Jottings from Kansas," *Dialect Notes,* V (1923), 245–246.

———. "A Word-List from Kansas," *Dialect Notes,* IV (1914–6), 101–114, 319–331.

Sackett, S. J. "Folk Speech in Schoenchen, Kansas," *Western Folklore,* XIX (1960), 277.

——— and William E. Koch. *An Instruction Manual for Members of the Kansas Folklore Society.* Hays, Kan.: Kansas Folklore Society, 1958. (A thirty-page mimeographed pamphlet concerned with collecting and publishing folklore from Kansas, with an essay on "Folklore and Fakelore" by Koch.)

———. "Proverbial Comparisons from Western Kansas," *Western Folklore,* XIX (1960), 10. (Twenty-nine items.)

———. "Signs of Death from Western Kansas," *Western Folklore,* XX (1961), 102.

———. "Signs of Rain from Western Kansas," *Western Folklore,* XIX (1960), 190.

Scheffer, Theodore H. "Geographical Names in Ottawa County," *Kansas Historical Quarterly,* III (1934), 227–245.

Scott, Robert. "What Happened to the Benders?" *Western Folklore,* IX (1950), 327–337.

Weigel, Lawrence A., and Nick J. Pfannenstiel. *German Folk Songs.* Hays, Kan.: Authors, 1956. (About 100 songs in German, collected in Ellis County. No music, no English translation.)

———. "German Proverbs from around Fort Hays, Kansas," *Western Folklore,* XVIII (1959), 98.

White, Mary Frances. "Strange Tales from Kansas." Doctoral dissertation, University of Denver, 1955. (Collected primarily from diaries, journals, and newspapers.)

―――. "Tall Tales in Kansas Newspapers," *Heritage of Kansas,* III (February, 1959) , 9–27.

Winters, Eleanor. "Folk-Say from Kansas," *The Aerend,* Winter, 1934, pp. 42–43. (Discusses "The Lane County Bachelor" and Frank Baker.)

Wyatt, P. J. "I'm Not Selling Anything: Some Folklore from Kansas." Unpublished Master's thesis, Indiana University, 1956. (Collected chiefly in Wabaunsee County.)

II

Carl, Sister M. Tharsilla. *A Survey of Kansas Poetry.* Seneca, Kan.: Courier-Tribune, 1938. (Contains a chapter on folksongs.)

Dick, Everett. "The Long Drive," *Kansas State Historical Society Collections,* XVII (1928) , 27–97. (Contains some customs, and seven of the most popular cowboy songs on the trail.)

―――. *Sod-House Frontier.* New York: Appleton-Century Co., 1943. (Includes some customs and tales.)

Hall, Carrie A., and Rose G. Kretsinger. *The Romance of the Patchwork Quilt in America.* Caldwell, Idaho: The Caxton Printers, Ltd., 1935. (Includes references to Kansas and a number of plates of quilt blocks found in the state or named after it.)

Harvey, Alexander M. *Tales and Trails of Wakarusa.* Topeka: Crane and Co., 1917.

Howes, Charles C. *This Place Called Kansas.* Norman, Okla.: University of Oklahoma Press, 1952. (Includes some lore and traditions.)

Inman, Henry M. *Tales of the Trail.* Topeka: Crane and Co., 1898. (Gives expansive "literary" treatment to several yarns of frontier life.)

Kansas: A Guide to the Sunflower State. (Federal Writers' Project of the Work Projects Administration.) New York: The Viking Press, 1939. (Contains a brief chapter on folklore.)

Lathrop, Amy. *Tales of Western Kansas.* Norton, Kan.: Author,

1948. (Mostly historical reminiscences collected in Norton County. Includes types of entertainment, celebrations, cures, customs, etc.)

Lawless, Ray M. *Folksingers and Folksongs in America.* New York: Duell, Sloan and Pearce, 1960. (Includes brief notes on Kansas folksingers.)

Lehmann, H. C., and P. A. Witty. *Psychology of Play Activities.* New York: A. S. Barnes, 1926. (Children's games in Kansas.)

Lowther, Charles C. *Dodge City, Kansas.* Philadelphia: Dorrance, 1940. (Contains many yarns told by old-timers, but no attempt at scholarly treatment.)

Meltzer, George. "Social Life and Entertainment on the Frontiers of Kansas, 1854–1890." Unpublished Master's thesis, University of Wichita, 1941. (Includes customs, bees, etc.)

Miller, Clifford D. "Social Conditions of Territorial Kansas." Unpublished Master's thesis, Fort Hays Kansas State College, 1936.

Pabst, Lettie Little. *Kansas Heritage.* New York: Vantage Press, 1956. (Contains several pages of beliefs and cures, some customs.)

Reinbach, Edna. *Music and Musicians in Kansas.* Topeka: Kansas State Historical Society, 1930. (A fifty-page monograph discussing immigrant songs, folksongs, state songs, and a list of Kansas musicians.)

Stephens, Kate. *Life at Laurel-Town in Anglo-Saxon Kansas.* Lawrence, Kan.: Alumni Association of the University of Kansas, 1920. (Contains a few interesting folksongs.)

Vestal, Stanley. *Short Grass Country.* New York: Duell, Sloan, & Pearce, 1941. (Some treatment of folkways and lore in Kansas, Colorado, Oklahoma, Texas.)

Wright, Robert M. *Dodge City.* Wichita: Wichita *Eagle* Press, 1913. (Contains many frontier yarns, but no attempt at scholarly treatment.)

P. J. WYATT
Kansas State Teachers College, Emporia

TITLE INDEX OF SONGS

A NOTE ON THE KANSAS FOLKLORE SOCIETY

The Kansas Folklore Society was organized in 1956 as a non-profit organization devoted to the preservation, publication, and study of folk materials and local history in Kansas and adjoining areas. The idea for this collection of Kansas folklore was conceived by the executive committee of the society, on which sit representatives of most of the major colleges and universities in the state, and the task of preparing the studies and papers which comprise the volume was assigned to various members. Membership now exceeds two hundred persons, who come from all walks of life.